HIDDEN MINORITIES

The Persistence of Ethnicity in American Life

Edited by
Joan H. Rollins

UNIVERSITY
PRESS OF
AMERICA

D1260816

Copyright © 1981 by

University Press of America, Inc.

P.O. Box 19101, Washington, D.C. 20036

Printed in the United States of America

ISBN (Perfect): 0-8191-2053-7
ISBN (Cloth): 0-8191-2052-9

Library of Congress Catalog Card Number: **81-40137**

To My Parents

Helena Golen Heller and John Heller

and My Children

Michael, Diane and Valerie Rollins

iii

ACKNOWLEDGEMENTS

The Rhode Island College Faculty Research Fund provided support for typing of the manuscript. Special thanks go to Sandra Whipple for her expert typing of the final copy of the book.

The Introduction benefited from the critical comments of Dr. Richard Sauber, Dr. Ellen Ginsburg and Dr. Carmela Santoro.

Finally, a debt of gratitude is owed to the authors of the chapters who specifically wrote their papers for this book and who were so patient in waiting for publication arrangements to be made.

TABLE OF CONTENTS

PREFACE

This book is dedicated to the greater understanding of ethnic groups in our midst. To further this goal of knowledge of American ethnicity, the editor and authors of <u>Hidden Minorities</u> are donating all proceeds from the sale of this book to the Ethnic Studies Project at Rhode Island College to be used for further research. None of the papers in this volume have been previously published. They have been written specifically for this book, albeit by authors who have a longstanding research interest in the groups about which he/she writes.

Ethnicity is an ideal meeting ground for interdisciplinary cooperation. The editor and authors of this book represent different disciplines -- social psychology, anthropology, sociology, history and international education. All of these perspectives are necessary in order to unravel the complexity of ethnic identity, acculturation and assimilation in American life. Further interdisciplinary cooperation is called for in focusing on specific research problems both in studying one ethnic group in a comparative analysis of the ethnic experience.

Culture, social structure and personality are mutually determinative. Migrants carry at least part of a culture with them. An it should be kept in mind that acculturation is a two way process with at least some elements of the migrants' culture becoming part of American culture and/or of the subcultures of other ethnic groups present in the contact situation. The structural conditions and processes that maintain ethnic diversity also maintain dominant and subordinate relations. But acculturation and assimilation are dynamic processes and institutional changes go hand in hand with cultural changes. Changes in personality structure and self identity occur as a result of and impetus to the cultural and institutional changes.

ix

Ethnic groups are transformed by the economic and political climate of the times. The opportunities for ethnic upward social mobility have largely been the result of a general increase in living standards for the American population as a whole and a shift from a preponderance of unskilled labor jobs to white collar jobs brought about by technological change. Certain political climates are more or less favorable to different ethnic groups depending on their occupational position and other interests. In turn, ethnic group patterns are still very evident in voting.

During the 1980's ethnicity will continue to be a salient factor in American life. An article on the front page of yesterday's New York Times (August 23, 1981) cites 1980 census data to support the claim that a tide of immigrants from Southeast Asia, Cuba, Ethiopia and the Soviet Union as well as Taiwanese, Samoans, Koreans, and uncounted legal and illegal aliens from Latin America and elsewhere is reshaping the social, economic and political life of California. The presence of new immigration enhances the ethnic group consciousness of not only those groups whose ranks are swelled by the new members, but also of other ethnic groups present in the culture. America is a heterogeneous society and there is a need for more empirical data on ethnicity.

August 24, 1981   Joan H. Rollins

x

INTRODUCTION

Ethnic Identity, Acculturation and Assimilation

Joan H. Rollins

The purpose of this volume is to focus on hidden minorities, ethnic groups which function beneath the strata of the dominant groups which have primary influence in the political and economic spheres. The historical role, present social status and identity claims of New England ethnic groups about which little or nothing has appeared in social science literature are examined. Chapters have been written for this book on Narragansett Indians, Mohegan and Scatacook Indians, Portuguese (Azoreans), Cape Verdeans, Armenians, Syrians and Lebanese and French-Canadians. Very few journal articles or books have been published about most of these groups, and very few papers presented at national meetings.

But they have a significance beyond their numbers in that their experiences in New England provide a microcosm for the study of acculturation and assimilation in America. New England still constitutes a heterogeneous community where the ethnic groups are set apart by racial differences and/or by surname and symbols of group unity. They share common "compulsory" institutions (schools and other public facilities) but differing cultural practices and reference groups (Smith 1960). The boundary maintaining mechanisms both of the white Anglo-Saxon, Protestant sector of society and of the ethnic groups themselves have implications for social mobility of these groups. Because of the lesser power and prestige of these groups in the society, their ethnic identification is related to slower assimilation and lower social status in most cases.

This book also provides a contrast between experiences of white and nonwhite minorities. The three nonwhite minorities discussed in this book, Cape Verdeans and Narragansett, Mohegan and Scata-

1

cook Indians have the added burden of being neither
black nor white in a society which Machado points
out (in the chapter on Cape Verdeans) operates with
a binary (black/white) system of classification.
An important focus of the papers on both Cape Verdeans and Narragansett Indians deals with their
struggle to be recognized as separate groups since
they are rejected by white society and don't want
to be labeled as black.

The papers on other ethnic groups highlight
the fact that being white in America is not sufficient for complete acceptance. Research carried
out by the author in Rhode Island on third generation college students of Portuguese, Polish, French-
Canadian, Jewish, Irish, and Italian ancestry revealed that these students still maintained social
distance toward the other groups (all white). The
Triandis (Triandis and Triandis 1960) social distance scale was used to measure prejudice toward
each of the ethnic groups in the study. The social
distance scores were largely the result of the college students indicating an unwillingness to date
or marry someone of the other ethnic group. Most
of the students would accept other ethnic group
members, for example, as coworkers, neighbors or
someone from whom to rent property. Table 1 shows
the relationship between the extent of prejudice
toward each group by the other groups in the study
(Received Social Distance Index) and the degree of
prejudice that group indicates toward the other
groups (Given Social Distance Index). Higher numbers indicate a greater degree of social distance.
Statistically, no relationship was found between
the social distance received by an ethnic group
from other groups included in the research and the
social distance that group displayed toward the
other ethnic groups.

TABLE I

RELATION BETWEEN SOCIAL DISTANCE RECEIVED BY
AN ETHNIC GROUP AND SOCIAL DISTANCE
GIVEN BY THAT GROUP

Ethnic Group	Received Social Distance Index	Given Social Distance Index
Irish	50	47
Italian	52	117
French-Canadian	74	74
Polish	79	102
Yankee	97	69
Jewish	137	195
Portuguese	177	61

NOTE: $r = .027$, df = 6, t = .483, p > .05

(Rollins, 1973, p. 226.)

There was, however, a significant correlation
co-efficient of .77 obtained between the degree of
social distance received by a group and the ethnic
identification of that group as measured by the Own
Categories card sort (an indirect measure of ethnic
identification) (Rollins 1973). On the other hand,
there was no relationship between social distance
shown by a group toward other groups and ethnic
identification.

As expected, the extent of identification with one's own group is influenced
by prejudice and discrimination toward the
group . . . . On the other hand, no simple
or consistent relation was found between
the degree of prejudice directed toward an
ethnic group included in this study, and
the social distance that the group showed

3

toward other groups (Rollins, 1973:228).

The research would seem to indicate that barriers from the outside in the form of prejudice, turn one inward toward the ethnic group and heighten identification with it. But despite warnings concerning ethnic studies degenerating into ethnocentrism and intergroup conflict, this research indicates that a high degree of ethnic identification can exist apart from either isolation within one's group or hostility toward other groups.

Social distance may be viewed as the psychological component reflecting conflict between groups. A conflict framework postulates a dominant and subordinate group(s). Ethnic stratification is based on vested interests of a group, the shared objects in which some groups have an established claim.

> In particular, we suggest that ethnocentrism, competition, and the relative power of the groups involved constitute a set of variables which are necessary and sufficient to explain the emergence of ethnic stratification, which is perhaps the most common outcome of initial contact. (Barth and Noel 1975:29).

Differential power of the ethnic groups as well as conflict and ethnocentrism are necessary for the establishment of ethnic stratification. Change will only come as a result of change in the relative coersive power of the ethnic groups involved.

Socio Historical Perspective

The historical perspective in each chapter traces the ethnic group in both its homeland and American society in order to explain the present maintenance of ethnic culture and identity. Each of these chapters illustrates the thesis that American society represents neither cultural pluralism nor a melting pot. Pluralism exists when each group maintains a separate and distinct culture. In its more clearcut form, pluralism can be seen in Canada and Switzerland. Each group agrees to tolerate and preserve the differences that separate them. Although each group agrees to retain its culture, tolerance of each other's value systems is necessary in order to establish and maintain superordinate national unity (Broom et al. 1954).

Within any given society, there may be a single uniform culture characterized by a similarity of action patterns, ideational systems, and social structure. A plural society on the other hand, is one containing culturally distinct groups which practice differing institutional systems although living adjacent to one another under a common government. Intermediate between the culturally homogeneous society and the plural society are societies which are socially and culturally heterogeneous. "A society the members of which share a common system of basic or "compulsory" institutions but practice differing 'alternative' and 'exclusive' institutions is neither fully homogeneous nor fully plural" (Smith 1960:767). The papers in this book would support Smith's model of a heterogeneous American society.

Only by tracing the history of diverse minority groups in American life can we hope to derive general principles of ethnic identity, acculturation and assimilation. Ethnicity is still strong in America sixty years after mass migration from Europe ended. What are the dynamics of ethnicity? Why is ethnic culture and identity maintained? To answer these questions each of the papers in this book traces the mosaic of ethnic experience for a particular group within southern New England. The excellence of scholarship in this volume is reflected in the fact that three of the authors, Handler (Azoreans), Machado (Cape Verdeans) and Stone (Armenians) spent long periods of time studying their respective groups in their native land as well as following their experiences in America. Only by first observing the immigrants in their homeland can one fully assess the impact of the new culture. Since it is also true that migrants are not a cross sectional representation of the population of their homeland, it is important to determine the regional, social class and other attributes that characterize the typical migrant. The book therefore serves a two-fold purpose: 1) to provide information about the ethnic groups; and 2) to compare the reactions of differing groups in the same contact situation in order to provide some insight into general patterns of ethnic identity persistence and its obverse acculturation and assimilation.

With the exception of the Native Americans, the minority groups described in this book are new minorities, the peak of their immigration being in the twentieth century, and in the case of the Cape Verdeans and Portuguese, the peak of immigration occuring during the past decade. They are ethnic minorities by virtue of their ancestral origin and common culture.

Groups whose members share a unique social and cultural heritage passed on from one generation to the next are known as ethnic groups. Ethnic groups are frequently identified by distinctive patterns of family life, language, recreation, religion, and other customs that cause them to be differentiated from others (Rose 1974:13).

Barth (1969) considers ethnic boundaries to be the critical aspect of ethnic groups which accounts for the persistence of ethnic identity. He distinguishes four necessary characteristics of an ethnic group: 1) largely biologically self perpetuating; 2) shares fundamental cultural values; 3) makes up a field of communication and interaction; and 4) has a membership which identifies itself, and is identified by others, as constituting a category distinguishable from other categoeies of the same order (Barth 1969:10-11). A strong ethnic boundary would be reinforced by social organization, defense mechanisms, language, biology, and ecology (Molohon, Paton and Lambert 1980).

6

Having a strong ethnic boundary serves to perpetuate the ethnic group.

> The characteristics and symbols that set off one category of people from another are not relics from the past but a result of the creative process involved when people take on different or reaffirm the same, ethnic attributes. When people declare themselves, by their behavior, as entitled to a particular ethnic label, they are creating ethnic boundaries anew. . . . Behavior properly labeled as ethnic can draw boundaries to enclose or exclude those with whom one is interacting (Hicks 1977:18).

All of the chapters in this book illustrate the changes in ethnic boundaries across different historical periods and as a result of interaction with other groups in America.

A transformation rather than a transplantation of the ethnic culture occurs with immigration. Handler points out that the Portuguese-American had an identification with his island in the Azores not as a Portuguese or even an Azorean before coming to America. So that what results for the immigrant is a new identification as a Portuguese-American. A new culture is also established which combines Portuguese and American aspects. For example, linguistically the same sentence may combine Portuguese and American words. A new group identification and cohesiveness emerges in American society as a result of the perceptions and attitudes which are exhibited toward them by other groups and a new culture emerges which combines degrees of the old and the new.

Although an ethnic group is often conceptualized as homogeneous and the process of acculturation and assimilation of the group seen as a monolithic process, it is not. Because of the multiple groups to which the immigrant is exposed in American society through the mass media and also through social interaction in job, school or other public

7

settings, the typical immigrant (and American for that matter) learns values and traditions of not only Anglo-American culture, but of aspects of other ethnic cultures to which he is exposed. The norm in American society is to have multiple reference groups.

Acculturation and Assimilation

The intensive study of acculturation in anthropology did not really take place until the 1930's. At that time, anthropologists began to recognize that culture was constantly changing and that much of the change could be attributed to contact with peoples holding different values and customs. In 1936, a sub-committee of the Social Science Research Council, composed of Robert Redfield, Ralph Linton and Melville Herskovits, prepared an "Outline for the Study of Acculturation" which defined the term and the field of study. The following definition of acculturation was proposed:

> Acculturation comprehends those phenomena which result when groups of individuals having different cultures come into continuous first-hand contact, with subsequent changes in the original cultural patterns of either or both groups (Herskovits 1938:310).

In addition to the definition itself, a note was appended which clarified the relationship of acculturation to other similar processes. Acculturation was to be considered one aspect of culture change, and assimilation to be considered a final phase of acculturation. The definition of acculturation thus excludes the process of socialization by which the individual gains the skills and modes of thought of his own culture. The methodology of studies of acculturation requires documenting the time the contact took place, the circumstances bringing it about, the nature of the relations between the two groups (whether friendly or hostile), the role of the individuals concerned and those

8

aspects of the culture which were accepted and which were rejected.

Again in 1953, the Social Science Research Council sponsored a seminar to review the research that had been conducted during the 15 year interim and to make a thorough theoretical analysis of the process of acculturation. Four of the five participants the sociologist Leonard Broom and the anthropologists Bernard Siegel, Evon Vogt and James Watson, subsequently wrote a paper entitled "Acculturation: an exploratory formulation" in which they delineated four principal facets of the acculturation process.

(1) the characterization of the properties of two or more autonomous cultural systems which come into contact; (2) the study of the nature of the contact situation; (3) the analysis of conjunctive relations established between the cultural systems upon contact; and (4) the study of the cultural processes which flow from the conjunction of the systems (Broom et al. 1954: 975).

The properties of the cultural systems which have relevance for acculturation are the boundary-maintaining mechanisms, the degree of flexibility of the internal structure and the functioning of the adjustment mechanisms in the system. The United States can be considered a relatively open system where migrants from diverse cultures have been admitted since its inception. In contrast, closed cultural systems such as that of the Southwestern Pueblos will admit few outsiders and impose strong sanctions on those who do not adhere to the main values of the culture. Boundary maintaining mechanisms may also include the relative restriction of the knowledge of the customs and values of the culture to in-group members, ritual initiation, the cultivation of ethnocentrism, territorial isolationism and legal barriers. Many of these mechanisms may not come into use, however, until after contact with an alien culture.

9

The sizes of the contacting populations and their other demographic characteristics are also important variables in determining the nature of the acculturation. At one extreme is the process of transculturation which occurs when one individual becomes detached from his cultural group and enters into the society of another, accepting the values, customs and ideas of the second group. The determinant of which culture will be dominant and which subordinate in the contact situation is not, however, usually a question of size of population. The more technologically advanced culture, even when it is in the distinct minority, is usually able to exert control in the contact situation.

Linton (1963) made the distinction between directed and nondirected culture contact situations. In directed culture contact, there is effective control including sanctions by members of one society over another. The superordinate society also usually has an interest in changing the conduct of the members of the subordinate culture in anywhere from a single aspect of behavior to the whole range of cultural behavior. Thus the members of one society are subject to controlling influences from their own culture and another.

Contacts which occur without control of one society by another fall into the non-directed category. There is interaction between the members of the cultures in contact, but one does not have a superordinate position over the other. The type of contact situation is crucial in setting the pattern of transfer from one culture to another. In the non-directed type, innovations from the other culture are integrated into the culture in terms of its own values and principles. Whereas in the directed type, the society is interested in bringing about changes in the other and regularly brings to bear definite sanctions on the members of the other society (Spicer, 1961).

The immigrant experience in the United States has largely been one of directed culture contact. The expectation, at least for the European immi-

10

grants was that they would be rapidly acculturated and assimilated. They were shamed and ridiculed for their "foreign ways". But if the process of Americanization was insurmountable for the first generation, the public school system was pressed into service to Americanize the immigrant's children. The cultural duality faced by the second generation creates a chasm between the child and the immigrant parents. Irving Child (1943) in his book on Italian Americans in New Haven, points out that the second generation is in a conflict situation. Identifying with one group or the other (Italian or American) influences such various aspects of one's world as area of residence, choice of friends, political attitudes, relations with fellow employees and employer and even choice of spouse and religious affiliation and practices. More recently, ethnic differences are tolerated and even glorified, so it is somewhat easier for the immigrant and her children to preserve her cultural heritage and at the same time participate in the basic institutions of the American core culture.

Acculturation is a process which may be both an individual and a group phenomenon, obviously acculturation at the individual level having been influenced by acculturation at the group level. Dominance of one culture over the other is a significant factor in determining the direction and degree of acculturation. A positive orientation by the acculturating group or by the out-group toward the acculturating group are not necessary prerequisites, nor is change in reference group orientation necessary for acculturation (Teske and Nelson 1974).

Assimilation may be viewed as the final stage of the acculturation process.

However, the assimilation process differs from acculturation in at least two specific respects. First, whereas acculturation does not require out-group acceptance, assimilation does require such acceptance. Second, unlike acculturation, assimilation requires a positive orientation toward the

out-group. Furthermore, it requires identification with the out-group (Ibid.:359).

The melting pot conceptualization of American society, which was dominant in both social science and
popular thinking for most of this century until well
into the 1950's, had the underlying assumption that
all groups would be assimilated. ". . . the assimi-
lationist paradigm then came under growing attack
in the 1960's as evidence began to accumulate that
ethnicity was far more persistent than the melting
pot model would permit . . . ." (Young 1976:7).

The political scientist Parenti (1967) noted
that the surprise that ethnics continue to vote as
ethnics in spite of increasing assimilation is due
to failure to distinguish between acculturation and
assimilation. Although ethnics have acculturated
in many ways by the second generation, having
adopted many American styles and customs, they have
not assimilated. He points out the importance of
making the distinction between cultural and social
systems as Talcott Parsons has urged.

. . . the cultural is the system of beliefs, values, norms, practices, symbols and
ideas (science, art, artifacts, language,
law and learning included); the social is
the system of interrelations and associations among individuals and groups (Parenti
1967:718).

A failure to assimilate may be due to factors outside of the group as well as within. Many a second
generation American Jew, believing himself, unlike
his immigrant parents, to be fully acculturated in
American ways, aspired to membership in the social
cliques, clubs and institutions of white Protestant
America.

But, alas, Brooks Brothers suit not-
withstanding, the doors of the fraternity
house, the city men's club, and the country club were slammed in the face of the
immigrant's offspring. And so the rebuffed

12

one returned to the homelier but dependable comfort of the communal institutions of his ancestral group (Gordon 1961:273).

Glazer and Moynihan (1963) note that exclusion of Jews from the clubs, neighborhoods, and high prestige schools was greatest during the 1920's and 1930's with a relaxation of this systematic discrimination occurring after 1945. In New York City of the 1960's only certain social and golf clubs and high society remained closed to the Jew. Jews, they noted, however, were still not integrated into the Christian community. According to Gordon (1961) the motif of the American pattern has been behavioral assimilation (or acculturation) without integration in the primary structures and relationships.

According to Moore (1981) it was the ethnics themselves that provided the impetus to lay to rest the melting pot myth.

Minority activism of the 1960's not only attacked social and economic barriers directly, but their intellectuals destroyed the 'melting pot' concept (Moore 1981:276).

For nonwhite minorities such as blacks, Chicanos and American Indians, the situation seemed to be more one of colonial and post-colonial treatment. The reception that an immigrant group faces in American society depends in part on the economic factors operating in the society at the time of peak immigration and at later stages of adjustment to that society.

It is ironic that the great diversity of American minorities is just now beginning to be noticed -- just as their cultures and diversity are beginning to be lost in the urban industrial world that has characterized America since World War II. Their fate is now inextricably linked both to that industrial world and to the cities themselves. An immigrant history becomes an industrial, urban history, modi-

13

fied more or less by federal and local actions and by the economic climate for the urban industrial base (Moore 1981:295).

It is for this reason that Glazer and Moynihan (1963) characterize ethnic groups in New York City as being primarily interest groups for social, political and economic activities.

An Interactionist Theory of Acculturation and Assimilation

An interactionist theory takes into account the physical, sociocultural and psychological factors operating upon and within an immigrant group. Such a theory can account for the great diversity of facts found when one reviews the empirical literature, such as the more rapid assimilation of some immigrant groups as compared with others in the same host society. Various factors in the new situation have differing relative weights for each group; for example, some groups for reason of color face greater discrimination than other groups. Some immigrant groups are initially more divergent from the dominant culture in language and cultural norms than are others, thereby lengthening the acculturation process.

Taft (1953, 1957) developed a social psychological model of acculturation and assimilation. The emphasis in his theory is on changes in attitudes, frames of reference, beliefs, role expectations, reference groups and ego involvement. His focus is on the individual in the process of assimilation, whether it be assimilation due to immigration or social mobility, religious conversions, imprisonment, internment and rehabilitation, army induction, starting at a new school, beginning a new job or joining a new social or residential group.

To this process of assimilation, Taft applies the concept of an interactionist frame of reference. In this context, he conceives of assimilation as ". . . the process by means of which persons ori-

14

ginally possessing heterogeneous frames of reference converge towards common frames of reference as
a result of social interaction (Taft 1953:49).
This definition is based on Sherif's experimental
paradigm of norm formation, the autokinetic study,
and Newcomb's theory that the most distinctive
characteristic of a group is the shared norms which
he called "shared frame of reference". Extending
this concept a little further, just as individual
members share norms prescribing different roles, a
converging of norms through interaction may pre-
scribe different role behavior for different individuals in various sub-groups of the society.

Taft states that there have traditionally been
two views of assimilation, monistic and pluralistic.
Monistic assimilation involves complete identification of the minority group with the standards and
values of the dominant group. Despite lip service
to the melting pot myth which implies that each
group changes the stew, the monistic assumption
underlies the assimilation process in the United
States. Highest status is accorded to the white,
Protestant Anglo-Saxon elements of the population
who have maintained cultural domination since colonial times. Although other immigrant groups have
contributed greatly to the progress and development
of America, they have not changed the basic cultural
patterns or primary institutions of American society.

The Melting Pot or Pluralism?

According to Gordon (1967) the ideal type of
the melting pot model is a cultural blend in which
large scale intermarriage has taken place and the
immigrant stock has entered into the cliques, clubs
and primary groups of the society and influenced to
some extent the social structures of the larger culture. Identification assimilation would also have
taken place in the melting pot. Gordon concludes
that America is not a melting pot; the cultures of
the diverse ethnic groups have not melted into one.
Gordon argues that even descendents of ethnic groups
such as the Scotch-Irish, German Protestants, Swedes

15

and Norwegians, who have been absorbed into the
white Anglo-Saxon Protestant sector of society
through this process of intermarriage have not altered the structures of white Protestant society as
a true melting pot concept would require. Culturally assimilation has meant loss of the immigrant
group's identity and transformations of their cultural heritage into Anglo-Saxon patterns. But
aside from the above groups, assimilation has not
taken place in American society. The sociologist
Ruby Jo Reeve Kennedy (1952) postulated the "triple
melting pot", in which Protestant, Jewish and Catholic nationalities were separately assimilating.
This separate melting is more truly occurring within
the Protestant and Jewish "pots" than in the Catholic one, as evidenced by the research reported in
this book on the French-Canadians and Portuguese,
both Catholic groups who still maintain their separate ethnic communities and culture. Groups that
are racially different such as the Mohegan and
Scatacook Indians, Narragansett Indians and Cape
Verdeans described in this book retain separate
sociological structures. (The outcome of all this
in contemporary American life is thus pluralism --
but it is more than "triple" and it is more accurate-
ly described as structural pluralism than as cultural
pluralism, although some of the latter also remains)
(Gordon 1975:249). The viewpoint of pluralism is
that each side is entitled to maintain its own culture.

A Heterogeneous Society

        Smith (1960) has developed a theory of plur-
alism which rests on his definitions of and distinctions made between culture and society. According to Smith, interdependent institutions which
comprise a common system of institutions are the
core of a culture. "Each institution involves set
forms of activity, grouping, rules, ideas and values.
The total system of institutions thus embraces three
interdependent systems of action, idea and value,
and of social relations" (Smith 1960:767). Examples

of institutions are kinship, government, educational, religious and economic systems. Each of these systems contains subsystems; thus under the kinship system would be included marriage, family, levirate, and extended kinship forms. Subsystems form institutions and interdependent institutions form a common system comprising what in Malinowski's terms could be considered a cultural whole. Societies in Smith's framework are ". . . territorially distinct units having their own governmental institutions" (Ibid.:766).

In Smith's framework a plural society would be one which although living under the same government would have differing institutional systems. The United States would therefore not be a plural society according to Smith. America better fits his definition of a heterogeneous society which shares certain "compulsory" institutions such as the judicial and educational systems but has differing "alternative" institutions such as religious and cultural institutions.

Morris (1967) criticizes Smith's conceptualization of a plural society as being based on a definition of institutions which is a mixture of both cultural and structural criteria. In addition since Smith included "kinship, religion, property and economy, recreation and certain odalities" as institutions which are part of the core culture, Morris says there was very little left outside of the cultural core. Morris further criticizes Smith for not clearly stating when variations within the institutional core of a society are sufficient to make a society plural as opposed to heterogeneous.

Formal models of groups, particularly the jural form which describes rules of recruitment into groups and the rights and duties of membership of groups, are unable, according to Morris, to adequately handle social change. In order to better handle structural alteration, he emphasizes process and analyzes groups in terms of transactions or relationships of incorporation, which are relationships of sharing in a joint interest with

17

some members of the society, and in relationships of transaction, based on inequality.

Groups that are culturally and linguistically different may not be elements in the same stratification system, but may be related in a kind of "federal" plural society such as is found in Switzerland. In other societies, however, where racial and cultural diversity exists, the groups are part of the same social stratification system. Where racial and cultural differences are only of secondary importance in the ordering of relationships within the society, it would not be considered a plural society.

Brown (1965) and other social psychologists and sociologists point out that Negroes in America have a separate and parallel social stratification system. For Caucasians, however, the United States, including New England, would not be considered a plural society in Morris' model, because members of all ethnic groups are part of the same general social stratification system. Factors such as education, income and occupation have greater relative weight in determining social status in New England than does ethnic group affiliation. It does, however, appear to be true in New England that members of certain ethnic groups may find more barriers to social mobility than others.

Both conditions in the host society and differences within the ethnic group must be taken into account in explaining social mobility. All immigrant groups do not begin in society at the lowest occupational rung and gradually move up. The working opportunities during the historical period in which the group arrived and the educational and occupational skills of the immigrants determine the occupational position and concentrations of the immigrant group. The occupational choice and residence of an immigrant group was also influenced by the presence of friends and relatives. Occupational concentration such as French-Canadians in the textile industry further served to facilitate similarity of life style, class interests, work

18

relationships and common residential areas.

Some theorists raise the question of whether the ethnic community is a product of its common ancestral culture, or rather held together by current common social milieu and economic plight.

Much that has been written about race, ethnicity, social class and community has centered around the issue of the importance of culture in determining life styles. Our review of this literature suggests that much of it is based on empirically untested assumptions about the importance of the portable heritage which a group brings from one place or generation to another. We suggest that a more parsimonious explanation of ethnic and community behavior will be found in the relationship of the ethnic community to the larger macroscopic structure of the society -- occupation, residence and institutional affiliation (Yancy, Eriksen and Juliani 1976:399).

While "consciousness of kind" in this case ethnicity, is certainly heightened by similarity of social class, occupation and residence, they are not necessary prerequisites for the existence of an ethnic sub-culture. ". . . a group can maintain ethnic social cohesion and identity while lacking an ecological basis" (Parenti 1967:718). New adjustments in ethnic organization and communication take place such as the use of the automobile and telephone to maintain extended family ties. Even when middle class status has been attained, these in-group social patterns seem to give ethnicity an enduring nature. Ethnic sub-cultures may persist and evolve new structures despite dramatic changes such as moves to suburbia and professional status.

Personality System

In addition to the social and cultural system in the process of acculturation and assimilation,

19

one must take into account the personality system. "Just as social assimilation moves along a different and slower path than that of acculturation so does identity assimilation or rather non-assimilation enjoy a pertinacity not wholly responsive to the other two processes" (Ibid.:723).

In our theoretical perspective, then, the individual is the primary focus of cultural learning, new ideas, and the social and ecological constraints affecting behavioral choices and decisions. Naturally, the anthropological observer is practically always interested in going well beyond the individual actor to describe and explain larger processes of cultural evolution, social movements and microcosm-macrocosm relations. In some situations the articulation of individuals to well-organized social groups is clear and unambiguous; most of the time, however, researchers in complex societies have had to deal with bewildering complications in the linkages between individuals and social systems (Pelto and Pelto 1975:13).

Network analysis provides a methodological strategy for studying these complex interaction patterns in modern society. The social network provides a mapping of the most important social relationships for the individual. It is these networks which reveal the extent of ethnic ties even when the individual does not share an ecological base with other ethnics nor is any longer culturally different from members of American society.

Hicks (1977) considers ethnicity to be an attribute of role just as age and sex. "By role we mean the behavior society expects or exacts from an individual according to his position in the social system" (Hicks 1977:2). By considering ethnicity within the framework of role analysis, the focus no longer has to be the ethnic aggregate, but may be the person's role. As Hicks points out, in some situations ethnicity may be the person's most salient

20

attribute, but in others, it may be irrelevant or
even forbidden to be considered such as in "equal
opportunity employment".

The personality characteristics of the individual and his socio-cultural roles also mediate
the acculturation and assimilation process. Role
may effect the degree of contact with the new culture. Also, the degree of similarity between the
role in the old and the new cultures or the necessity for changing roles, as is frequently the case
with occupation, affect the rate of acculturation.

The anthropologists Caudill (1949) and Spindler and Spindler (1958) went beyond the use of de-
scriptive techniques to include personality data
obtained from adaptations of projective techniques
such as the Rorshach and TAT. Caudill studied the
psychological characteristics of the highly acculturated Ojibwa Indians of Lac du Flambeau Ojibwa
showed similarities in personality patterns to the
aboriginal Ojibwa (whose characteristics were
pieced together by the anthropologist from reports
of explorers in the 17th and 18th centuries) and
the present-day, relatively unacculturated Canadian Ojibwa (on whom the anthropologist Hallowell
obtained Rorshach data). Characteristic of both
the aboriginal and unacculturated Canadian Ojibwa

> . . . were a detailed, practical, noncrea-
> tive approach to problems, a high degree
> of generalized anxiety, an emphasis on re-
> straint and control, an emotional indiffer-
> ence to things, a lack of warm interper-
> sonal relations, a wariness and suspicious-
> ness, and a great deal of aggression and
> hostility covertly expressed in sorcery
> (Caudill 1949:425).

The social structure of the Flambeau, however,
has apparently broken down, permitting the overt
expression of aggression in physical violence rather than in sorcery as in the past. An interesting additional finding was that the comparison of
the Rorshachs of the acculturated Canadian Ojibwa

21

and the TAT's of the Flambeau children show a sex difference in adjustment to acculturation favoring the females. This difference has roots in the traditional Ojibwa culture in which the woman had less heavy responsibilities and were less anxious.

Spindler and Spindler (1958) made one of the first systematic attempts to analyze sex differences in acculturation, in their study of Menomini Indians of Wisconsin. Rorshach tests were administered to 68 males and 61 females, all over 21 years of age. In addition, a schedule of 23 sociocultural indices were obtained for each subject and used for placing subjects on an acculturative continuum. The model psychogram for the Menomini male was one of "disturbance, tension and diffuse anxiety, and decrease in emotional controls" which was not present in the psychogram of the females. Sociocultural factors could account for these differing reactions of males and females to acculturation. Menomini culture was traditionally male oriented with rigidly defined "instrumental" roles such as hunting, warfare and ceremony. Women's roles were more flexible. In her "expressive" role as wife and mother, there is greater continuity with Western culture so that the woman does not face as much conflict in culture change. Although acculturating Menomini males continue to take instrumental roles of community leadership and provide a living for their families, the content of these roles has drastically changed.

He must learn to be punctual in his arrivals and departures, and run his daily and weekly cycle by the clock and calendar. He has to learn the accumulation of property and money is the way to 'get ahead' and he has to learn that getting ahead in this fashion is the most important thing that a man can do. There are no precedents for these and many other expectations in traditional patterns of instrumental roles for males in Menomini culture (Spindler and Spindler 1958:230).

In addition to learning new patterns and goals which are in conflict with his traditions, the Menomini male faces the prejudices of whites towards Indians in his daily life. Women, on the other hand, continue to perform their habitual roles, Spindler and Spindler thus attribute the anxiety, tension and breakdown of emotional controls found in acculturating Menomini male to the role conflict.

For the Azorean immigrant, the role of women changed much more than that of men. The wife in the Azores did not work outside of the home, but the typical Portuguese immigrant wife works in paid employment. Yet Handler, in the chapter on Azoreans, notes no personality disruption or disorganization due to the more drastic role change of the Azorean immigrant woman compared to that of the immigrant man.

Most psychologists who have studied ethnic groups have focused on prejudice and discrimination or comparisons of intelligence test results. There is a need for further research on modal personality patterns of different ethnic groups and changes in these patterns with acculturation and assimilation. Anthropologists, such as Caudill and Spindler and Spindler (cited above) have used projective techniques which are subject to bias in interpretation. The use of standardized personality tests comparing immigrants and their children and grandchildren would provide greater reliability and validity in the study of personality change accompanying acculturation and assimilation. Further research is needed on ethnic groups based on representative sampling.

The role of the primary group in culture change has also been a focus of attention in studies of North American Indians. Bruner (1956) put forth the thesis that the differential degrees of acculturation among the Mandan-Hidatasa Indians of the village of Lone Hill in the Missouri River Valley is related to the orientation of the nuclear family. He found the interaction of two factors, the presence or absence of a white model through

interrmarriage and the direction in which the family
was consciously trying to socialize the child, to
be a basis for the differences in degree of acculturation and assimilation or have an anti-assimi-
latory effect.

Hidden Minorities

It is evident from the ethnic groups described
throughout this book that the two most important
forces in supporting the ethnic culture and rein-
forcing ethnic identity are the family and the
church.

The primary reason for Portuguese immigration
is to improve the family's economic situation. Very
often the Portuguese immigrant brings his family
with him (in addition to wife and children, frequently parents, aunts and uncles, etc.). The first
year here the Portuguese family lives very frugally.
They often squeeze grandparents, children, aunts,
uncles, etc. into a three room apartment. A sub-
stantial amount of money is saved in this first year
alone and some of it finds its way back to other
relatives in the Azores who soon join them in America. The Portuguese-Americans are very religious and
most, even to the third generation, observe at least
one feast day a year, the Holy Ghost feast. They
are very sincere in their Catholic beliefs which are
displayed in regular church attendance. The Portuguese are a hard working, law abiding, religious
group of people who are maintaining subcultural
practices through identification with family and
church.

The Cape Verdean shares with Portuguese a
desire to work hard and provide a better life for
his family than he can in the arid Cape Verde Islands, but he has the added burden of being colored
in a predominantly white society. My own research
on Cape Verdeans bery mucy supports Machado's thesis (in the chapter on Cape Verdeans) that they want
to maintain a separate racial category for themselves as Cape Verdean and neither be considered

black nor white. But, the identity problem for Cape
Verdeans is more than the black/white issue. They
are also an ethnic group with a distinctive culture
-- spoken language, food, music and cultural customs which they wish to preserve.

Running through all of these papers is the
theme of identity. Bouvier characterizes the French-
Canadians' struggle to maintain their identity as
"survivance," which focuses on religion, language
and culture. And for survivance, second generation
French-Canadians sacrificed the upward mobility in
education and occupation characteristic of other
second generation Catholics -- the Poles, Irish and
Italians. The barriers to upward mobility and acculturation were therefore largely internal to the
ethnic group. Perhaps in part because of the proximity to Canada and the ease of visiting relatives
there, the French-Canadians, my research has shown,
are the most likely of the immigrant groups in
Rhode Island to maintain their language into the
third generation.

Bouvier (in the French-Canadian chapter) men-
tions Hansen's Law - "What the son wishes to forget; the grandson wishes to remember" (Hansen 1964)
and notes that for French-Canadians it did not hold
true. The second generation French-Canadian stayed
close to the ethnic community in residence, language
and culture, but that the third and fourth generations are acculturating. My own research based on
interviews and questionnaires administered to first,
second, and third generation members of many ethnic
groups -- the ones included in this book as well as
others such as Poles, Italians, Irish and Jews
found no evidence for Hansen's law for any of the
groups. All of the ethnic groups show a progressive loss of language, observation of special holi-
days and cultural customs of the ethnic group. Intermarriage also increases with each progressive
generation further diluting the ethnic cultural
identity and practices. Nevertheless, ethnic identity and some cultural practices, particularly those
relating to religious observances and food and
patterns of social distance toward other ethnic

25

groups, persist into the third generation.

Rather remarkable, in view of their small numbers and many generations of culture contact is the survival of the Native American groups included in this book, the Mohegan and Scatacook Indians and the Narragansetts. Perhaps this can be accounted for by Lieberson's theory (1961) which points out that ". . . subordinate migrants appear to be more rapidly assimilated than are subordinate indigenous populations. Further, the subordinate migrant group is generally under greater pressure to assimilate, at least in the gross sense of 'assimilation' such as language than are subordinate indigenous populations" (Lieberson 1961:908).

The lesser pressures on Indians to assimilate, combined with their residence in rural areas of their states, have been contributing factors to their continued identity and existence. With some romanticism of the Indian in white society, some of the existence of symbols of Indian culture and history have also been preserved by the white society.

The history and culture that an immigrant or indigenous group possess, how their culture and skills "fit in" with the social and economic structure of the dominant culture and the barriers or aids to acculturation that they meet are all determinants of the rate and nature of the assimilation process. The initial cultural differences between Native American groups and the American core culture are much greater than between immigrant groups and the American culture. The Armenians, in particular, have evidenced certain values congruent with American society which have made for more rapid socioeconomic mobility than for the other groups discussed in this book. A number of parallels can be drawn between the Armenians and Jews. The strongest tie that binds Armenian Americans is their history of persecution and attempted genocide by the Turks. In this country they have exhibited a high value for education, which according to informants in the Armenian community, has led to approximately 90% of the third generation being college graduates. The

26

Armenian Students' Association of America provides scholarship grants and interest free loans to many young people of Armenian descent. Another characteristic shared by Armenian Americans and other successful American ethnic groups such as Jews and Japanese is a low birth rate.

The Harvard Encyclopedia of Ethnic Groups notes that it is their very affluence and success in American life, however, which poses a threat to the continuence of Armenian culture in America.

Greater affluence, mass culture, and almost universal education as far as college in the years after World War II sharply transformed the Armenian family ethos. The next generation adopted middle and upper-middle-class American values. The Californians were generally more thoroughly assimilated than the Easterners, but studies of individual parishes indicated that 60 to 70 percent of all third-generation Americans intermarried -- raising troubling prospects for future ethnic preservation (Mirak 1980:143).

Like the Armenians, the Syrians and Lebanese had mass migrations around the turn of the century and the early decades of the twentieth century. Unlike the Armenians, however, they have had large families through the first and second generations and a much lower percentage of college graduates through the third generation than the Armenians. A high birth rate depresses the rate of socioeconomic mobility and may be one of the reasons for the slower economic and educational progress of the Syrians and Lebanese as compared with the Armenians.

The Syrians and Lebanese have clustered in cohesive communities not only in New England cities sucy as Providence, Pawtucket and Boston, but also throughout the country in larger cities such as Brooklyn, New York, Detroit, Cleveland and Los Angeles. In all of these cities, the focus of Syrian and Lebanese social life is the family and the

27

church. Any event of personal life such as a birthday or anniversary is a cause for an extended family gathering. Cultural traditions are also carried on at social festivals, usually through the church or sometimes some other organizations such as the Arabic Education Foundation. Like most other immigrant groups the language is usually not spoken by the third generation, but the food and music are still very much a part of their experience. Intermarriage was a virtual taboo for second generation Syrians and Lebanese as was moving out of the ethnic community, but many of the third generation are marrying non-Arabs and moving to the suburbs, but are still maintaining ethnic ties, primarily through the extended family and church.

Conclusions

The research reviewed serves to point out certain principles which are basic factors in the acculturation process. Of importance in acculturation in varying circumstances is the primary group which serves as an anchorage for the individual and which may either facilitate or impede acculturation. When the primary group has had greater contact with the dominant culture through intermarriage and favorable acceptance, it serves to facilitate acculturation. Where the primary group, because of discrimination toward the ethnic group or other factors seeks to preserve the ethnic identity and culture it serves to impede acculturation. Even in the latter case, however, it may be functional for the individual in preventing him from having to face the conflicts encountered in rapid acculturation, particularly if the new culture is quite different from the old.

Another generalization that can be derived is that acculturation increases with progressive removal in time and generation from the ethnic culture. The longer the immigrant group is in the new culture or the more distant the generation from the immigrant one, the greater the degree of acculturation and the greater the likelihood of assimilation occurring.

28

On the basis of limited data, it appears that there may be continuity in personality characteristics in acculturation, although with changes in social structure, the form of expression of certain impulses and emotions may change. The role the individual plays such as sex role and occupational role and the extent of change in the role in acculturation mediate the rate of acculturation and the degree of disturbance experienced by the individual.

Cross currents of assimilation and pluralism still swirl in American society. The persistence of ethnic identities and sub-cultures proved the melting pot a myth. On the other hand, there is nonetheless significant acculturating, and even assimilating occurring with succeeding generations and sharing in the basic institutions of society by all ethnic groups which stamps as false the concept of American pluralism. America is a diverse or heterogeneous society. Finally, the basic institutions such as the educational institution are beginning to appreciate that diversity. In a recent issue of Theory Into Practice Pratte states:

> This issue explores the state of cultural pluralism and education . . . the spirit amounts to the value belief that differences between cultures are to be celebrated rather than denied, distorted, or used as justification for invideous comparisons between cultures. The positions taken are in general accord that the educational system should be responsive to the fact that the United States is culturally diverse . . . there has been and probably always will be a multiplicity of American cultures and the core or pluralistic education embraces recognizing and prizing diversity, developing greater understanding of other cultural patterns, developing greater understanding of all cultures and developing positive and productive interaction among students . . . pluralistic education is a humanistic concept, prizing diversity, human rights, social justice,

29

and alternative life styles of all people (Pratte 1981:1).

The persistence of ethnic identity cannot be explained entirely at the socio-cultural level. Much of the explanation is at the psychological level; ethnicity provides a sense of security and of continuity with the past. It provides a definition of self -- who I am and who my people are and have been, where we came from and what our characteristics are, what kind of people we are and what our values are. It provides a stable anchorage in a rapidly changing world. Also, since the loss of ethnic culture progresses from one generation to the next, remembrances of the ethnic culture and its observances and remembrances of childhood. One remembers the grandparents who spoke the language and perhaps were not even bi-lingual, one remembers their tales of the old country, or if a Native American the stories of the Indian way of life. To maintain the ties with one's childhood is also to maintain the ties with one's ethnicity and ancestral past.

REFERENCES CITED

Barth, Ernest A. T. and Noel, Donald L.
1975 Conceptual frameworks for the analysis of
race relations: An evaluation. In Norman R.
Yetman and C. Hoy Steele Majority and Minority: The dynamics of racial and ethnic
relations (2nd Ed.) Boston: Allyn and
Bacon.

Barth, Frederik
1969 Ethnic Groups and Boundaries. Boston:
Little Brown.

Bogardus, Emory S.
1924-1925 Measuring social distances. Journal
of Applied Sociology. 9:299-308.

Broom, L., Siegel, B., Vogt, E., and Watson, J.
1954 Summer Seminar on Acculturation: Acculturation An Exploratory Formulation. American Anthropologist, 56:973-1002.

Brown, Roger
1965 Social Psychology. New York: The Free
Press.

Caudell, W.
1949 Psychological Characteristics of Acculturated Ojibwa Children. American Anthropologist, 51:409-427.

Child, Irving R.
1943 Italian or American? The Second Generation in Conflict. New Haven: Yale University Press.

Glazer, Nathan and Moynihan, Daniel P.
1963 Beyond the Melting Pot: The Negroes, Jews,
Italians, and Irish of New York City. Cambridge: The M. I. T. Press and Harvard University Press.

Gordon, Milton M.
    1961 Assimilation in America: Theory and Real-
        ity. Daedalus 48:263-285.
    1967 The Nature of Assimilation and the Theory
        of the Melting Pot. In E. P. Hollander and
        R. G. Hunt (Eds.) Current Perspectives in
        Social Psychology. (2nd Ed.) New York:
        Oxford University Press.
    1975 Assimilation in America: Theory and Real-
        ity. In Norman R. Yetman and C. Hoy Steele
        Majority and Minority: The Dynamics of Racial
        and Ethnic Relations. (2nd Ed.) Boston:
        Allyn and Bacon.

Hansen, Marcus Lee
    1964 The Immigrants in American History. New
        York: Harper and Row.

Herskovits, M. J.
    1938 Acculturation: The Study of Culture Con-
        tact. Gloucester, Mass.: Peter Smith

Hicks, George L. and Leis, Philip E. (Eds.)
    1977 Ethnic Encounters: Identities and Con-
        texts. North Scituate, Mass.: Duxbury Press.

Kennedy, Ruby Jo Reeve
    1952 Single or Triple Melting Pot: Intermarri-
        age in New Haven, 1870-1950. American Journal
        of Sociology. 58:56-59.

Lieberson, S.
    1961 A Societal Theory of Race and Ethnic Rela-
        tions. American Sociological Review, 26:
        902-910.

Linton, Ralph
    1963 Acculturation in Seven American Tribes.
        Gloucester, Mass.: Peter Smith.

Mirak, Robert
    1980 Armenians. In Stephen Thernstrom (Ed.)
        Harvard Encyclopedia of America. Ethnic
        Groups. Cambridge: Belnap Press of Harvard
        University Press.

Moore, Joan W.
  1981 Minorities in the American Class System.
  Daedalus 275-299.

Morris, H. M.
  1967 Some Aspects of the Concept Plural Society.
  Man, new series 2:169-184.

Parenti, Michael
  1967 Ethnic Politics and the Persistence of
  Ethnic Identification. The American Political Science Review. 61:717-726.

Petto, Pertti J. and Petto, Gretel H.
  1975 Intra-cultural Diversity: Some Theoretical Issues. American Ethnologist. 2:1-18.

Pratte, Richard
  1981 This Issue Theory Into Practice. 10:1.

Rose, Peter I.
  1974 They and We: Racial and Ethnic Relations
  in the United States. 2nd ed. New York:
  Random House.

Smith, M. G.
  1960 Social and Cultural Pluralism. Annals of
  New York Academy of Science. 83:763-785.

Spindler, L. and Spindler, G.
  1958 Male and Female Adaptations in Culture
  Change. American Anthropologist. 60:217-233.

Taft, Ronald
  1957 A Psychological Model for the Study of Social Assimilation. Human Relations. 10:141-
  156.
  1953 The Shared Frame of Reference Concept Applied to the Assimilation of Immigrants.
  Human Relations. 6:45-55.

Teski, Raymond H. C. and Nelson, Bardin H.
  1974 Acculturation and Assimilatiin: A Clari-
  fication. American Ethnologist. 351-367.

Triandis, Harry C. and Triandis, Leigh M.
  1965 Some Studies of Social Distance. In I. D.
    Steiner and M. Fishbein (Eds.), Current
    Studies in Social Psychology. New York:
    Holt, Rinehart & Winston.

Yancey, William L., Eriksen, Eugene P., and Juliani,
  Richard N.
  1976 Emergent Ethnicity: A Review and Reformu-
    lation. American Sociological Review. 41:
    391-403.

Young, Crawford
  1976 The Politics of Cultural Pluralism. Madi-
    son: The University of Wisconsin Press.

NARRAGANSETT IDENTITY PERSISTENCE

William S. Simmons

According to the 1970 United States census,
10,872 persons identified as Indian live in the
six New England states. Many of these, the exact
figures are not known, are Indians of non-New
England ancestry who migrated to urban centers such
as Boston and Providence; about a third of the total
New England Indian population live on reservations,
of which there are now nine, or in communities such
as Charlestown, Rhode Island, Mashpee and Gay Head,
Massachusetts, and Mohegan, Connecticut, where native American enclaves have existed since before
Puritan times until the present (Taylor 1972: 176,
226-230). Outside the State of Maine, the Indian
inhabitants of New England no longer speak the ancestral Algonquian languages, and are economically,
socially, as well as culturally similar to the general population. In the southern part of Rhode
Island, mainly in Washington County, live some four
to five hundred people who are of a mixed Indian,
African, and European racial background, who live
dispersed throughout the majority White and minority
Black community, and whose names, religious beliefs,
occupations and life-styles are essentially similar
to those of other working class people in the area,
yet who consider themselves to be American Indian
of the Narragansett Tribe. In the last three hundred and fifty years the Narragansett, like most
Native American groups of the earliest settlement
areas, evolved from a community with unambiguous
claims to race, language, and culture, to a population which protects a precarious Indian identity,
the authenticity of which is challenged frequently
by Whites, Blacks, and more culturally distinctive
Indians. The purpose of this essay is to establish
the connection between the well-known Narragansett
Tribe of the earliest contact period and the population which identifies itself as Narragansett today.
In particular I have focused on a limited number of
events and institutions which I think were critical
in the transformation of the one into the other over

the course of the last three and one-half centuries.
I have drawn primarily upon documentary sources,
but also from fieldwork at three recent Narragansett ceremonies, discussions with Narragansett informants, and the published work of other anthropologists. The most notable of these is Professor
Ethel Boissevain of Lehman College of the City University of New York who has been conducting field
research in the Narragansett community for more
than twenty years. (Since this article was written
Boissevain (1975) Campbell and LaFantasie (1978)
Sainsbury (1975), and Simmons (1978) have written
important pieces on Narragansett culture and history.

The first encounter between the Narragansett
and a European was in the spring of 1524 with the
Italian navigator Giovanni da Verrazzano who wrote
of them: "These people are the most beautiful and
have the most civil customs that we have found on
this voyage. They are taller than we are. . . the
face is clear-cut. . . the eyes are black and
alert, and their manner is sweet and gentle, very
much like the manner of the ancients" (Wroth 1970:
138). The first European settlement on their ter-
rain was that by Roger Williams and the English
founders of Providence in 1636, followed by the
Antinomian settlement on Aquidneck Island in 1638.
Roger Williams' early American classic <u>A Key Into
the Language of America</u>, the most important source
on New England Indians in the seventeenth century,
was written mainly about the Narragansett. Having
permitted the English to settle within their territory they allied themselves with Puritan soldiers
of Massachusetts Bay and Connecticut in their war
against the Pequot in 1637, thus strengthening the
English foothold in southern New England and for-
ever foregoing the possibility of a unified local
response to English colonization. Because of their
location outside the boundaries of the United Puritan Colonies, their political and military autonomy,
and the peculiar religious views of Roger Williams
who was the most prominent minister in their midst,
the Narragansett were not pressured to convert to
Christianity and actively discouraged those mission-

aries who attempted to convert them (Williams 1881).
By 1675, with much of their territory sold or "mort-
gaged," the Narragansett chiefs, or sachems, became
embroiled in a conflict that began between the
English of Plymouth Colony and the Wampanoag sachem
Philip of Mount Hope. The United Colonies demanded
that they surrender Wampanoag women and children
refugees, which they refused to do. On December 19,
1675, the United Colonies attacked and overwhelmed
the Narragansett retreat, deep within a swamp in
what is now South Kingstown, Rhode Island, and by
the end of 1676, less than seventy Narragansetts
remained of an estimated four to five thousand persons at the start of the War (Hubbard 1865:II:55).
Most had been killed, died of starvation, or sold
out of the country into slavery. The English believed Indian culture to be the creation of the
Devil and the Narragansett to be the Devil's principal tool in preventing their settlement on New
England soil. The Narragansett rejected that interpretation of themselves and suffered the greatest
violence that Puritan armies and writers could un-
leash. Cotton Mather wrote in his Magnalia Christi
Americana that: ". . . we can hardly tell where
any of 'em are left alive upon the face of the
earth" (1820, II:336). In 1676 the English began
moving into the vacated Narragansett lands and the
survivors submitted to long periods of indenture-
ship to colonial families (Easton 1858:175; Gookin
1854:270-273; Staples 1843:170-171).

Those who survived the war merged with a small
neighboring group, the Niantic, who because they
followed a nominal pro-Puritan policy were not destroyed. The Narragansett and Niantic populations,
particularly the ruling families, had been linked
always by intermarriage, and the combined population became known as Narragansett. Neither Rhode
Island nor Connecticut exercised much control over
the affairs of this now powerless tribe and allowed
them to inhabit a large territory between Kingston
and Westerly, Rhode Island, under the hereditary
leadership of a lineage of Narragansett-Niantic
sachems. By 1696, free roaming Indians were considered to be a social nuisance, and the Rhode

Island Assembly passed an act which prohibited
Negro slaves and Indians from being abroad after
nine o'clock in the evening, because, according
to the wording of the act, they had committed
"divers thefts and robberies" (Laws of the Colonial and State Governments 1832:53). Within a few
years the General Assembly met to determine with
the sachem and his five man council, "what may be
a sufficient competence of land for him and his
people to live upon" (Report 1880:15), and in the
following year, 1709, the sachem quit-claimed to the
Colony all former Niantic land except a 64 square
mile tract in what is now Charlestown, which the
tribe kept as its reservation. From the time of
the creation of this reservation the Colony's
legislature exercised complete control over the
tribe, although the hereditary sachem and council
continued to regulate many internal affairs until
late in the eighteenth century when the last hereditary sachem died. In 1713 the Colony passed an
act forbidding tribal leaders to sell reservation
lands and in 1718 passed an act to protect Indians
from being sued for debt, the wording of which indicates that the reservation community was be-
leagured by poverty, exploitation, and liquor (Laws
of the Colonial and State Governments 1832:54).

Despite their social and moral decline as perceived by English neighbors, the massive erosion of
their social and kinship institutions, and their
increasing involvement in the colonial economy as
servants and artisans, the Narragansett-Niantic
community maintained faith in their traditional
religious practitioners, known as pow-wows and continued to reject the religious symbols of the dominant culture. In 1713 the missionary Experience
Mayhew of Martha's Vineyard visited the reservation
and recorded in his journal this exchange with the
ruling sachem:

> On November the 3d . . . I returned
> to the Narragansett Country; and on the
> next day; having obtained two Interpre-
> ters, one English man, the other an Indi-
> an that had lived with an English master,

I treated with Ninnicraft the Sachim there,
about the affairs I went upon.

. . . He demanded of me why I did not
make the English good in the first place:
for he said many of them were still bad:
He also told me that he had seen Martha's
Vinyard Indians at Rhode Island, that
would steal, and these he said I should
first reform before I came to them. He
further objected that the English there at
Narragansett were divided, some keeping
Saturday, others Sunday, and others not
keeping any day; so that ye Indians could
not tell what religion to be of, if they
had a mind to be Christians (1896:110).

In 1738, another minister, Reverend John Callender of Newport, commented upon their resistance
to Christian teaching and exhibits then current
racial, cultural, and class assumptions:

After the war, they were soon reduced
to the condition of the laboring poor, without property, hewers of wood and drawers of
water; and there is no more reason to expect religion should, by human means, thrive
among such people, than among the lazy and
abandoned poor in London. The few that have
lived much together, on Ninigret's lands,
have had several offers of the gospel, as
the Narragansetts had before; and at present
the Congregational minister at Westerly is
a missionary to them, and encouraged by an
exhibition from the Scotch Society for propa-
gating Christian knowledge. . . . (1838:139).

Callender continued:

The strange destruction of this people
now since the wars ceased, and within mem-
ory, is very remarkable. Their insuperable
aversion to English industry, and way of
life, the alteration from the Indian method
of living, their laziness, and their uni-

39

versal love of strong drink, have swept them
away in a wonderful manner. So that there
are now (1738) above twenty English to one
Indian in the Colony (Ibid., 141).

The Congregational minister mentioned by Callender was Joseph Park who had been sent to Narragansett country in 1733 by the Commissioners of the
New England Society for the Propagation of the Gospel. The reservation community population was at
this time about 350 persons. Park preached to the
Narragansett for nine years without much effect until that remarkable surge of religious enthusiasm
known as the Great Awakening affected the English
colonies. Park recorded some details of the Narragansett conversion to Christianity in a series of
letters, from which the following passages derive:

> . . . the Power of GOD began to be most
> remarkable among <u>the Body of them</u> upon
> <u>Feb. 6, 1942, 3</u>. When upon the <u>Lord's Day</u>,
> a number of <u>Christian Indians</u> from <u>Stoning-</u>
> <u>ton</u> came to visit the <u>Indians</u> here: I went
> in the Evening after the publick Worship of
> God to meet them, and preach a <u>Lecture</u> to
> them.

> The LORD gave me to plead with him
> that his Kingdom might be seen coming with
> Power among the <u>Indians</u>. The <u>LORD</u> I trust
> began to answer even in the Time of <u>Prayer</u>.
> After which we sung an <u>Hymn</u>. The Glory of
> the LORD was manifested more and more. The
> <u>Enlightened</u> among them had a great Sense of
> spiritual and eternal Things: A SPIRIT of
> <u>Prayer</u> and Supplication was poured out upon
> <u>them</u>; and a SPIRIT of <u>Conviction</u> upon the
> <u>Enemies</u> of GOD.

> I attempted to preach from 2 Cor. 6.2,
> but was unable to continue my Discourse by
> reason of the <u>Outcry</u>. I therefore gave it
> up: And as I had Opportunity offered a Word
> of Exhortation, as the Lord enabled me. I

spent the Evening until late with them
(Prince 1744:208).

For the English, the Great Awakening represented a break from the reasoned preaching style and
orderly behavior of the congregation, to an emotional preaching style and ecstatic behavior on the
part of the congregation, such as shouting, crying,
and fainting. Accounts of the time indicate that
the enthusiasm transcended cultural and racial
boundaries and that Whites, Blacks, and Indians
participated in the revivals. For the English and
Puritan Indians it seemed to provide a renewal of
religious convictions. For the Narragansett, Pequot, Mohegan, and Montauk, most of whom had persisted until this time in shamanism, the Great
Awakening initiated a major cultural transformation.
Park wrote of the Narragansett: "They have for-
saken their _Dances_ and drunken Frolicks, appear
sober and serious, very diligently attend the preaching of the _Word_ of God and _Prayer_" (Ibid., 209).
With conversion they showed an increased interest
in coping with the heretofore devasting reality of
Euro-American domination through education and
moral reform:

> Their Faith and Hope in GOD encour-
> ageth and quickeneth them in Duty to ob-
> tain the Promises of the good Things of
> this Life, and of that which is to come.
> So that there is among them a Change for
> good respecting the _outward_ as well as the
> _inward_ Man. They grow more decent and
> cleanly in their outward Dress, provide
> better for their Households, and get
> clearer of debt (Prince 1945:26).

> Especially they have been kept per-
> fectly free, for ought that has appeared
> to me, from the Sin of Drunkenness, the
> Sin which so easily besets them. Many of
> them say that they have no Desire after
> strong Drink. . . They manifest great Sor-
> row of Heart, for their Brethren and Kins-

41

Men . . . ., when they hear of their drink-
ing and quarrelling. . .

Ever since the Lord has been gracious-
ly among the Indians manifesting his Power
and Glory; they have been desirous of a
School among them, that their Children and
all such as can, might learn to read (Ibid.,
27).

In the Great Awakening, which for a time held
some promise of dissolving social and racial boundaries, the Narragansett shed their tribal deities
and committed themselves to the boundless God of
Christian mythology. Through conversion they seem
to have gained some control over self-destructive
behavior and aspired, both symbolically and practically, to integrate more successfully within
colonial society.

For two years the Narragansett converts met
with Park's English congregation until in 1745 they
withdrew, apparently because White members disap-
proved of the Indian style of exhorting. In 1746
the Indians ordained a Narragansett minister over
themselves and shortly thereafter created the distinctly Narragansett Church, which one authority
described as, "of the Freewill Baptist order, with
a leaning toward Adventist views" which under a
succession of Indian ministers continues into the
present (love 1899:195). Thus, participation in
the rituals of Colonial society was followed by a
withdrawal into a sect, the beliefs and rituals for
which they recombined from local Protestant traditions, but the community of participants was exclu-
sively Indian. The Church grounds became the site
of what is known as the August Meeting, held once
each year on the second Sunday of that month. The
August Meeting was and continues to be an occasion
for dancing, games, feasting, and reunions with
friends and relatives, and persons from other northeastern tribes. According to Roger Williams, the
harvest ritual of the pre-conquest Narragansett
also involved dancing, feasting, and games, and was

attended by large numbers of people (1973:231).
The eighteenth century August Meeting seems to be
a continuation of that event.

An account written by the Reverend Joseph Fish
of Stonington, Connecticut, of his journey to Narragansett country in 1771, indicates that by that
time the zeal, asceticism, and aspirations of the
Awakening aftermath may have dissipated, and that
the Narragansett were committed to their minister,
Samuel Niles:

> I felt my self in a very low Frame
> much discouraged about this Indian Mis-
> sion, at seeing the Indians so generally
> despise their privileges -- Set no store
> at all by the blessed Institution of a
> preached Gospel. The Care that Christ
> takes of them in Sending Messages of
> Grace to them, and ordering the holy
> Scriptures to be read, is Slighted by
> almost all of them. They had rather fol-
> low That Ignorant, proud, conceited, ob-
> stinate Teacher, poor <u>Sam Niles</u>, than at-
> tend regular preaching of Sound Gospel
> Doctrine. Rather follow some their work,
> and then their pleasures, Idleness, Drun-
> kenness or any way of Serving the Devil
> and their Lusts, than to Spend an hour or
> two in hearing the precious Truths of the
> Gospel (Fish 1771:9).

Their decline in morals as described by Rever-
end Fish was cause for concern also to members of
the Indian community. In the years preceding the
American Revolution a movement began among the
Narragansett, Mohegan, and other Great Awakening
Indian converts, which was reminiscent of the
Puritan emigration to the wilderness of the New
World. Largely through the inspiration of the
Mohegan Indian minister Samson Occum, they made
plans to move west from New England to the less
densely settled lands of the Oneida Iroquois in
northern New York, where they intended to estab-
lish a Christian New England Indian town on the

Connecticut town government model. By this move they planned to unite the serious Christians into one community to be named Brothertown, discard the hereditary form of government which had functioned often at the expense of the tribe, remove themselves from the influences of immoral English and backsliding Indians, escape the relentless efforts of Whites to obtain their resources, and obtain better land than that which they then possessed. (For accounts of Narragansett land disputes in the eighteenth century see Arnold (1896) and Campbell and La Fantasie (1978).) The Oneida granted a large tract for this purpose in 1774, and added a purifying condition of their own: "With this particular clause or reservation that the same shall not be possessed by any persons deemed of the said Tribes who are descended from or have intermixed with negroes and mulattoes" (Love 1899:222). As the Puritans who emigrated to New England did so in part to convert the Indians there, so Samson Occum felt that the Iroquois needed the living example of a Christian Indian community for their betterment. They went in two moves, the first in 1775 and the second between 1783 and 1785. Many Narragansetts from the reservation participated but how many is difficult to determine. From Brothertown, New York they moved again in the 1830's for similar reasons to Brothertown, Wisconsin, where the community of Christian New England Indians finally came to rest. One can surmise that those who left were the most Christian of the least racially mixed, and that their exodus changed the racial and social milieu in the Tribal center. The story of those Narragansett who moved west is beyond the scope of this paper (see Commuck 1859).

By about 1780 the last hereditary sachem in Rhode Island died, and in keeping with post-Revolutionary democratic values, the Tribe began electing a Governor or President and council officers once each year. Indian-Black intermarriage required a formal definition of boundaries for voting membership in the Tribe. "An Act Regulating the Affairs of the Narragansett Tribe of Indians" passed in 1792, states that, "every male person of twenty-one years, born of an Indian woman belonging to said

44

tribe, or begotten by an Indian man belonging there-
to, of any other than a negro woman, shall be entitled to vote" (Report 1880:19).

The Narragansett language dropped out of use
after about 1825 and by the middle of the nineteenth century all members of the Tribe possessed
Black and White as well as Indian ancestry. The
State Commissioner of the Tribe described mid-nineteenth century reservation conditions:

> The general condition of the tribe at
> present, compared to what it was . . . has
> . . . improved . . . now, they are provided
> with comfortable dwellings, are well clad,
> and have proper supplies of food. If they
> have not, as a community, become more in-
> dustrious, they make better use of their
> earnings than formerly, when three fourths
> were spent for intoxicating liquors. The
> young men generally work out, by the month,
> on farms, . . . some few go to sea. There
> are but few members of the tribe who follow
> farming exclusively . . . Quite a number
> are masons, stone cutters, and wallers, and
> command good wages for their work (Report
> 1858:6).

Next, the State began efforts to abolish the
Tribe as a legal and political entity, and according to the report of a committee to the Rhode Island
General Assembly in 1867, the Tribe resisted these
efforts:

> A majority of the Indians, including
> the governing class, were evidently opposed
> to changing the existing relations to the
> State. They wished to be let alone in gov-
> erning themselves. They objected to being
> taxed, to being subject to the draft, and
> especially to being made liable to be sued.
> They professed to be indifferent to the
> privileges of citizenship and to set a low
> value thereon (Commission 1883:13).

45

Members of the Tribe expressed their reasons for continuing tribal relations on the reservation at the detribalization hearings in 1879. In their statements which are published _verbatim_ a number of Narragansett indicated that they preferred to live as a protected community on their ancestral property, that they resented being considered as drunks, liars, paupers, and thieves, and that they considered detribalization to be the final phase of dispossession by the White colonists. The speakers referred to themselves and were referred to alternately as Indians and "colored," and foresaw no advantage to being colored citizens. That racial mixing made them less Indian was denied by Daniel Sekater, a council member:

> We have now here a little mite of property that belongs to the Narragansett Indians, conveyed to them by their foreparents, and it belongs to them; and it does seem to me that they ought to have the handling of it as they see fit . . . Some argue that they ought to come out as citizens because they are mixed up with others. There are /Negroes/, it is true -- perhaps more /Negroes/ than anything else. But other classes are mixed up with other nations just as well. There is hardly one that can say, 'I am a clear-blooded Yankee' (Report 1880:38).

The council however agreed to quit-claim to the State all common, tribal, and vacant lands, except the site of the church, with its graveyard and August Meeting ground, and in 1880 the State passed, "An act to abolish the tribal authority and tribal relations of the Narragansett tribe of Indians," by which members acquired citizenship status, the Tribe as a legal body was dissolved, and the residential community broke up. The detribalization commission determined that 302 men, women, and children were entitled to a share of the sale of reservation lands.

Narragansett detribalization was one incident in a widespread national effort to encourage Indians to be property owning citizens rather than protected members of a tribe. This effort culminated in the passage of the General Allotment Act in 1887, the thrust of which was to grant citizenship, break up tribal governments, and encourage individualistic economic adaptations. That the Narragansett had ceased to exist in official minds is evident in the Rhode Island census for 1885 which lists 199 Indians in the State but lists none in Charlestown, because the Town Clerk of that town denied that the residents of the former reservation community were really Indian (Perry 1887:408-409).

Following detribalization the Narragansett never were again a physically bounded community, but persons who identified with the name continued to live in the vicinity of the former reservation and the Church and August Meeting persisted as the focus of shared values and kinship. United States Government Indian policy changed again in the 1920's and 1930's in the direction of greater respect toward Native American society and culture -- a direction which culminated in the Indian Reorganization Act of 1934. The Narragansett retribalized as a private corporation immediately following the passage of this act, and offered membership to all persons able to demonstrate lineal ties to members of the Tribe as defined at its dissolution in 1880. In 1935 and 1936 a number of Narragansett published a magazine Narragansett Dawn which contained articles on Tribal history, traditions, and folklore, and statements to remind readers that the Narragansett exist. The reconstituted Tribe through its elected officers encouraged attendance at the Church and sponsored a number of ceremonial events such as the Harvest Meeting, a Pilgrimage to the site of the 1675 Great Swamp defeat, and particularly the August Meeting (re-named the Narragansett Pow Wow) which has become a well-attended, money-making event. As the August Meeting became the publicity oriented Pow Wow the participants retained much that is traditional -- the place and timing of the event, the services in the nearby Church, and the

47

johnny cakes and clam chowder that are as Indian as they are Yankee in southern Rhode Island. The modern Pow Wow is becoming more markedly ethnic. Indian dances, either self-invented or adapted from those performed by other groups, Indian clothing such as Plains area headresses and beadwork, and names specifically introduced for this occasion, replaced the square dancing, conventional clothing, and mainly English names of earlier years. Recent participants are attempting to recreate seventeenth century clothing and implements as best these can be reconstructed from museum and ethnohistoric sources. The Pow Wow now is the most important public assertion, to the news media, the surrounding non-Indian community, and members of other Tribes who attend, and whose events they attend, that the Narragansett exist and that they are Indian. Participation in the Pow Wows of other northeastern groups such as the Long Island Shinnecock provides opportunities to extend this assertion to wider audiences and to establish a network of relationships with persons whose cultural and racial histories resemble their own. This identity is a source of recognition and pride to its adherents and it is the symbol of as well as the basis for a range of social commitments which unite them. Whether and to what extent it provides economic advantages over other non-Whites in their local communities is a question to be researched. Narragansett Indian is a local identity, however, which is confined mainly to the few rural communities where they live and to the northeastern Pow Wow circuit. Maintenance of this identity now involves an increased interest in cultural authenticity, and requires an increasingly deliberate denial of the history of inter-racial and inter-cultural synthesis which long has been taking place.

REFERENCES CITED

Arnold, James
   1896 A Statement of the Case of the Narragan-
       sett Tribe of Indians. Newport: Mercury
       Publishing Co.

Boissevain, Ethel Lesser
   1952 Narragansett Pow Wow - 1951. The Archeo-
       logical Society of New Jersey 5:12-14.
   1963 Detribalization and Group Identity: The
       Narragansett Indian Case. Transactions of
       the New York Academy of Sciences, Series II,
       25(5):493-502.
   1968 From Pagan to Protestant: A Case History
       and Comparative Analysis of Conversion in
       Colonial New England. New Jersey Academy of
       Science, The Bulletin 13(1):66-70.
   1975 The Narragansett People. Phoenix: Indian
       Tribal Series.

Boissevain, Ethel and Ralph Roberts
   1974 The Minutes and Ledgers of the Narragan-
       sett Tribe of Indians, 1850-1865, Man in the
       Northeast 7:3-28.

Callender, John
   1838 An Historical Discourse, on the Civil and
       Religious Affairs of the Colony of Rhode Is-
       land (1739). Collections of the Rhode Island
       Historical Society IV. Providence.

Campbell, Paul R. and Glenn W. La Fantasie
   1978 Scattered to the Winds of Heaven -- Narra-
       gansett Indians 1676-1880. Rhode Island His-
       tory 37:66-83.

Commission on the Affairs of the Narragansett Indians
   1883 Providence: E. L. Freeman and Co.

Commuck, Thomas
   1859 Sketch of the Brothertown Indians. Collec-
       tions of the State Historical Society of Wis-
       consin IV:291-298. (Reprinted by the Society,
       1906).

Easton, John
    1858 A Narrative of the Causes Which Led to
        Philip's Indian War on 1675 and 1676 (1676).
        Albany: J. Munsell.

Fish, Joseph
    1771 Eighth Book of Accounts, Indian Affairs,
        Narragansett. Manuscript in the Collections
        of the Connecticut Historical Society, Hart-
        ford.

Gookin, Daniel
    1854 Indian Children Put to Service 1676. New
        England Historical and Geneological Register
        VIII:270-273.

Hubbard, William
    1865 The History of the Indian Wars in New
        England from the First Settlement to the Ter-
        mination of the War with King Philip, in 1677.
        2 Vols. Samuel G. Drake, ed. Roxbury:
        W. Elliot Woodward. (Reprinted: Kraus, New
        York, 1969).

Laws of the Colonial and State Governments
    1832 Washington: Thompson and Homans.

Love, W. DeLoss
    1899 Samson Occum and the Christian Indians of
        New England. Boston: The Pilgrim Press.

Mather, Cotton
    1820 Magnalia Christi Americana . . . (1702).
        2 Vols. Hartford: Silas Andrus.

Mayhew, Experience
    1896 A Brief Journal of My Visitation of the
        Pequot and Mohegan Indians . . . 1713. In
        Some Correspondence Between the Governors and
        Treasurers of the New England Company in Lon-
        don and the Commissioners of the United Colo-
        nies in America . . . to Which are added the
        Journals of the Rev. Experience Mayhew in
        1713 and 1714. London: Spottiswoode.

Narragansett Dawn
  1935-1936 Princess Redwing, ed. Oakland, R. I.

Perry, Ames
  1887 Rhode Island State Census, 1885. Provi-
    dence, R. I.: E. L. Freeman & Son.

Prince, Thomas
  1744 The Christian History . . . For the Year
    1743. Boston: S. Kneeland and T. Green.
  1745 The Christian History . . . For the Year
    1744. Boston: S. Kneeland and T. Green.

Report of the Commissioner on the Narragansett Tribe
  of Indians
  1858 Providence: Knowles, Anthony, & Co.

Report of the Committee of Investigation
  1880 Narragansett Tribe of Indians. Providence:
    E. L. Freeman & Co.

Report of the Commission on the Affairs of the Narragansett Indians
  1881 Providence: E. L. Freeman & Co.

Sainsbury, John
  1975 Indian Labor in Early Rhode Island. The
    New England Quarterly 48:378-393.

Simmons, William
  1978 Narragansett. In Handbook of North American
    Indians: Northeast, XV. William Sturtevant,
    series, ed., Bruce Trigger, vol. ed. pp. 190-
    197. Washington: Smithsonian Institution.

Simmons, William and George Aubin
  1975 Narragansett Kinship. Man in the Northeast.
    9:21-31.

Staples, William
  1843 Annals of the Town of Providence. Provi-
    dence: Knowles and Vose.

Taylor, T. W.
    1972   The States and Their Indian Citizens.
        Washington: U. S. Government Printing Office.

Williams, Roger
    1881   Christenings Make Not Christians (1845).
        Providence: Sidney S. Rider.

Williams, Roger
    1973   A Key Into the Language of America /1643/.
        J. J. Teunissen and Evelyn J. Hinz, ed.
        Detroit: Wayne State University.

Wroth, Lawrence C.
    1970   The Voyages of Giovanni da Verrazzano
        1524-1528.   New Haven: Yale University Press.

MOHEGANS AND SCATACOOKS:
Minority Indian Groups in Connecticut

Ethel Boissevain

The purpose of this chapter is two-fold.
First, my intention is to document the colonial
period emergence of these two groups as tribes in
the written records and to delineate their histories, again as revealed by written records. This
will be prefaced by a short description of the
lifeways of the Indians before the white man came
and followed by a short description of their lifeways in the late 1970's into the 1980's.

Secondly, my purpose is to demonstrate that
Indian tribal life is not and has not been as sta-
tic as various records and tribal lists would have
us believe. Indeed, the post-colonial and contemporary accounts of these tribes reveal a dyna-
mism that has enabled them to adapt themselves and
accommodate their lives without sacrificing Indian
identity to the ever-increasing and dominating white
man. It must not be forgotten, though, that the
present status was achieved through conflict, hard-
ship, privation and poverty. Also, the present
group status is so unsatisfactory for the Scatacooks that they are working toward an improved relationship with the state of Connecticut, as will
be discussed later. (The name Scatacook is spelled
variously in the literature as Scatticook, Shagti-
coke and Schaghticoke, or other).

The Indians of New England are most obviously a
numerical minority and in Connecticut where the two
tribes in question have always lived we find that:
of over three million people there were 2,222 Indians in Connecticut, which is .07% in 1972. The
state maintains four reservations which together
include 804 acres (Taylor 1972:176). In descending
order this acreage includes 400 acres for the Scati-
cook reservation with no residents, 220 acres for
the Eastern Pequot reservation, with 11 residents,
184 for the Western Pequot reservation with two

residents, and "one lot" for the Golden Hill reservation, near Trumbull, with two residents in 1972 (Taylor 1972:226). The Mohegans are considered a community of 150 people in New London County, Connecticut (Taylor 1972:228).

It is a common belief that the Indian communities of today and those mentioned in colonial reports existed in pre-colonial times and also enjoyed a very ancient existence. However, both the Scatacooks and Mohegans came into being as tribes after the colonists had been in New England for some years.

To begin with, we must look into the question of what is a "tribe." The term comes to us through the Latin "tribus" which was applied by the Romans to Germanic groups. It was applied to Indian groups by the European colonists with the expectation of certain internal leadership and an accepted spokesman. Further research has shown that Indian groups on which the term "tribe" was imposed did not always have the expected qualities, including central authority, but the term tribe became imbedded in the writings.

This demands a working definition of "tribe" and I will attempt one for post contact-colonial times in New England: a group of people who share a common language, share a common territory (which may have subdivisions) over which there is a recognized (by colonists) leader or spokesman. This is indeed vague and this is the problem. Recent ethnological theorists (Julian Steward, Elman Service et al) have drawn up specific differences between bands, tribes and chiefdoms.

Accepting their arguments, much of southern New England was occupied by bands, while southeastern New England but for outer Cape Cod was occupied by chiefdoms. We must remember that any group to which a name could be applied was called a tribe by the colonists. Thus, the Niantics, Massachusetts, Narragansetts, Wampanoags and Pequots were called tribes.

According to 20th century ethnologists a band
is a small group with weak or no leadership that
occupies contiguous territory. There are certain
expected social regulations concerning marriage and
family obligations. They were hunters and gather-
ers of wild animals and plants. Socially and economically they were egalitarian in position and
material wealth. There is good reason to believe
that many of the "tribes" of Connecticut, especially western, were of this order of socio-economic
lifeway.

We can jump from this style of socio-economi-
cal life to the chiefdoms of southeastern New England. Here have been found (Speck 1928b:11-18,
based on colonial writers) Indian communities in
which a certain person, the chief, or "king" according to some colonial writers, had some autocratic power. It was one of these who "received"
colonial governors. They always seemed to display
authority and power. According to these arguments,
the chiefdoms of southeastern New England were the
Wampanoag, Massachusetts, Narragansetts, Niantics
and Pequots.

A certain amount of inequality among the members of a chiefdom was recorded by the colonists
(Gookin 1674(1):141, 154 and Mayhew quoted in Banks
1911:38-39, Williams 1643:120-122). The chief had
the right to exact tribute (mostly in food stuffs)
from lower chiefs (Speck 1928:18) and assumed the
duty of providing for widows, orphans and physically injured members of his tribe (Governor Edward
Winslow of Plymouth Colony as quoted by Nathanael
Morton 1803:489).

But there is a question as to what extent the
chiefs' assertions or commands were obeyed. For
example, such a chief could not expect to be obeyed
or followed into battle by all his tribesmen; certain subchiefs could refuse to fight with him
(Speck 1928b:18).

The following pages will contend that the Mohegan tribe of Connecticut was an offshoot of the

Pequots who were a chiefdom. (They should not be confused with the Mahicans to their north and west.)

In the 1630's, among these near-autocratic chiefs was Sassicus, the chief of the Pequots of the area of Groton, Connecticut, son of Wokigwooit, His sister married Uncas, son of Oweneco, the "Mohegan Pequot" (Peale 1939:50). There is a question as to what Mohegan-Pequot meant to the Indians at that historical period. There are speculations concerning how independent the Mohegans were from the Pequots. One speculation is that they were a clan group, with the appelation Mohegan which means "wolf." This should not be construed as totemism since there is no record of this practice in southern New England. One thing is certain: according to Frank Speck and J. D. Prince, the Pequot and Mohegan languages are identical and should be referred to as Pequot-Mohegan (Speck 1928a:207).

The socio-political implication of the language unity is important in that it means a closeness if not a total cultural and "tribal" oneness of the two groups. A glance at the map of tribes and dialects of the eastern Algonquian language made by Swanton and Michelson in 1913 reveals that tribal groups in very close geographic proximity spoke different dialects and Mohegan and Pequot were linked as one, the Y dialect (Swanton, J. and Truman Michelson, the 28th Annual Report, Bureau of American Ethnology, Washington, D. C., 1913).

This linguistic closeness is important in the following thesis. It has become apparent that the Mohegan tribe had no separate identity prior to 1640 (Speck 1909:184). This seems to be the sequence of events that led to the origin of the Mohegans as a tribal entity:

In 1637 the Pequots were attacked by the English with the aid of Narragansetts and some other Indian groups. The reasons on the part of the English for this attack were to destroy their power since they had been interfering with the English and Dutch trade. The important thing is that the

English attack on the Pequot fortified village near present New London has become a notorious massacre. The English and their Indian allies attacked at or before dawn, threw firebrands into the very flammable village with its wooden palisade and thus caused the burning to death of an unknown number of Pequots. Estimates run into the hundreds (Mason 1826:141). Although we will never know actually how many men, women and children were killed in that brief attack, the strength of the Pequot tribe (or chiefdom) was from then on broken. There were a few survivors who fled westward and we will hear more about them in the part of this paper about the Scaticooks.

Probably somewhat before this massacre of Pequots, Tatabam, daughter of Pequot chief, Wopigwooit, and sister of his son Sassicus, married Uncas, the son of Oweneco, known as a Mohegan-Pequot. Thus the Pequot chief was the brother-in-law of Uncas (Peale 1939:50).

There are no written details, but it looks as though the Mohegan-Pequots with Uncas as a leader took advantage of the devastation of the Pequots proper and established themselves near present Norwich, Connecticut a few miles north of the Pequot "capital," which was in or near present Groton,

From then on the Mohegan's policy seems to have been to side with the English in Colonial-Indian wars, and to consider themselves and be considered as a separate tribal entity by the colonists. This became a new tribe born from the pressures and devastations of the presence of Europeans in southern New England.

A famous example of the Mohegans' siding with the English occurred in 1643 in a warring dispute between them and the Narragansetts. The Mohegans were aided by the English. Miantonomi, the nephew and co-chief of the Narragansetts' elder chief Canonicus was captured in Mohegan controlled territory near the Connecticut River. The English wanted to do away with him. Evidently the Mohegans

provided for his execution. This was, to us, a
bizarre method of "rubbing out" a person. The Narragansett co-chief, Miantonomi, was being marched
back eastward to his home territory when suddenly
his head was cracked by a tomahawk from behind. An
anthropological question is whether this was a culturally accepted method of execution or whether it
was a special ruse of the moment (Chapin 1931:49).

Further, in the famous Great Swamp Fight in
Narragansett territory in 1675 some Mohegans, number unknown, fought on the side of the English
(deForest 1851:281-282 paraphrasing Hubbard, 1865:
112-121.).

Despite or maybe because of the initial Mohegans' siding with the English colonists, they as
well as other southern New England Indians constantly lost land. Uncas and his successors, whose
names were European first names with Uncas as a
surname (the same was done by the Niantic-Narragan-
setts using Ninigret as a surname) sold land to the
English continuously.

The political and land sale affairs of the Mohegans in the 17th and early 18th centuries is complex and very involved with the rivalry of the
English and Dutch colonists and traders. As in
the case of other Indian tribes, the Indians deeded
large tracts of land for cloth and manufactured
clothing and trinkets. These transactions are sum-
marized in Arthur L. Peale's "Uncas and the Mohegan-Pequot," 1939 and in John W. deForest's "History of the Indians of Connecticut," 1851. Their
data in turn is taken from original colonial papers
and documents.

Uncas and his hereditary successors seem con-
tinually to have made exchanges that were disas-
trous to the tribe to the point that in the 18th
century the Mohegans were a poor and depressed
minority. They owned too little land to be prosperous farmers and they were untrained in well-paid
skills. In 1769 Ben Uncas the sachem died and no
successor agreeable to the Indians and colonists

could be found. From then on the tribe was directly under the colony.

Since Uncas and his heirs made such disadvan-
tageous sales to the English throughout the 17th
century we may ponder: were they really so naive
for so long or were they ever trying to curry the
favor of the English? The Mohegan chiefs seem to
have adopted the pattern of behavior of the surrounding older chiefdoms whereby the chief made the
sales with little or no evidence (in the records at
least) of consultation with the tribal members.
(cf Speck 1928b:16-28). The colonial governments
took sides chiefly in succession-disputes to their
advantage and it is possible that the chiefs believed that they would gain advantages by complying
with the wishes of the colonial governors who
seemed stronger at the moment.

During these years and later the Mohegans,
like other Indian groups in southeastern New England, became increasingly acculturated to European
living habits, notably in use of firearms, clothing,
and house types. By about 1850 the wigwam had been
superseded by the frame house. The Pequot-Mohegan
language also slowly went into dis-use but it and a
few crafts survived into the 20th century in a
small measure (Speck 1904 and 1928a).

To go back to other general trends and important events in Mohegan conversion to Christianity
and this necessarily brings us to the life of one
of their most famous members, Samson Occum. Indian
resistance to Christian preachers was very strong
in the 17th and early 18th centuries. This was, no
doubt, in part due to general ideological antipathy
which is expressed in the writings of Reverend
Experience Mayhew in his itineraries of trips to
Pequot and Mohegan country in 1713 and 1714 as a
missionary (Mayhew 1896:98-126). This was also due
in part, especially in Mohegan territory, to the
fear on the part of the chief that if the Indians
agreed to the preachings that they would not pay
tribute to the chief (Drake 1851:177).

Some Indians in southern New England who had
become servants of the whites complained that if
they attended Christian services their masters
would send constables after them (Mayhew 1896:110).
This of course led Mayhew to exhort the whites to
teach their Indian servants more about Christianity. His contacts with Indians in 1713 and 1714
were failures as far as arousing enthusiasm about
being converted to Christianity goes but practically a bargain was struck: that the adults would
hear the preachers if schools for the children were
instituted, which the Indians wished (Mayhew 1896:
126).

An especially important individual in the conversion of the Mohegans and of other Indians was
Samson Occom, born in the town of Mohegan in 1723.
He has become one of the most famous of New England
Indians because of his gigantic endeavors and
successes in the achievements of his goals. He
did, however, suffer from reversals, defeats and
exploitations. His parents were non-literate and
spoke only Pequot-Mohegan, but he was attracted to
European mores and religion. For this interest and
craving he found his way to Eleazor Wheelock's
School.

This school itself had modest beginnings.
Eleazor Wheelock was "settled over" a church in a
part of present Lebanon, Connecticut and taught
English and classics to "several young men." Into
this company Samson Occom was accepted. He lived
in his own wigwam in the precinct of the school and
received instruction. He must have been brilliant,
certainly in language learning, since he acquired
Latin, Greek, and some Hebrew, not to mention English which itself was a second language to him.
After some years of missionizing among the Montauks of eastern Long Island, one of the many societies for the Propagation of the Gospel sent him to
England to preach and thereby raise money for the
movement to teach Christianity to Indians. This he
did with tremendous success. He was astonishingly
well-received in England and Scotland by audiences
during the years 1765-1768 as well as by the English

king, nobility and especially the Earl of Dartmouth.

Despite his practical glorification in England and Scotland, he came home to Mohegan territory to face severe disappointments. Some of these were within the family but more important for the purpose of this paper was his chagrin that the Wheelock School for Indians was to be moved to New Hampshire. There it took the name of Dartmouth College due to the financial contributions of the Earl of Dartmouth. But as Occum had pointed out, there were few Indians living in that region and so very few would be benefited. (The summary above is taken mostly from W. de Loss Love, "Samson Occom and the Christian Indians of New England," Boston: Pilgrim Press, 1899).

It is tempting to expand on the life of Samson Occom as a person. How he reflects the changing lifeways of the Mohegan Indians is the subject that is really pertinent to this paper. He certainly was influential in persuasion by his preachings and his habits to bring about change of Indian lifeways to the English style. The same may be said of his influence in the adoption of Christianity by the southern New England Indians and the Oneidas of present New York State. He suffered from the latent lack of trust in an Indian on the part of his white superiors both before and after his trip to England and Scotland. For example, a white man accompanied him on his trip to the British Isles. Although he was entusiastically acclaimed by the English and Scottish and collected surprisingly high sums of money for Wheelock's School for Indians, $60,000, little of it ever benefited Indians.

A very important contribution to Indian life on the part of Samson Occom was the emigration of several Mohegans, Narragansetts and Montauks in 1775. It is unknown whether he organized this migration out of New England because of the rebuffs he received from the white clergy superiors or because the population pressure was so severe that his course was the only logical way out of an in-

61

tolerable situation. Their destination was land within the Oneida's control in present New York State.

On their way they encountered the American Revolution and were harrassed and finally retreated eastward to Stockbridge, Massachusetts. After the war years they, with others, returned to Oneida and founded the community, Brotherton. Their model of town government was the Connecticut Town Plan. Here Samson Occom died in 1792. (The summary above is based on Love. This biography includes enriching data on Indian mores of Mohegans and other Indian communities in southern New England. It is sympathetic to Samson Occom as a person but does exhibit some "white man superiority" sentiments concerning Indians in general, not unusual for its time, published in 1899.)

Although the controversial issues of the American Revolution affected the Indian tribes of New England little or not at all, an unknown number of Indians did volunteer to join the armed forces of the colonists. The deaths of some of them, though absolutely few, certainly added to the temporary decline of the strength of southern New England tribes.

Likewise, Occom's emigration to Oneida country and the subsequent emigration to Wisconsin was a drain on the vigor of the Indians of the regions from which they came.

Thus Samson Occom was an influential person in at least three ways: as a famous preacher in England and Scotland he made the Mohegans and Indians in general known and appreciated by the outer world; he converted, or was close to doing this, Indians of southwestern Connecticut which led to further acceptance of the Indians on the part of the dominant majority of whites, and, lastly, he organized and led a group from southern New England to New York state, where he died. The out-migration certainly had immediate beneficial results for his followers in gaining their livings. But a broader and longer termed beneficial result to the Indians was a step in the direction of pantribalism, the attitude of brotherhood among all Indians and a unity that supersedes former inter-tribal animosities. If only this thinking had been prevalent in New England in the 17th century, the demise of the Indians might not have occurred or certainly would not have been so rapid and thorough.

Coming to the 20th century, the research and time spent by Frank G. Speck among the Mohegans in the early years of the 1900's, published in 1903, 1904, 1909, and 1928 has yielded invaluable insights and data, large and trivial, concerning the turn-of-the-century affairs of the Mohegans.

From these papers, as well as from a few other sources, we glean the following information.

The Mohegans never had a real reservation, although de Forest uses the word "reservation" and there were colonial overseers (de Forest 1851:471-473). Yet they have maintained a concentrated population around Montville, Connecticut, a few miles north of Norwich. They formed a Mohegan Indian Association at Mohegan, Connecticut in 1920 "to preserve the integrity of the tribe and for social and legal aims" with 49 Mohegans enrolled (Speck 1928b:213). In a compendium on State Indian reservations and communities they are listed as Mohegan Community in New London County, Connecticut with 150 as population (Taylor 1972:228).

That they are integrated into the large community there is no doubt. The interesting question is their maintenance of identity and how this is achieved. For one thing, there is the close proximity of residence of the 150 people who are probably relatives, but this is hardly enough to maintain a tribal identity. An important focus is the Congregational Church at Montville, Connecticut in a central location of the Mohegans' residences. This was built in 1831 as the result of prodigious efforts on the part of certain Englishwomen who taught the Indians and petitioned the legislature and

63

missionary societies for money for the building and for the salary for a permanent preacher (de Forest 1851:480-485). It is at present attended and administered by whites as well as Indians.

The Mohegans have eschewed such pan-Indian activities as holding a Pow Wow, increasingly prevalent in New England since the 1920's among tribal groups and pan-tribal associations. They have, however, had a September harvest festival that is not particularly Indian in flavor in front of their church at Montville.

To fill in the thinking of the Mohegans in the very early 20th century, we refer to the 1928 paper by Frank Speck, describing and discussing a recently found diary of Fidelia Fielding, a Mohegan who died in 1908 (Speck 1928: 205-258). She may have been the very last of the Mohegan language speakers. The diary consists largely of trivia of weather and animals seen and then sometimes refers to religion and other thoughts concerning the supernatural. Mrs. Fielding was Christianized but still related to the aboriginal Indian beliefs.

More broadly, it reveals at least three important things: that in the very early years of the 20th century or shortly earlier the Mohegan language was alive enough for someone to write it, although she may not have had anyone left with whom to converse; that such a person had enough formal education in the European sense to write using the English alphabet; that although living alone, she was watched over and aided by relatives in respect to food and fuel getting and social diversions. The diary manuscript was given to the Heye Foundation (Peale 1930:47).

Probably the Mohegans were at their lowest ebb around mid-18th century. By then they had sold too much land to the English to live as aboriginally or by farming, and yet they had not yet become well enough educated in English skills and lifeways to earn comfortable livings.

I find that the early Mohegan siding with the English from the 1600's became a traditional pattern of behavior in later centuries. It is reflected in some of the choices that Samson Occom made and in the present eschewing of Indian "nativistic" behavior in the form of Pow Wows. Also the Mohegans are not the exclusive managers of the Protestant church in their community.

There is a museum in Montville, near the church, which holds the collection of and is cared for by sister and brother Gladys and John Tantiguidgeon. They are descendants of a Mohegan family that is named in 18th century documents. Gladys Tantiguidgeon has written a number of articles on Indian beliefs and ideologies concerning weather lore, medicinal practices and Indian folklore in general.

For all their being a poor minority in the 18th and 19th centuries, attention is quickly drawn to the tribe and its hereditary chiefs in a Royal Burial Ground in Norwich, Connecticut. There is a granite obelisk on which "Uncas" is engarved. This was erected in 1840; before, in 1833, President Andrew Jackson came to the area and laid the foundation for it. Nearby are inscribed stones with dates of the 18th century hereditary chiefs, descendants of Uncas (Peale 1930:8-9). To add to the adulation of Uncas, Buffalo Bill (William Cody) and at least two Sioux chiefs visited this memorial to Uncas on July 2, 1907. They circled the grave on horseback, sang a war chant, placed a wreath and sounded taps (Peale 1930:27). The cutting and erection of the memorial stones must have been a considerable expense. Certainly the Indians themselves could not have afforded it at that time. Why the citizens of the Norwich areas went to this trouble and expense to memorialize the 18th century chiefs of the Indians tribe who sold land to their ancestors at proverbially ridiculously low prices can only be surmised. One assumption is that it was a romantic gesture to express gratitude to the Mohegans who had aided the colonists against other Indians who had been enemies. Why otherwise would

65

Andrew Jackson, who signed the bill to expell the Cherokees from their homeland in the Carolinas and Georgia ever visit and lay a foundation stone for an Indian memorial?

Now we must shift attention to western Connecticut to investigate the history of another present day tribe that owes its existence in part to the Pequot massacre of 1637. It, like the Mohegans, was not a tribe with a name before the 17th century. This is the present Scatticook, or Schagticoke tribe, with spelling variations, whose reservation is in western Connecticut near present Kent and the border of New York State but whose members now reside throughout Connecticut and Massachusetts as well as in various other states. In contrast to the Mohegans, they are a tribe with a reservation of 400 acres (Taylor:226) but with very few tribal residents on it. As of early March, 1981 however, there are three Indian occupied homes and a tribal office. The office and homes are said to be nice looking clapboard (Personal communication from State House, Hartford, Connecticut, March 10, 1981).

Unlike the chiefdoms of the southeastern coastal area of New England, the Indian communities west of the Connecticut and especially along the Housatonic River were small and loosely organized groups. In present anthropological terminology they would be called bands. It seems to have been the colonists, Dutch and English, who gave the groups tribal names and even introduced the term for them: "Wappanger Confederacy." This group of bands was no confederacy in the sense of groups willing to join in wars against a common enemy.

Rather, Waban, Wapan or Wa means in eastern Algonquian languages: light, or white and refers to light from the east, hence from the east where the first light of days comes from. Hence, Wampanoag: eastern Indians, or, so Wappanger confederacy means a group of tribes or bands on the east -- Inger is a Dutch plural ending: so Wappanger means something like people from the east,

66

meaning east of their contact base with Dutch speaking settlements along the Hudson River (Smith, de cost 1948:36).

The language in this Housatonic area was phonetically closer to the Munsees of the Delawares and Hudson River Algonkians, then to the Pequot-Mohegan dialect of Algonkian (Loskiel 1794: 19). However, it was not different enough from the Algonkian of the Pequot-Mohegan variety for mutual understanding.

Most of our knowledge of the early history of this area is derived from the writings of the Moravian missionary, George Henry Loskeil, published in English in 1794 as well as from John de Forest's "History of the Indians of Connecticut," 1851, who based his history on Connecticut's Indian Papers and local town records.

There seems to have been a community by the name of Pachgatgoch, one of several, on the west side of the Housatonic River a few miles east of the New York - Connecticut border near present Kent, Connecticut. Into its original population came an unknown number of Pequots and possibly other Indians retreating westward before the advancing whites, especially the punitive forces following the Pequot village massacre at Groton, Connecticut, of 1637. There is a romantic account of how a Pequot chief, Mauwehw, from the southern Housatonic area saw from a mountain top a large area uninhabited and invited various Indians to join him in this undisturbed land (de Forest 1851: 407-409, paraphasing a missionary, Jonathan Barber).

Probably it is more realistic to assume that migrating Pequots and other Indians were accepted into the area by native Indians. An interesting question is whether the Pequots, used to chiefly authority, instituted more organized socio-political life. De Forest believes that the name Mauwehw was probably Indianized Mayhew (But why?) and that this man became chief of a settlement later known

67

as Scatacook (deForest 1851:409).

This missionaries' accounts of Pachgatgoch, one of the settlements in the Scatacook area, begin in 1740. According to Loskiel, a young and venturesome German Brother of the United Brethren among the Indians of North America, Christian Rauch, found his way from New York City to an Indian community by the name of Shekomeko, a few miles north east of Poughkeepsie, New York, also near Kent, Connecticut. Here, after his share of vicissitudes, he began to gain converts (Loskiel II 1794: 10-14).

He was soon joined by other Moravian missionaries, some with their wives. These missionaries housed themselves, dressed and ate in the Indian style and also worked for the Indians for small payment (Loskiel II 1794:37). In 1743 some Indians from Pachgatgoch walked from their town 20 miles to Shekomeko to hear the Brothers preach, while the missionaries themselves walked from one Indian settlement to another. Finally the Pachgatgoch group received a missionary of their own who with his wife were housed "in the abode of the captain of the town" (Loskiel II 1794:38).

We must not believe that the missionaries' efforts were all crowned with success. Many Indians hated and ridiculed them. Also a number of the white settlers hated them because they were bringing about temperance which led to Indian caution in making land sales. Some Indians from the vicinity of Freehold reported that they were offered rum if they would kill Brother Christian Rauch (Loskiel II 1794:37, 51).

This peaceful relationship might have lasted for years but for the white settlers' desire to rid the area of the Moravians. For one thing they wanted the Brethren to swear allegiance to King George of England. The Brethren were pacifists and would not serve in the militia nor actually take any oath. When brought to trial in Rhinebeck, New York the leader of the Brethren favorably impressed the justice and the court, was acquitted and given a certificate to prevent their injury from the mobs that gathered (Loskiel II 1794:59-62). Still the white settlers wanted to rid their area of the Brethren and passed acts in the Assembly in 1744 that prohibited the Brethren from instructing the Indians and demanded that all suspicious persons take an oath of allegiance or be expelled (Loskiel II 1794:63). Of course, the missionaries were suspected persons because they would not take oaths so they and some of their Indian converts left western Connecticut and nearby New York on a trek for resettlement in Bethlehem, Pennsylvania where land was provided by the Moravians there.

By 1749 these strong feelings seem to have died down and Brethren again visited Pachgatgoch and other Housatonic Indian settlements. In Pachgatgoch a school house was built and in 1754 the missionaries reported over 100 in their congregation.

In 1755 the Indians were again under suspicion on the part of the white settlers. This time some of the whites believed that the Brethren and their Indian followers were in league with the French in the French and Indian War. In 1759 recruiting parties took young Indian converts from the Moravian mission towns and the Pachgatgoch became dispersed during the war (Loskiel II 1794: 192, 230).

During these years of the mid-18th century, land transactions in the form of rentals or sales to individual colonists went on with the Indians constantly the losers. Besides the legal transactions there were encroachments and trespasses. When petitioned for land in 1752, the Connecticut Assembly granted the Indians, called Scatacook in these transactions, 200 acres to use and farm but to remain in the possession of the Colony (deForest 1851:415). Earlier, 2000 acres were reserved for them "in the mountains" (deForest 1851:413). Finally, a white man overseer of the Scatacook tribe as appointed by the Colony in 1757 but he and

69

his successors seem to have done them little if any good. Petitions on the part of the Indians were reviewed by committees but as in the case of 1786, the reports were most unsympathetic toward the Indians of the Scatacook area who then numbered fewer than 75 (deForest 1851:415-418). The committee even refused a school for the 20 children of school age because of the small number of them and because they were "kept in such a wild savage way" (deForest 1851:418, quoting from Connecticut Colonial Records, Vol. XII).

From 1800 to 1850 further land was sold, some of it to defray the expenses of the remnants of the tribe, about 50 in 1849. It was around 1800 that the tribe was in its worst condition of poverty and despair. Some of those who could, moved away. Their then 2000 acre reservation "in the mountains" was mostly uncultivatable and of use almost only for hunting and firewood. In 1938 there were four families on it amounting to 14 individuals (Cornwall 1939: no page number). Anecdotes gleaned in 1938 reveal a somewhat migratory life of fishing expeditions for some, coupled with a subsistence of farming or gardening for others (Cornwall 1939: no page). In 1972 there were no residents (Taylor 1972:226) but in March 1981, three Indians occupied homes and an office are located on the reservation (personal communication, March, 1981).

Although loss of useful land, early deaths and out-migration nearly destroyed the Indian culture and reduced the population drastically, the tradition of being a Scatacook is definitely alive among descendants. Their number is unknown because of residence in different parts of New England where they are employed in various occupations. At Pow Wows throughout New England, though, Indians identify themselves as Scatacooks.

In the 1970's a great effort was made to strengthen this identity. A Schaghticoke Tribe was incorporated in the early 1970's and held a Pow Wow in Randolph, Massachusetts, the home city of one of the prime movers of the tribal incorporation, Princess Necia Hopkins. Indians of various New England tribes participate. One of their main objectives is to make an Indian Culture Center of the reservation. They are uneasy about its being unoccupied by Indians and especially by the State's permission to non-Indian people to erect trailers and mobile homes in the tract (personal communication from Princess Necia Hopkins).

Returning to the opening remarks of this paper, we can see that the few descendants of these tribes have adjusted in different ways to the devastating effects of the Europeans in Connecticut. Yet their will to maintain Indian identity has never been lost and has expressed itself in different ways.

The Mohegans have their church (shared by whites), the graveyard in Norwich with its granite memorials to hereditary chiefs, and the Indian Museum of the Tantaquidgeons -- but no reservation land. The Scatacooks are more dispersed, have no large stone memorials, but still have their reservation.

Numerically both groups are very much of a minority, as stated earlier in 1972 all Indians of Connecticut totalled about 2,200 (Taylor:176), but thanks to a romantic interest in Indians in the mid-19th and especially the 20th centuries they are not as unknown or hidden as they might be.

The Royal Cemetery in Norwich with the imposing obelisk to Uncas, other stones to subsequent Uncases, and more recently the Tantaquidgeon Indian museum are all attention attracting and interesting evidences of Mohegan life. In the nearby State Park are remains of Fort Shantok from which the Mohegans, aided by the English, fought off the Narragansetts in 1643. These memorials have all been erected and cared for at state or private white man group expense. For example, a stone to one of the last contenders to the chiefdomship was erected by the Boy Scouts of America. There are also a few remains of the Wheelock Indian School and the Bible

71

used by Samson Occom is proudly owned by the Daughters of the American Revolution of Norwich, Connecticut.

The Scatacooks, as pointed out earlier, did not have the "glamor" of the early Mohegans, with their autocratic hereditary chiefs, nor did they have a Samson Occom. However, they participated in Pow Wows wearing Indian regalia and hold a Pow Wow of their own, in Massachusetts. Again, as a small minority, they are making themselves visible and are occupying their reservation in a small way in 1981 which may increase over the years.

Both of these tribal groups stem from the 17th century, yet both in their own way have adapted to the dominant whites. It is not a finished story, especially for the Scatacooks.

REFERENCES CITED

Chapin, Howard M.
   1931   Sachems of the Narragansetts. Providence,
      Rhode Island: Rhode Island Historical Society.

Cornwell, M. E.
   1939. The Schaghticokes, Descendants from our
      First Americans. Kent, Connecticut: In-Kent
      Associates.

deForest, John W.
   1851   History of the Indians of Connecticut from
      the Earliest Known Period to 1850. Hartford:
      W. J. Hammersley.

Hopkins, Necia
   Personal communications.

Hubbard, William
   1815   A General History of New England. In Massa-
      chusetts Historical Society Collections, 2nd
      Series, V-VI.

Loskiel, George Henry
   1794   History of the Mission of the United Breth-
      ren Among the Indians of North America. Part
      II. Printed for the Brethren's Society for
      the Furtherance of the Gospel. London, England.

Love, William de Loss
   1899   Samson Occom and the Christian Indians of
      New England. Boston: The Pilgrim Press.

Mason, John
   1826   A Brief History of the Pequot War. In
      Massachusetts Historical Society Collections,
      2nd Series, VIII.

Mayhew, Experience
   1896   Journals 1713, 1714. In Some Correspon-
      dence Between the Governors and Treasurers of
      the New England Company in London and the Com-
      missioners of the United Colonies in America.
      London: Spotteswoods & Co.

73

Peale, Arthur L.
1930 Memorials and Pilgrimages in the Mohegan
Country. Norwich, Connecticut: The Bulletin
Co.
1939 Uncas and the Mohegan-Pequot. Boston:
Meandor Publishing Co.

Smith, de Cost
1948 Martyrs of the Oblong and Little Nine.
Caldwell, Idaho: Caxton Printers.

Speck, Frank G.
1904 A Modern Mohegan-Pequot Text. American
Anthropologist, Vol. 6, No. 4.
1909 Notes on the Mohegan and Niantic Indians.
Anthropological Papers, American Museum of
Natural History.
1928a Native Tribes and Dialects of Connecticut:
A Mohegan-Pequot Diary. American Bureau of
Ethnology, Annual Report, Vol. 43.
1928b Territorial Subdivisions and Boundaries
of the Wampanoag, Massachusetts and Nauset
Indians. Indian Notes and Monographs, Museum
of the American Indian, Heye Foundation, No.
41-48.

Swanton, J. and Truman Michelson
1913 Bureau of American Ethnology, 28th Annual
Report. Washington, D. C.

Taylor, T. W.
1972 The States and Their Indian Citizens.
United States Department of the Interior,
Bureau of Indian Affairs. Washington, D. C.:
Government Printing Office.

Vaughn, Alden T.
1965 New England Frontier -- Puritans and Indians. Boston: Little, Brown & Co.

Winslow, Edward
1855 Account of the Natives of New England,
1624. Quoted in Morton, Nathaniel, New Eng-
lands Memorial. Boston: Congregational
Board of Publication.

THE FRENCH-CANADIANS OF NEW ENGLAND

Leon F. Bouvier

Introduction

The purpose of this paper is to present more
information on a relatively small ethnic group not
well known to most Americans, due to their preponderance primarily in New England. These French-
Canadians are sometimes confused with the Acadians
of Louisiana and the French-Americans who migrated
directly from France to the United States.

The Acadians originally traveled from France
to what is now Nova Scotia and were deported by the
English to Louisiana and other southern colonies in
1755. The French-Americans were among the earliest
Europeans of the Catholic faith to migrate to the
new world. Their arrival dates from about 1800,
and they settled mostly in New York and Pennsylvania. The Protestant Huguenots also came to this
area at about the same time.

The French-Canadians came to what is now the
Province of Quebec in the early part of the seventeenth century. Many still reside there and constitute an important force in Canada. The people
with whom we are concerned here are those who migrated south from Quebec into New England during the
nineteenth and early twentieth centuries.

I. The Historic Background

Less than a century after Jacques Cartier
landed at New Foundland in 1534, there were several
tiny settlements in what is now Nova Scotia and
Quebec. In fact, the present city of Quebec dates
back to 1608. By the early eighteenth century, an
organized community of Frenchmen existed in the
eastern part of New France. The populating of Quebec roughly parallels the settling of New England
by the Pilgrims and the Puritans.

Following the defeat of Montcalm by Wolfe and the British in 1759, the French population in North America faced a severe crisis. Henceforward they were to be subservient to a Protestant and English-speaking monarch. Placed on the defensive by this course in history, the French-Canadians determined to keep their three most cherished possessions: religion, language, and customs. This attitude, traditionally known as "survivance" became the dominant theme in their way of life.

In Canada, the French have successfully preserved their culture in a North American English sea. This nationalistic and religious tenacity has also been an important factor in the Americanization of these people after their migration south.

The emigration of French-Canadians to the United States began before the American Revolution. Many fought for the colonies in this war of liberation. In appreciation for their services, Congress gave these volunteers a tract of land in upper New York State which became known as the Refugee's Tract. After the insurrection of 1837 in Quebec, there began a new movement. Some of those defeated in that short ill-fated uprising sought refuge in Vermont, and this led to the founding of the first small French-Canadian settlement in New England. This remained but a minor migration until after the Civil War. It was then that the largest movement of people occurred.

A number of reasons account for the migration south of the border. Most important were the unprecedented industrial prosperity in New England; the inborn love of traveling common to most Canadians; and a desire for high wages. As a result, many French-Canadians settled in the numerous mill towns then mushrooming throughout New England. By 1900 there were 810,105 persons of French-Canadian parentage in the United States, of whom 508,362 lived in New England (U. S. Census of Population: 1950). This fairly large minority group resided in the midst of a predominantly Protestant Anglo-Saxon majority. The only other Catholic group of any

76

significant size in New England at the time was the Irish who greatly outnumbered the French-Canadians, and who had arrived at an earlier date. The migrants from Quebec were faced with a double disadvantage. They were, at one time, both a religious minority among Protestants, and a minority within the Catholic Church. Furthermore, they were handicapped by speaking a foreign language; the first such group of numerical importance to migrate to New England. Once again it was necessary to struggle to preserve their French culture, religion, and language. "Survivance" was at stake!

The French-Canadians whether living in Quebec or in New England were and still are devout Catholics.

The parish was the basic social unit of French Canada, religiously, scholastically, and municipally; and it played an equally vital role at least in the first two aspects, among the French-Canadian immigrants in New England in the last century (Wade 1950:163).

Any study of the French-Canadians in the United States must, of necessity, include a close look at the historical development of the parishes, especially in New England. The church played an important role in the French-Canadian attempt to "survivance."

As early as 1814 small communities of French-Canadian families existed in Winooski, Vermont, and Woonsocket, Rhode Island. By 1820 some had migrated to Worcester, Massachusetts; by 1832 to Manchester, New Hampshire; by 1833 to Lewiston, Maine, and Southbridge, Massachusetts. However, prior to 1850, these communities were minute with the possible exception of the Winooski-Burlington neighborhood. Madawaska, near the northern tip of Maine, had a large settlement in the early part of the nineteenth century. However, this parish was under the Canadian hierarchy until 1870. The French centers of Vermont were under joint Canadian-American juris-

77

diction. That is, they were subject to Bishop
Cheverus of Boston (this diocese then included all
of New England), but through an agreement with Bishop Plessis of Quebec, the latter furnished an
occasional priest to administer to the needs of the
French-speaking Vermonters (Wade 1950: 165-167).

The first French-Canadian parish in New England
was probably St. Joseph's of Burlington founded in
1850, despite the vehement opposition of the Irish-
Catholics in the area. This rivalry was typical of
what was to follow throughout the latter part of
the nineteenth century and early twentieth century
between these two Catholic ethnic groups.

The Irish Catholics began immigrating to New
England shortly after the potato famine of 1845.
Although regarded as "Papists" by the Protestants,
they gradually assimilated into the community.
This was made easier by English being their
language. Though Catholic, they at least shared
some customs and the language of the Anglo-Saxon
majority. As the French-Canadian migration grew in
size, the Irish began fearing this new competition.
Their use of a foreign language gave new impetus to
the anti-papist fears of the Protestants who had,
by this time, reluctantly accepted the Irish Catholics. This resulted in new difficulties for the
Irish in their relations with the ruling "Yankees."
The new foreign group was also an economic threat
to the Irish because they were willing to work
longer for less pay. Furthermore, the earlier immigrants tended to look down at the most recent newcomers. The French-Canadians occupied the lowest
social class, while the Irish moved up the stratification ladder. There were also some basic tem-
peramental incompatabilities between the French-
Canadians and the Irish, and all this led to a demand for separate French-speaking parishes. Although these two were Catholic, they differed in so
many ways that clashes were inevitable.

The conflict which developed in many other sections of the nation as new immigrants insisted on
their own ethnic churches led to the Cahenslyism

movement. Father Peter Cahensly and others demanded of Rome, that dioceses in the United States be set up along nationality rather than territorial lines. The newcomers from Europe would then be served by pastors of the same background, and they would confess their sins and listen to sermons in their native tongue.

The earliest German Catholics had little difficulty in establishing their own parishes, but those who came later, settling in localities where the Irish were already dominant, found themselves in churches they could not regard as their own. The plight of the Italians and Slavs, who began to arrive toward the end of the century, was even more painful, since the Irish church they found in America appeared to them even more remote from what they had been accustomed to at home and what they so longed to re-establish in the New World. 'The result was a struggle, parish by parish, between the old Catholics and the new, a struggle that involved the nationality of the priest, the language to be used, the saints' day to be observed, and even the name of the church' (Herberg 1955:158).

The American-Catholic hierarchy was split over this issue of English-speaking or ethnic churches. Some favored the quick assimilation of foreign Catholics to eliminate differences in language and tradition. Others favored conserving the nativist customs under priests of the same ethnic stock. In 1889 the Catholic Council of Baltimore stressed that "It must always be remembered that the Catholic church recognizes neither north nor south, nor east nor west; nor race nor color." That Congress held that "national societies, as such, have no place in the Church of this country; after the manner of this Congress, they should be Catholic and American" (Wade 1950:185). Although this has gradually become the policy of the church, it was violently opposed for many years by French-Canadian leaders. A com-

promise evolved whereby English-speaking parishes
were established and ethnic churches were superim-
posed on a temporary basis. Many of these still
exist, though some are disappearing as the Americanization process continues. However, the new
concern with ethnic identity is contributing to a
revival of interest in these parishes and the recent decision of the American bishops to allow more
Masses to be said in the "vernacular" will no doubt
intensify this interest. However, at the time of
the Congress of Baltimore, many feared that this
new policy would soon eliminate the French-Canadian
parishes which had been established in New England.
"Survivance" it was predicted would die due to
Irish opposition. The fear was unfounded, and, to
this day, numerous French language parishes are to
be seen throughout New England.

> The French parish has remained the
> bulwark of the French-American's remark-
> able resistance to complete cultural fu-
> sion in the American mass, while the
> French-American's record in industry,
> government, and military service has re-
> futed the nineteenth century nativist's
> dire forebodings that the establishment
> of national parishes meant the end of the
> Republic. Frictions there have been,
> still are, and presumably will be in the
> future, but the French-American has be-
> come as typical of New England as the
> Yankee and the Irish, and has notably
> enriched it religiously as well as other-
> wise (Wade 1950:191).

By the middle of the twentieth century French-
Canadians were established in the six New England
states. Yet, of all ethnic groups in that area,
they had resisted Americanization the most.

> They have retreated into narrow ghet-
> toes confining themselves to ingroup ac-
> tivities to avoid the major unpleasantness
> of community life and to shun open compe-
> tition on unfair terms with those who

discriminated against them economically,
politically, educationally, and socially
(Foley 1960:11).

The results of this self-imposed segregation
and the intense desire for "survivance" will be
evident in the statistical studies to be analyzed
later. The principle of "survivance" which had
been imbedded in the minds of these people ever
since the fall of Quebec remains strong to this
day. Their devotion to the Roman Catholic faith
has kept them united, and because of this, the
clergy has been in a position to keep the hopes of
"survivance" alive.

II. The Demographic Study

Most United States French-Canadians live in
New England. Determining the exact size of the
population of an ethnic group is not easy. No universal agreement exists on the definition of a person of foreign ancestry. Is it limited to those
persons living in the United States who were born
in a foreign country? Does it include their children? How about the siblings of a mixed marriage,
as when the father or the mother is of foreign
birth? Do third generation Americans belong to a
foreign ethnic group?

As statistics must be comparable to be useful, and as this study compares French-Canadians to
other groups, the definition of the United States
Bureau of the Census serves as the sole guide.
Foreign stock, according to the Bureau, consists of
the foreign-born and the native born of foreign or
mixed parentage. All data in this thesis are based
on this definition and, therefore, third generation
Americans are not considered foreign stock. The
third generation "immigrant", though affected by
Hansen's law, is primarily an American (Hansen
1945). Generally his first language is English;
his customs are American; even his religion has become Americanized.

The members of the third generation
have no reason to feel any inferiority
when they look around them. They are
American-born. Their speech is the same
as that of those with whom they associate.
Their material wealth is the average possession of the typical citizen. The third
generation, in short, really managed to
get rid of the immigrant foreignness, the
hopelessly double alienation, of the generation that preceded it; it became American in a sense that had been, by and large,
impossible for the immigrants and their
children (Herberg 1955:43-44).

A second definitional problem affects the French-
Canadian group. Through the 1950 census, all Canadian foreign stock residents of the U. S. were sub-
divided into "French-Canadian and All Other." Beginning with the 1960 Census this subdivision was
eliminated. Thus, it is no longer possible to turn
to official U. S. Government publications to determine how many French-Canadians live in the U. S.
Indeed, in the 1980 Census even questions on the
second generation were eliminated -- the concept of
foreign stock no longer exists in the Census of the
United States.

In 1950 the white population of the U. S. totalled 134,477,365. Of these 23,578,374 were
native-born of foreign or mixed parentage, and
10,095,415 were foreign-born. Thus, approximately
25 percent of all white Americans were of foreign
stock. In that year there were 238,409 French-
Canadians born in Canada, and 519,495 born in the
United States of foreign or mixed parentage or
757,904 persons of French-Canadian stock. Thus,
French-Canadians made up about 1.5 percent of the
American population and 2.3 percent of the foreign
stock (U. S. Census of Population 1950).

New England is the home of most French-Canadians. According to the 1950 Census, of the
757,904 French-Canadians in the United States,
551,116 lived in New England. The remaining

82

206,000 were distributed among the remaining states
with only Michigan having a French-Canadian community of any meaningful size. (See Table I.)

Any study of the French Canadians must necessarily be centered in New England. The site of the
original migration, it remains the traditional home
of these transplanted northerners. Reasons have
been cited for the mass movement south from Quebec
to the New England states. These include a strong
desire for better living conditions which would be
acquired as a result of steady mill wages. However, this movement was not unopposed in Canada.
At first, it was thought to be but a temporary migration. These young men and women certainly would
soon return to their native land. When this assumption was proven incorrect, government agents
were sent to the numerous mill towns of Massachusetts and Rhode Island in an attempt to lure back
these French-Canadians with free transportation and
land in Canada.

When the exodus could no longer be
ignored, about the middle of the century,
the Quebec clergy launched agricultural
colonization movements for the migrants
who were to be established either in the
province or in the American midwest since,
as day laborers in cities and factory
towns they lost everything that Canadians
held highest: religion, language, nationality -- all of which might be preserved
under the American as well as the British
flag if the emigrants were concentrated
in farming communities and preferably in
the West where society was still in the
process of formation (Wade:1950:169).

The great Canadian Northwest was still wilderness 100 years ago, and its tremendous growth did
not get under way until well into this century. If
the venturesome French-Canadians were to remain
farmers, the alternatives were either their own
native province of the American Midwest, which, by
then, was already well populated. A concerted ef-

83

TABLE I. NATIVITY AND PARENTAGE OF THE FOREIGN WHITE STOCK
BY STATES: 1950

State	Total Foreign White Stock	Foreign Born White	Native White of For. Par.
Alabama	46,378	13,813	32,565
Arizona	156,399	45,594	110,805
Arkansas	33,479	9,289	24,190
California	2,982,388	985,333	1,997,055
Colorado	244,897	58,987	185,910
Connecticut	964,354	297,859	666,495
Delaware	48,304	13,844	34,460
Dist. of Col.	120,332	39,497	80,835
Florida	336,991	122,731	214,260
Georgia	51,405	16,730	34,675
Idaho	88,427	19,407	69,020
Illinois	2,684,567	783,277	1,901,290
Indiana	400,980	100,630	300,350
Iowa	482,637	84,582	398,055
Kansas	217,997	38,577	179,420
Kentucky	75,973	16,068	59,905
Louisiana	116,124	28,884	87,240
Maine	245,477	74,342	171,135
Maryland	313,005	84,440	228,565
Massachusetts	2,272,919	713,699	1,559,220
Michigan	1,967,465	603,735	1,363,730
Minnesota	1,022,641	210,231	812,410
Mississippi	25,269	8,314	16,955
Missouri	403,865	92,050	311,815

84

State			
Montana	168,184	43,119	125,065
Nebraska	299,168	57,273	241,895
Nevada	34,795	10,530	24,265
New Hampshire	191,664	58,134	133,530
New Jersey	2,013,656	630,761	1,382,895
New Mexico	60,621	17,336	43,285
New York	6,803,774	2,500,429	4,303,345
North Carolina	46,334	16,134	30,200
North Dakota	241,442	49,232	192,210
Ohio	1,578,548	443,158	1,135,390
Oklahoma	84,461	18,906	65,555
Oregon	309,042	83,612	225,430
Pennsylvania	2,830,289	776,609	2,053,680
Rhode Island	387,429	113,264	274,165
South Carolina	24,148	7,503	16,645
South Dakota	173,752	30,767	142,985
Tennessee	51,210	15,065	36,145
Texas	932,280	276,645	655,635
Utah	135,149	29,844	105,315
Vermont	96,423	28,753	67,670
Virginia	128,920	35,070	93,850
Washington	633,421	191,001	442,420
West Virginia	110,820	34,586	76,235
Wisconsin	1,059,349	218,234	841,115
Wyoming	53,490	13,290	40,200
TOTAL	33,750,653	10,161,168	23,589,485

TABLE I. NATIVITY AND PARENTAGE OF THE FRENCH-CANADIAN FOREIGN STOCK
(CONTINUED) BY STATES, 1950

State	Total French-Canadian	Foreign Born	Native of For. Par.
Alabama	201	71	130
Arizona	547	197	350
Arkansas	311	106	205
California	22,005	7,990	14,015
Colorado	1,176	311	865
Connecticut	52,290	16,900	35,390
Delaware	266	81	185
Dist. of Col.	978	373	605
Florida	4,403	1,808	2,595
Georgia	248	98	150
Idaho	774	249	525
Illinois	11,581	3,196	8,385
Indiana	1,938	598	1,340
Iowa	1,496	346	1,150
Kansas	1,086	226	860
Kentucky	285	105	180
Louisiana	518	173	345
Maine	89,919	28,329	61,590
Maryland	969	359	610
Massachusetts	226,289	69,479	156,810
Michigan	48,921	15,786	33,135
Minnesota	11,357	2,482	8,875
Mississippi	124	39	85
Missouri	1,174	329	845

Montana	2,307	727	1,580
Nebraska	873	178	695
Nevada	504	179	325
New Hampshire	79,735	24,930	54,805
New Jersey	6,666	2,306	4,360
New Mexico	210	50	160
New York	48,454	18,254	30,200
North Carolina	386	136	250
North Dakota	2,714	634	2,080
Ohio	5,163	1,713	3,450
Oklahoma	625	160	465
Oregon	3,671	1,171	2,500
Pennsylvania	3,374	1,114	2,260
Rhode Island	67,298	19,163	48,135
South Carolina	198	58	140
South Dakota	978	213	765
Tennessee	218	68	150
Texas	1,559	524	1,035
Utah	544	139	405
Vermont	35,585	12,485	23,100
Virginia	1,315	280	1,035
Washington	7,198	2,508	4,690
West Virginia	242	77	165
Wisconsin	8,942	1,642	7,300
Wyoming	289	69	220
TOTAL	757,904	238,409	519,495

Source: Department of Commerce, Bureau of the Census, special report of 16th Census, Nativity and Parentage of the White Popula-tion – Gen. Char., U. S. Census of Pop.: 1950, Vol. IV, Part 3A.

fort was made to send French-Canadians to this farm belt where it was expected that they would remain French in culture, religion, and language.

At all times the fear that a loss of language would result in a loss of faith was prevalent. The Roman Catholic clergy of Quebec was convinced that this would happen. French-Canadians shared the opinion that "survivance" should be maintained whatever the sacrifice. Many felt that this would be lost in the New England mill towns, with their many Protestants and Irish Catholics. As Marcus Hansen lucidly explains in The Immigrant in American History, this brave experiment in the west failed because of the desire of the French-Canadian for a steady income -- an income available at his doorsteps in New England. Although "survivance" was most dear to the hearts of all French-Canadians, economic necessities forced them to migrate to New England. There, remembering the warning of their Quebec relatives, the struggle for "survivance" would continue with more intensity.

His French-speaking neighbor was due for another role, a fate the more surprising in view of the rural nature of his background and training. In 1840, there was every indication that the pioneer qualities he had developed in cutting his way back from the St. Lawrence would be put to service in the new lands of the West. Colonies of French-Canadians were formed in Illinois, Michigan, and Wisconsin, and to observers these settlements seemed the beginning of an emigration from Quebec which would rival any that the neighboring province could send out. But many circumstances of society and economic life made it difficult for the young Frenchman to take a permanent leave of the parental roof. The young British-Canadian had only one obligation and that was to relieve his parents of the burden of his support. The young Frenchman, however, felt obliged to contribute to the cash income that was be-

coming increasingly necessary in the economy of the household. What he desired was
a job with wages, good hard cash delivered
into his hands on Saturday night. When the
opportunity for such payment arose within
what to his sturdy legs was walking distance, the attraction of the West dimmed
(Hansen 1948:187-189).

Within the New England states, French-Canadians settled as near to Quebec as possible, or they
established a home in towns where mill employment
was available. Table I shows that Massachusetts
in 1950 contained more Americans of French-Canadian stock than any other state -- 226,289. However,
these people represented a larger portion of the
population in the three northernmost states -- 15
percent in New Hampshire; 10 percent in Maine; 9.5
percent in Vermont. Rhode Island, like Massachusetts, a textile state, had 67,298 French-Canadians,
8.5 percent of the population. Connecticut, with
only 52,290 French-Canadians making up 2.6 percent
of the total, had the smallest representation in
New England. Connecticut is the furthest removed
from Quebec, and also, in the nineteenth century,
it had fewer textile mills than either Massachusetts or Rhode Island.

Where is the capital of American French-
Canada? This is a disputed question among several
New England cities. According to the 1950 Census,
seven cities with populations of more than 100,000
had sizable French-Canadian minorities. In Massachusetts, Fall River had 15,217 in a population of
111,963; New Bedford had 12,633 out of 109,189;
Springfield had 11,055 out of 162,399; Worcester
11,036 of 203,486. Hartford, Connecticut had 7,837
French-Canadians in a total population of 177,397.
Waterbury, also in Connecticut, had 5,497 out of
104,477. Providence, Rhode Island had 7,779 out of
248,674. Thus, it would appear that Fall River is
the "capital" because it has both the largest population and the highest percentage of these people
in the United States. Nevertheless, several smaller
cities can also lay claim to being the "capital."

These include Lewiston and Biddeford in Maine; Manchester and Nashua in New Hampshire; Southbridge and Lowell in Massachusetts; and Woonsocket in Rhode Island. It is generally agreed that Fall River, Woonsocket, and Lewiston are the three most French-Canadian cities in the United States, but not necessarily in that order.

Where are the French-Canadians? Unfortunately, we are limited to 1950 statistics, but at that time most were living in New England, either near the Canadian border or in the textile centers of central and southern New England. Almost all of the above-mentioned cities are (or were before the southern textile movement) cotton and wool manufacturing towns. It is reasonable to assume that in 1981 these same cities remain the most "French-Canadian" in the nation.

III. Social Status in 1950

Are French-Canadians members of the upper class? Or, as one of the immigrant groups of the latter half of the nineteenth century, have they been relegated to the lower classes? Three criteria are employed to determine the social status of French-Canadians in 1950: educational attainment, average income, and occupational classification (Bouvier 1964:18-22).

The French-Canadians are compared to the overall national average in each of these categories. They are then contrasted to three other ethnic groups predominant in New England: Irish, Poles, and Italians. These were chosen because of their numerical strength in that area; the time of their migration to America; and their religious affiliation. In all these, there are similarities with the French-Canadians. It is well known that these minorities have often been in competition in the continuing struggle for social advancement. In comparing these four, attention will center on New England.

90

In 1950, the white population of the United States 14 years of age or more had completed an average of 10.1 grades; the native born had completed 10.4 grades; the native of foreign or mixed parentage 10.3; the foreign born 8.2 grades. Foreign born French-Canadians had attended school for an average of 8.2 years and the second generation 8.9. For the Italians, it was 5.3 and 10.3; for the Poles 6.0 and 10.1, respectively. The educational level attained by the Irish nationally was 8.4 for the foreign born, and 10.6 for the second generation. The foreign born among the French-Canadians are on an equal level with other groups educationally. However, the second generation tends to fall behind. Educationally, the second generation of the other nationalities, anxious to become "Americanized," forges way ahead of their parents. On the other hand, "survivance" has kept the second generation among the French-Canadians close to its parents and the French language. Table II shows this very clearly.

TABLE II. MEDIAN SCHOOL YEARS COMPLETED
BY PERSONS 14 AND OVER: 1950

	Foreign Born		Native Born of Foreign or Mixed Parentage	
	U. S.	N. E.	U. S.	N. E.
United States whites	8.2	---	10.3	----
French-Canadian	8.2	7.6	8.9	8.8
Irish	8.4	8.3	10.6	11.4
Italian	5.3	5.2	10.3	10.5
Polish	6.0	4.8	10.1	10.5

Source: Department of Commerce, Bureau of the Census; special report of the Sixteenth Census, Nativity and Parentage, U. S. Census of Population; 1950, Vol. IV, Part 3A.

91

It must be realized in Table II that although first and second generation data appear to represent fathers/mothers and sons/daughters, these are all 1950 data. They do reflect the improvements between generations but not over time.

In New England, a similar pattern emerges. The French-Canadian there achieved 7.6 grades among the foreign born, and 8.8 grades among the second generation. Contrasted to this, the Irish attained 8.3 and 11.4 grades, respectively; the Italians 5.2 and 10.5; the Poles 4.8 and 10.5. It is especially noteworthy that the Italians and the Poles, coming later than the French-Canadians, and from foreign-speaking European countries, registered meaningful educational gains in the second generation. The Irish, having arrived earlier and with no language barrier, were slightly higher on the educational ladder. They, too, had a sizable increase from the first to the second generation. French-Canadian offspring gained 1.2 grades as compared with 3.1 for the Irish; 5.3 for the Italians; and 5.7 for the Poles. This minor increase among French-Canadians is perhaps attributable to their desire to keep the French tradition alive in the family. Once the children had graduated from the French-speaking parochial school, there was great fear that a public high school education would result in the loss of the faith, the culture, and the language.

The second criterion of social status is mean earnings of persons 14 years of age and over -- again, as determined by the 1950 Census.

In 1950 the median income of the white population of the United States (14 years and up) was $2,053. The native born had an income of $1,938; the foreign born, $2,181; and the native of foreign or mixed parentage, $2,314. The foreign born French-Canadian median was $1,958, and the second generation averaged $2,010. Nationally, the Irish had incomes of $1,970 among the foreign born, and $2,309 for the second generation; the Italians, $2,301 and $2,293, respectively; the Polish, $2,267 and $2,476. Again the French-Canadians were slightly below the national average and below the other three national groups. Because of the reliance on median average, these statistics may have only limited value. A relatively large population between ages 14 and 18 would result in a lower median income; a small number in that age group would yield a higher median. This may partially explain the higher income for Italians of foreign birth than for their offspring. Aside from them, all others reported a higher income for the second generation.

New England statistics are similar to those for the entire nation. Table III, shows that the second generation French-Canadian income was lower than the comparative incomes of the Irish, the Italian, and the Poles. The tremendous increase in the income of the second generation Irishmen is noteworthy. Otherwise, differences are not significant.

TABLE III. MEDIAN INCOME OF ALL PERSONS
FOURTEEN YEARS AND UP IN NEW ENGLAND, 1950

	Foreign Born	Native Born of Foreign or Mixed Parentage
United States whites	$2,181	$2,314
French-Canadian	1,867	1,948
Irish	1,560	2,219
Italian	2,141	2,081
Polish	2,016	2,207

Source: Department of Commerce, Bureau of the Census; special report of the Sixteenth Census, Nativity and Parentage, U. S. Census of Population; 1950, Vol. IV, Part 3A.

The third criterion utilized to determine social status is occupational classification.

The employed population was divided into nine
occupation classes similar to those used by the
Bureau of Census. These were then given propor-
tionate value, that is, nine for the professional
class, eight for the farmowners, seven for the
managers, and so on. These values were then multi-
plied by the percent of the total employed in that
given category.

Thus, if four percent of the total employed
French-Canadians were professional, the group received 36 points in that class. This was done for
each class. The total was the score of that ethnic
group. The higher the score, the greater the proportion of upper level occupations. Combined
scores for the two-generation "foreign stock" were
also calculated. The scoring for this combined
group gives a better picture of that particular
ethnic group's employment level than do separate
computations for first and second generation.

The white population of the United States had
a score of 540. Broken down into groups according
to parentage, the native born had 541; the combined
score for the foreign stock was 514. The national
French-Canadian total (foreign stock) was 479. As
for the other groups, the Irish foreign stock
scored 526; the Italian, 481; and the Polish, 486.

The New England results are indicative of the
reluctance of the French-Canadians to move into
the American melting pot. The scoring for the combined two generations was: Irish 526, Polish, 481,
Italian 478, French-Canadian 463. However, the
scores for the foreign born were Polish 464,
French-Canadian 452, Italian 414, Irish 408. The
difference can be explained by studying the second
generation results: Irish 539, Italian 486,
Polish 485, French-Canadian 464. This follows the
same pattern as that observed in education. The
foreign born French-Canadians were just behind the
Poles on the occupational score, and ahead of the
Irish and the Italians. However, the second generation failed to keep pace with these other new
Americans and was last of the four groups. This

94

naturally follows from the statistics on education.
The foreign born parents feared sending their children to English-speaking schools. Unless finan-
cially able to send them to secondary school in
Quebec, these offspring usually entered the textile
mills of New England after completing their elementary training in the French parochial schools.
The idea of "survivance" was so imbedded in the
minds of these people that they preferred seeing
their children accept low class jobs than risk losing the religion, and language of their ancestors
in English-speaking high schools and colleges. On
the other hand, the second generation Poles and
Italians and especially Irish made a determined effort to become "Americanized." This usually involved receiving a public secondary education.

The national status of French-Canadians is
higher than it is in New England. As most of these
people live in the six northeastern states, it becomes apparent that the few who have migrated to
other sections have been quite successful in becoming "Americanized." These French-Canadians have
not been influenced by the "survivance" ideal due
to their being isolated from the majority. This is
evident after examining the occupational classification of French-Canadians outside New England.
Their overall score on the index was 527. Among
the foreign born 9.4 percent were professionals,
and 11.2 percent of the second generation fell into
that class; well above the national average.

From these studies two general conclusions
follow as of 1950: First, among most French-Canadians who reside in New England, the second generation has failed to keep pace with the other ethnic
groups in the Americanization process. This may be
due to the intense desire to keep the mother tongue
and the French culture, and to the fear that loss
of these would ultimately lead to the loss of the
cherished Roman Catholic faith. Second, among the
few French-Canadians who have settled in other sections of the country, the ideal of "survivance" has
not been an influencing factor, and they have remained above the national average on the occupa-

tional scale.

The latter group, however, is extremely small,
and the concern here is with the French-Canadians
of New England. There the picture is clear. "Survivance" -- that theory which evolved from the historic struggles both in Quebec against the English
and in New England against the Irish -- was successful at least to the mid-Twentieth Century. It
kept the second generation "French." However, the
price paid for this ideal was great. The French-
Canadians in the United States lost one generation
in the process. While the second generation Poles,
Italians, and Irish were becoming "Americanized"
though maintaining their Roman Catholic religion,
the second generation French-Canadians were remaining French-Canadian in language and culture.

IV. The French-Canadian Today

Is the third generation abandoning, or at
least compromising, the ideal of "survivance?"
It is difficult to find empirical data that can
shed any information on this subject. As noted
earlier, the Census Bureau defines "foreign stock"
as the first and second generations, and since 1950,
no separate data have been gathered on French-Canadians.

The French-Canadians of New England lost one
generation in the process of maintaining "survivance." The third generation, therefore, roughly
parallels the second generation among the other immigrant groups. By observing the activities of
these Americans and comparing them to the third
generation French-Canadians, some conclusions may
be reached concerning the progress of these people
as they strive to enter the great American melting
pot.

As the new immigrant broke away from the ancient European traditions, he (seldom she!) often
entered the field of politics. Here he could be
recognized by his fellow Americans. Here he could

assist his own group by speaking of its problems. The Irish soon mastered the science of politics and became powerful enough to be reckoned with even before this century. The Italians have made spectacular advances in government over the past thirty years. A number of governors of New England states have been of Italian ancestry. For many years the senior United States senator from Rhode Island was a second generation Italian. The Polish-Americans have not been as successful in this area. Nevertheless, there have been some notable exceptions, former Senator Edmund Muskie of Maine, for example.

The French-Canadians, until recently, have been notable by their absence from civic affairs. Their insistence on banking together and keeping the old traditions and language made it extremely difficult for any member of their group to be successful politically on the state level. Even in cities with large French-Canadian populations, there was a reluctance to participate in government.

This may be changing. The names of French-Canadians in New England state politics appear more and more frequently in the nation's press. As late as 1940 this was a rare occasion. Representative Aime Forand of Rhode Island gained prominence in 1960 with his federal medical aid program. Today, Rhode Island, Connecticut and New Hampshire have French-Canadian congressmen. A recent governor of Rhode Island was of French-Canadian parentage as was a recent senator from Alaska -- a French-Canadian born in Massachusetts. In recent years, more French-Canadians are participating in government throughout New England -- a phenomenon that has developed primarily since the second world war. It is strong evidence that the third generation is finally moving into the general population.

When the younger members of this group leave the self-imposed ghetto-like neighborhoods, many eventually marry persons of different ethnic backgrounds. A glance at the marriage announcements in any large New England newspaper attests to this

97

fact. This, too, is a step away from the principles inherent in "survivance." The partners in
such a mixed marriage usually change their parish
affiliation and join the territorial English-
speaking Catholic Church. As this movement accel-
erates, it is possible that the ethnic parish may
eventually disappear from the New England scene.

Nevertheless, a recent survey in Rhode Island
clearly indicates that of all major Catholic ethnic groups in that state, French-Canadians remain
the most devoted to their religion (Bouvier and
Rao 1975:141-146). When asked about the frequency
of communion, over 20 percent of all adult female
French-Canadians stated that they received communion at least once a week. This compared to the
Irish 12.1 percent and the Italian 7.9 percent.

The same study showed that French-Canadians
were much more likely than any other group to have
attended parochial school. Of all the French-
Canadians responding, 70 percent had had at least
some parochial school training, compared to 55
percent for the Irish and 20 percent for the Italians.

Since 1950, there is growing evidence that the
third (and fourth) generation French-Canadians have
broken away somewhat from the constraints imposed
by "survivance." Although an entire generation has
been lost in the process and cannot be regained,
French-Canadians may be the better for it. They
did not have to break away from old traditions to
be accepted as "Americans" as did many second generation Poles, Italians, and Irish.

Perhaps a different conception of "Survivance"
remains with today's French-Canadians. It is easy
for them to remember the traditions of their ancestors because their parents never did forget. On
the other hand, they have developed the desires
that could have been their parents' -- success in
the "American" way. Today, they are "Americanized," while maintaining their language and customs,
though to a secondary degree of importance. The

example set by fellow Americans of different origins has convinced French-Canadians that there is no danger of losing their faith, even if the French language and the French customs are neglected somewhat. Hansen's Law was mentioned earlier: "What the son wishes to forget; the grandson wishes to remember." Perhaps for French-Canadians it should read: "What the son never forgot, the grandson wishes to partly forget, and partly remember."

REFERENCES CITED

Bouvier, Leon F.
    1964 La Stratification Sociale Du Groupe Eth-
        nique Canadien-Francois Aux Etats - Unis.
        Researches Sociographiques. Sept.:18-22.

Bouvier, Leon F. and S. L. N. Rao
    1975 Socioreligious Factors in Fertility De-
        cline. Cambridge, Mass.: Ballinger Publish-
        ing Co.

Foley, Albert S.
    1960 Survey and Collation of Research in Inter-
        religious Relations. Unpublished paper,
        Spring Hill College.

Hansen, Marcus
    1947 The Problem of the Third Generation Immi-
        grant. Rock Island, Ill.: Augustana His-
        torical Society.
    1948 The Immigrant in American History. Cam-
        bridge, Mass.: Harvard University Press.

Herberg, Will
    1955 Protestant, Catholic, Jew. New York:
        Doubleday.

Department of Commerce, Bureau of the Census
    1950 Special Report of the Eleventh Census,
        Nativity and Parentage of the White Popula-
        tion -- Country of Origin; U. S. Census of
        Population: Vol. IV, Part 3A.

Wade, Mason
    1950 The French Parish and Survivance in the
        Nineteenth Century New England. Catholic
        Historical Review.

THE ARMENIANS OF NORTH AMERICA

Frank Andrews Stone

One day in 1922 a ship bearing many Armenian immigrants who had boarded it at Beirut, Lebanon docked in Providence, Rhode Island. Actually, its original destination had been New York, but that port had already received its quota of Armenian refugees for the month, so these new arrivals came down the gangplank in New England. Among them was a young widow, whom we will call Miriam Sarafian, and her nine year old son, Vahan. Their home had been a small town called Hadjin, located amid the Taurus Mountains in southern Turkey not far from the Syrian border. Miriam had been born in an outlying village where her father was the pastor of a little Protestant chapel established there as the result of the work of American missionaries.

Due to her family's connection with the American Mission, when Miriam finished the village elementary school, she was brought to Hadjin in order to attend the more advanced "Home School" that had been established there by the Protestants. Its purpose was to educate girls who would become the teachers in the extensive church-related school system which then served the Armenian and Greek Christian population of this part of the Ottoman Empire. As a result of having had this opportunity for learning, Miriam knew a little Armenian and some English, in addition to the Turkish that was commonly spoken by both Christian and Muslim villagers in this part of Turkey at that time.

After finishing her secondary level studies, at the age of sixteen, Miriam had been sent to teach in a remote Protestant village school. Her leadership potential, however, was soon evident. Miriam was then sent to a more advanced mission school located in the bustling Aegean port city of Smyrna (Today Smyrna is called Izmir and is the third largest city in the Republic of Turkey. The account of Miriam and Vahan Sarafian is a true case

study based on personal interviews with the informants, although their names have been changed
in order to protect their privacy.) for a year
of teacher training before coming back to teach
at the "Home School", her old alma mater. Soon
after taking over her duties in Hadjin, Miriam became aware of a handsome young Armenian physician
who had just begun practicing medicine there. The
doctor, whose name was Simon, had been graduated
from the lycee which the Mission sponsored in the
town of Tarsus, a community located on the Cilician Plain of southern Turkey. Simon had then
gone on to the Syrian Protestant College in Beirut
for his medical preparation. (Students from
southern Turkey who wished to study medicine at
this time either had to go to the capital, Constantinople, or to Beirut. The Medical School connec-
ted with the Syrian Protestant College in Beirut
was related to the same American organization that
also backed St. Paul's Institute, the school in
Tarsus. So it was natural that Simon would be sent
for medical training to Beirut. Syrian Protestant
College became today's American University of Beirut and St. Paul's Institute is now the American
School for Turkish Youth.) By 1911 he was back in
his hometown of Hadjin, bringing modern medical
care to this community of some 20,000 Armenians who
lived in a remote part of the Ottoman Empire.
Within a year, Simon and Miriam were married.

There had already been several periods of internal unrest for the Christian minorities of the
Ottoman Empire before this time. The vast Empire
over which the Turks had ruled for five hundred
years was in the process of breaking up. Many of
the peoples who had been forced to live under Ottoman control began to have aspirations of national
rebirth. England, France and Czarist Russia often
encouraged these movements; posing as the protectors of the various Christian minorities in Turkey.
During the late years of the nineteenth century
Turkey was ruled from the imperial capital at Constantinople (Istanbul) by a despotic Sultan, Abdul
Hamid II. Looking for a scape goat in order to
placate his Muslim subjects and fearing that the

Armenians in the Empire might obtain the support of the European powers to force him to grant them their basic civil rights, Abdul Hamid struck in 1895. He launched a program against the Armenian population in his realm, causing the death of more than 300,000 people. Again, in 1909, under the regime of the Young Turks who had finally overthrown Sultan Hamid, another 30,000 Armenians and Greeks were massacred in Cilicia when it was feared that they might lay claim to this region of the Ottoman Empire.

Simon and Miriam, therefore, were beginning their married life in troubled times. The future was unpredictable for them and the several million other Armenians who lived under Turkish rule. Nevertheless, their home was soon gladdened by the arrival of a son, Vahan, delivered by his physician father. Day by day, however, political conditions worsened. The Young Turk junta that now ruled the Ottoman Empire allied the country with Germany and Austria, the Central Powers in Europe. As the clouds of the First World War gathered, Ottoman subjects were conscripted into the army. Being a medical doctor, Simon was among the first men in Hadjin to be drafted. He was posted to the southern front and Miriam received a few letters from him. Then there was silence. Simon Sarafian was one person among the huge number of casualties incurred by the Turks. Miriam found herself a widow.

Her personal tragedy was compounded by a new program of mass deportation and extermination directed against the Armenian subjects of the Ottomans. Fearing a Russian invasion in which the local Armenians might aid their fellow Christians who lived under the Czar, and jealous of the powerful positions that Armenian merchants and intellectuals frequently occupied in Turkey, the junta in Istanbul was determined to settle the "Armenian Question" once and for all. Every Armenian in Asia Minor was ordered to march from their homes to a place of exile hundreds of miles away in the Syrian desert. The men were usually herded together and shot within a few days of setting out. Most of the women and children died of exposure and starvation along the way. Many of the girls were raped by the militia sent to supposedly guard the refugee convoys. As a result of this genocide, between one and two million Armenians lost their lives. There is hardly an Armenian American family that did not have its martyrs.

Somehow, Miriam and her little son, Vahan, survived the trek. They were able to escape and take refuge with some relatives in the Syrian city of Aleppo. When the war was finally over, Miriam was asked to go back to the town of Marash in Turkey, not too far from the ruins that marked the site where Hadjin had once been. Here the Mission was re-opening its Girl's School under the protection of the French, who now ruled this part of Turkey. Miriam would be able to support herself and her son by teaching at this institution. For a while, relative tranquility had returned and Miriam's new responsibilities kept her busy. But soon the Muslim Turkish population of the city began to chafe under the French occupation. The Nationalists were organizing themselves to drive the foreign powers from Turkish soil. Their leader was Mustafa Kemal, the only Ottoman general who had successfully fought against the Allies during the First World War. Turkish guerrilla forces now circled Marash, keeping up a steady barrage of gunfire aimed at the French troops and their Armenian allies. Then the French diplomats signed an agreement with the Nationalist Turks to withdraw behind the Syrian border.

Along with all the other Armenians in Marash, Miriam and Vahan woke up one snowy morning to discover that their French protectors had secretly decamped during the night. The town now lay defenseless. There was nothing else to be done but to again take to the road in order to escape from the wrath of the Turks. Leading her students and with her son strapped on her back, Miriam again made her way to Aleppo. A brother of her late husband's now lived in the United States and, with his help, Miriam was able to arrange for a passage to

America from Beirut for herself and her son.

Miriam was barefoot when she came down the gangplank onto American soil that day in Providence. The authorities on the ship had insisted on fumigating all of the immigrants' clothing for fear of disease and insects. When Miriam's only pair of shoes were returned to her, they were shrunken too small to fit her feet. So, clinging to Vahan's small hand and carrying the bundles that contained their only possessions, Miriam had difficulty climbing up onto the back of the open truck that transported the immigrants to Boston for customs inspection and their other landing formalities.

From Boston Miriam and Vahan made their way to Syracuse, New York, where the brother-in-law lived. There, Miriam found employment, first as a factory hand and later as a seamstress making alterations in a tailor shop. Vahan attended the American public schools and before long his mother enrolled for a night course at the local university. Miriam's aim was to prepare herself to be a social worker who could assist other refugees arriving from the Middle East and help them to adjust to their new lives in the United States. After earning her degree and becoming a qualified social worker, however, the depression began and Miriam couldn't find a job in her profession. Eventually she started a business repairing oriental carpets, and was able to support herself and her son as a rug merchant. Vahan became a university graduate and has had a successful professional career.

The tragic events that engulfed Miriam and Vahan only about sixty-five years ago, eventually bringing them to our shores, underlie the main waves of Armenian immigration here. Most of today's Armenian Americans arrived in the very late nineteenth or early twentieth centuries as refugees from their homeland. However, the first Armenians came to America in colonial days. Then, as in more recent times, they were usually exiles. Captain John Smith, for example, recruited Armenian artisans who knew how to make glass, soap and tar for the Virginia colony as early as 1618. They were also skilled at raising silk worms and weaving cloth from the thread they produced. All of the items that these original Armenian colonists knew how to produce were prized for trading with the Indians in order to obtain from them necessary raw materials.

A native of Persia known as "Martin the Armenian" is mentioned in several of the documents related to the colonial period. Although Martin was a naturalized British subject, he had to go to court in 1622 when the English customs officials tried to charge him a high duty on some tobacco that he was importing on the grounds that he was an alien. Martin later became a member of the Standing Committee of the Virginia Company of London. (This and subsequent data are based on M. Vartan Malcolm, The Armenians in America. Boston: Pilgrim Press, 1919 and on James H. Tashjian, The Armenians of the United States and Canada. Boston: Armenian Youth Federation, 1947.) Two other Armenians were brought over to Virginia from the Ottoman Empire in 1653 in order to work in the silk industry there. We also know that a Hungarian Armenian, Stephan Zadon, visited Cambridge, Massachusetts in 1682. He reported his impressions of the Massachusetts Bay Colony to the Archbishop of Canterbury, explaining that due to the Turkish military campaigns that were then raging in the Balkans, he wasn't able to go back to Hungary. The Church of England Missionary Society sent an Armenian clergyman, the Rev. Peter Tustian, to South Carolina in 1719. Tustian later moved to the Maryland colony, but there were probably other Armenian settlers in the Carolinas and Georgia during colonial times.

These pioneer Armenian Americans were very few in number. The next relatively small group of Armenians who reached America came in the middle of the nineteenth century. Their arrival was related to the sending of the first representatives of the predominantly Congregationalist American Board of Commissioners for Foreign Missions from Boston to

the Ottoman Empire in 1820. After traveling about
to survey conditions in the Sultan's realms, these
Yankee missionaries concentrated their educational,
medical and religious activities on the Christian
minorities of the Empire. Especially in the interior villages and towns of Asia Minor the Americans found many Arab, Armenian, Assyrian and Greek
Christians living in ignorance and poverty. The
American missionaries believed that if they could
enlighten and evangelize these members of the ancient orthodox and oriental churches, that these
native Christians would become the means of bringing the Gospel to the Muslims of Turkey. Protestant schools were opened all over the Anatolian
countryside. Many others were established under
Roman Catholic auspices as well. Soon the Armenian
Apostolic Church authorities also had to establish
schools in the Turkish interior in order to protect
their adherents from foreign influences. As a result of all this activity and ferment, a few young
Armenians began to come to the United States in order to complete their education.

Khachadour Osganyan, for example, a young man
who had studied at the famous Seminary begun by
one of the American Board missionaries named Cyrus
Hamlin at Bebek near Constantinople, came to the
City College of New York in 1834. Osganyan stayed
in America, becoming a writer for the New York
Herald Tribune. In 1857 he published The Sultan
and His People, the first book written in English
by an Armenian American and printed in the United
States. For the first time, American readers could
get a native point of view regarding conditions in
the Ottoman Empire, rather than depending exclu-
sively on missionary reports. Another young Armenian studied medicine at Princeton University in
1837, and the Rev. Haroutune Vahabedian was enrolled at Union Theological Seminary in New York
City in 1841. Vahabedian was later elected a Patriarch of the Armenian Apostolic Church.

At least fifty-five Armenians came to the United States between 1850 and 1870, usually on a temporary basis as students. After 1870, the movement

of young Armenians toward New England, northeastern and middle western colleges increased because of the extensive network of American missionary secondary schools that were operating all over Anatolia where there was then a large Armenian population. The Hartford Theological Seminary and Yale Divinity School, for example, educated many Armenians who often returned to serve the churches and schools of their Ottoman homeland. Eight young men were the founders of a flourishing Armenian community in New Jersey; while Massachusetts became another tiny center of Armenian American life with small communities developing in Boston, Lawrence, Lynn and Worcester.

Ever since medieval times the Armenians have lived as minorities within the major Empires that controlled the Caucasus and the Middle East. They were usually either subjects of the Persians, Russians or Turks. To avoid persecution and military conscription, as well as to further their commercial and productive enterprises, some Armenians had long lived outside of the traditionally Armenian regions. There were little colonies of Armenian diaspora in England, France, Hungary and Poland. Other Armenians lived in Egypt and the Balkans. There were even tiny Armenian settlements at Bombay, India and Singapore.

It was the perilous conditions and the massacres in Turkey after 1895, however, that forced thousands of Armenians to seek refuge outside the borders of the Ottoman Empire. Some of them fled to Russia, while others became exiles in Egypt and France. More than 70,000 Armenians, though, landed in the United States during the first four years after the Ottoman authorities began the campaign against them. These refugees usually settled along the East coast in Massachusetts, Rhode Island, Connecticut, New York, New Jersey or Pennsylvania. Although they had often left their homeland under duress, the Armenians who came to the United States at this time were often able to bring their goods, money and tools with them. Usually they had been skilled craftsmen, merchants or intellectuals in

Turkey, which aided them to adjust to the conditions that they found in the United States.

Worcester, Massachusetts was the chief center of Armenian culture in the United States at this time. The first Armenian Apostolic Church in the United States was established there in 1888. In 1892, the first Armenian Evangelical Church in America, the Church of the Martyrs, was also opened in Worcester. Armenians were coming to this industrial city because they could easily find work in the "wire mill" of the Washburn and Moen Company there. Even though the factory pay was low and these newcomers had to toil hard for long hours, no capital was needed in order to get jobs there and the work could be done by men who knew very little English. Probably one's relatives and friends from the same old country hometown would be in Worcester, who could help to assuage the loneliness of living in exile in a foreign land. Until around 1920 most of the Armenians living in the United States considered themselves to be temporary residents of the New World. They worked hard and saved as much of their wages as they could, in order to be able to go back to the homeland whenever conditions there improved.

It was the terror of the Armenian genocide in 1915 that undermined all of these hopeful aspirations for returning home. The influx of more Armenians into the United States was temporarily halted by World War I, but between 1920 and 1931 more than 26,000 more Armenian refugees got to America. They had often survived frightful experiences and many of them landed here virtually penniless. When America refused to accept the League of Nations mandate for Armenia and the tiny free Armenian Republic that had been established in the Caucasus lost much of its territory to the Kemalist Turks and then was taken over by the Soviets in 1920, the last expectations of going home faded among the Armenian Americans. It was now apparent that they were in the United States to stay and they turned their attention toward helping their fellow Armenians who were disemarking to begin their lives all

109

over again in America.

Several autobiographical and fictional accounts
well portray the experiences of this generation of
Armenian immigrants to America. One of the best of
them is Leon Surmelian's I Ask You, Ladies and
Gentlemen (Surmelian 1945). Viewed through the
author's own eyes as a sensitive youth who was
growing up in the Black Sea port of Trebizon when
the holocaust hit, his first hand experiences of
deportation and massacre are humanely described.
Surmelian succeeds in making the triumph of the
human spirit over inhuman disaster believable.
Another compassionate memoir of the era of tragedy
for Armenians in Turkey is Neither to Laugh Nor to
Weep by Abraham Hartunian (Hartunian 1968). The
author was an Armenian Protestant pastor in Turkey
between 1895 and 1922 who later wrote down his
recollections in Armenian. His manuscript was
eventually translated into English by his son,
telling about one family's experiences in the town
of Marash and later at the port of Smyrna. These
and other parallel accounts provide insights about
the conditions from which many Armenians had to
flee when they came to the United States.

Experiences of adapting and adjusting to the
new society are told in a number of other books.
By far the best known of these is William Saroyan's
My Name is Aram (Saroyan 1940. Mr. Saroyan died in
1981). Originally published in 1940, the Dean of
Armenian American writers here employs a great deal
of autobiographical material to produce this de-
lightful collection of vignettes about growing up
in Fresno, California during the 1920's. Due to
the similarity of its climate to that of the Cilician region of Turkey from which they had come,
southern California attracted many Armenian immigrants in the early twentieth century. They were
often farmers who were soon again growing citrus
crops, grapes and olives. If they couldn't afford
to buy much land, they were likely to engage in
truck farming, raising the lush egg plants, melons
and squash that had been so prized in the old country.

Most Armenian immigrants chose urban settings in the United States, however, and they have usually engaged in commerce, industry, services or trades. Richard Hagopian's novel, Faraway the Spring (Hagopian 1952. Hogopian also wrote another insightful novel about Armenian immigrants in America, Wine for the Living. New York: Scribners, 1956. On its pages the Aroian family faces the tragedy of having their two daughters choose to marry non-Armenian "odars."), for example, concerns the family of an Armenian factory worker. Poverty stalks their working class apartment in a walk up tenement in Chelsea, Massachusetts. Setrak Dinjian, the father, faces many problems and frustrations with which he is unable to cope. Although his wife is a simple village woman with little formal education, it is her determination that keeps the family together and somehow provides their basic necessities. Marjorie Housepian, on the other hand, recalls her formative years in an Armenian middle class extended family in New York City. One of her relatives runs an Armenian restaurant that is a focal point in their little ethnic community. Traditional Armenian customs such as the great respect that is accorded elders and the heritage of effusive hospitality for guests are carefully maintained in mid-Gotham. Yet, in A Houseful of Love (Housepian 1957) Housepian realizes that she is living simultaneously in the Armenian world of her ancestry and also in the contemporary English speaking environment that is all around her. Much of one's heritage can be maintained, but only by artfully adapting it to the conditions of the dominant American society.

Since the 1930's Armenian immigration to the United States has never ceased. Unfortunately, there is no accurate record of how many people are entailed because Armenian immigrants originated from a number of countries. Some of them still come from Turkey, but more of them begin their journey to America from Cyprus, Greece, Lebanon or Syria where they or their families re-located when they had to leave their original homes. Some come from other Middle Eastern countries such as Egypt,

Iran and Jordan; where there are Armenian communities. Others move on from France or Italy, or in some cases from places like Argentina, Brazil or Ethiopia. These lands have all served as way stations for the Armenian diaspora. The civil war in Lebanon during the last decade has forced many Armenians to seek refuge in the United States, and another group of Armenian immigrants have come here from Soviet Armenia.

By tracing one case of Armenian immigration to America, we can better understand the processes that are involved. A young Armenian graduate of a boy's mission school in Turkey was assisted to come to the United States for his college education by an American family in 1956. At this time the boy's family was living in the central Anatolian town of Kayseri, where they had moved from their original home in a village located in the vicinity of Yozgat. Once they had been prosperous landowners there and the male head of their family was the village headman. But in the turbulence during and after the First World War they had lost their property and been forced to re-settle as day laborers in the town. There the family could keep itself alive by plying trades such as brickmaking, iron mongering and tailoring. With their limited resources only one of their sons could be given an extended formal education, and he would have to study on scholarships.

After graduating from University in the United States that lad became a production engineer and married an American girl. Both of them worked in order to collect some money together with which to pay for the passage to America of one of the brothers still in Turkey. By now, the family had left Kayseri and moved to the Turkish metropolis and port city of Istanbul. Here the prejudice against them was less blatant on the part of their Muslim neighbors and they were also close to the foreign consulates and travel agents who could arrange emigration formalities. The son in America was now working for a corporation headquartered in New York, so the brother shared the couple's apartment in

112

Flushing. Trained as a tailor, he was soon working making alterations on the suits sold by a clothing firm in the city. Immediately, he too began saving money to bring over his wife and children.

Within a year another brother who was trained as a draftsman joined the other two in New York. Months later, the three brothers located a comfortable house in a Westchester County suburb where they would have more room and better schools for the children, who were now on their way over. The second brother's family joined him, and they also brought over a widowed sister and their father and mother. Next, a nephew came over from Turkey. He was just seventeen years old and had been attending an Armenian high school in Istanbul. He began the struggle to learn English during the next two years while he attended an American high school. Later, he went on to college; but by then his father and mother, together with their three other children had also emigrated from Turkey. So did another family of five close friends who originally hailed from the same village. In all, the single original immigrant who came to the United States in 1956 was responsible for making it possible for nineteen of his relatives and other people from the same community in the homeland to come here. Today their households form a small mutual support network, and most of the adults are employed in a family business. The process that has been described in this little case study is not at all unique. On the contrary, it is a common phenomenon as Armenians continue coming to the United States and Canada. With the assistance of their relatives and compatriots from the same town or village in the Middle East, the newcomers locate appropriate housing, find their first jobs, and begin the arduous struggle of adapting to America.

The Armenian Carpet

Who hasn't heard of Ara Parsegian, formerly the head football coach at Notre Dame University, or watched Mike Connors (Krikor Michael Ohanian)

113

star in <u>Mannix</u>? You have probably cheered sometime
when Garo Yepremian kicked a field goal for the
Miami Dolphins. Perhaps you have admired photo-
graphs taken by Yousuf Karsh, or enjoyed a per-
formance by Arlene Francis, actress and T. V. personality. This list could be much extended, but
these five celebrities are all North Americans of
Armenian descent. They are some of the more notable members of an ethnic group that is estimated
to number between 500,000 and 600,000 people in
Canada and the United States. The orientation and
institutions of these Armenian Americans reflect
the variations in the historical "carpet" composed
of all the movements in the past that have made an
impact on them. They participate in a shared consciousness that is the product of these complex
processes.

In the first place, besides the various centers of the Armenian diaspora that are located outside of the Caucasus and Asia Minor, four distinct
Armenian states have existed on the soil of the
homeland. Two of them, Greater and Lesser Armenia, were nations in antiquity. Greater Armenia
included fifteen provinces in a region that is east
of the Euphrates River surrounding the snow capped
slopes of Mount Ararat. Ararat is the mountain on
which Noah's ark is believed to have come to rest,
and although the Armenians are believed to have
originally been a lake culture around bodies of
water like Lake Van, Mount Ararat is today everywhere recognized as their national symbol. The
second ancient Armenian homeland was lesser Armenia, in the region just to the west of the larger
Armenian kingdom. It was wedged in between the
Greek kingdom of Pontus on the Black Sea coast and
Cappadocia to the south. Greater Armenia was in
the Persian sphere of influence during much of its
early history, while Lesser Armenia more often
found itself a Byzantine dependency. The Armenians
living in both of these states aspired to unity,
but the two were actually joined together only for
a short time during the reign of Tigranes the Great,
who ruled from 95 until 56 B. C.

Who were the natives of Greater and Lesser
Armenia; the ancestors of modern Armenians? The
traditional legend of their origin relates them to
Haik, son of Togarmah, which explains why Armenians
call themselves the "Hai" and their land Haiastan.
Actually, however, archeologists believe that the
origins of the Armenian people evolved through a
gradual social process. Apparently, proto-Armeni-
ans called Muschki entered this region twelve
centuries before the common era. Here they came
into contact with the Phrygians, and their vassals,
the Achchenazians and Arimaians. During the second
half of the seventh century B. C. another tribe
known as the Arimi also entered this same general
area, and it is claimed that the modern name,
Armenian, was derived from their appelation. These
various invaders didn't come into an empty land,
however, but rather slowly merged with the people
whom they found there. Eventually they produced a
new society known as Urartian in ancient Assyrian
inscriptions. Some of the ancestors of the modern
Armenians may also have originated in European
Thrace or possibly Thessaly, while the peoples whom
they encountered in eastern Anatolia were certainly
indigenous Caucasian tribes. So at the dawn of
their national history, some Armenians were blond
and fair skinned, others were dark haired and had
olive complexions. They were a blend of West and
East.

     Unfortunately, the little Armenian kingdoms
were placed at a geographical junction of many military and trading routes. The Armenians often found
themselves embroiled in the conflicts among their
more powerful neighbors. They were vassals of the
Medes when that empire was being attacked by the
Assyrians and Scythians. Armenian military units
fought in the Persian army that was defeated by
the Macedonians led by Alexander the Great in 333
B. C. Armenia was absorbed into the Macedonian
Empire, and later was part of the Seleucid Empire.
Similarly, at other times Armenians found themselves
pawns being fought over by Parthia and Rome. Later
they were in the midst of the struggle between the
Persian Sassanids and Byzantium. When the Muslims

resisted their Christian opponents from Europe at
the time of the Crusades, the Armenians sided with
their Christian compatriots. The Byzantine Empire,
however, a Christian state, conquered Ani, the Armenian capital, in 1045 A. D. The Byzantines, in
turn, were followed by the invading Seljuk Turks
who ended the political independence of Greater
Armenia in 1064. Armenia lay on the route of Tam-
erlane and his Tartar hordes in 1405, who left a
chain of smoking ruins in their wake. Then, in
1514, the Ottoman Turks under Sultan Selim I annexed most of the Armenian lands to their Empire
in order to create a buffer between themselves and
their Safavid Persian rivals. For more than a century the Persians and Turks fought each other to
devour the Armenian morsel, but the spoils were
finally divided between them in 1639. Alongside of
the larger Turkish Armenia, a smaller Persian-Arme-
nian dependency was formed.

The third historic Armenian state was established shortly after the Seljuk invasion of Greater
Armenia from the West, and the descent of the Mon-
gols on it from the East. Refugees moved to form
a small, free enclave called "New Armenia" along
the Mediterranean coast of Asia Minor, south of the
Taurus Mountains. This Cilician Armenia, founded
by exiles from Greater and Lesser Armenia, survived
for three centuries, from 1080 to 1375 A. D. Once
again, however, the Armenians found themselves a-
stride an international passageway that became the
battle ground where the Seljuk rulers of Konya confronted the invading Egyptian Mamelukes. This was
the corridor along which the Crusaders passed on
their way to retrieve the Holy Land, with Christians fighting Muslims. When the great Armenian
fortress capital at Sis (today called Kozan) fell
to the Mameluk invaders in 1375, Cilician Armenia
also passed into history as a free nation.

Cilician Armenia is particularly relevant to
our study because the majority of Armenian Americans in New England have patriotic ties with this
region. Although they have not been politically
independent for over six hundred years, the Cilician Armenians have never lost their devotion to

116

their homeland. At public gatherings of the Armenian Americans who trace their roots to this part
of Asia Minor no program is complete without sing-
ing Giligia (Cilicia) by Nahabed Rousinian (Quoted
from the 1976 Memoranda. New York: Prelacy of the
Armenian Apostolic Church of America. The references to Syria, Lebanon and Cyprus in the second
stanza indicate the places of refuge for many of
the exiles from the Cilician provinces after 1915.
Venice, Italy is an allusion to the famous monastery of the Mekhitarian Order there that played a
vital role in the Armenian renaissance during the
eighteenth and nineteenth centuries. "Parev" is
the Armenian greeting of salutation.).

Giligia

When the doors of hope are opened
And the winter has fled away from our land,
O beautiful land of our Armenia,
When its sweet days shine forth
When the swallow returns to the nest
When the trees put on their leaves,
I wish to see my Giligia
The country that gavest me the sun.

I saw the plains of Syria,
The mountain of Lebanon and its cedars.
I saw the land of Italy
Venice and its gondolas.
There is no island like our Cyprus
And indeed no place is more beautiful
Than my Giligia
The country that gavest me the sun.

There is an age in our life
When all desires come to their end,
An age when the soul
Aspires to its memories.
When my lyre becomes cold
Giving a last "parev" to love
I wish to fall asleep in my Giligia
The country that gavest me the sun.

117

After their independence had been lost both in Cilicia and in the eastern provinces, the Armenians living under Ottoman rule chafed because of the many restrictions that were placed on the Sultan's Christian subjects. They were termed the "raya" or sheep by their Muslim overlords, and like sheep they often were fleeced. Some Armenians dreamed of achieving a degree of autonomy under the auspices of their co-religionist, the Russian Czar. Others hoped to obtain some European backing to obtain more freedom. They thought that the Pope, France, or possibly Great Britain might come to their aid. The Russians did take over much of the Transcaucasus in the early years of the nineteenth century when their Empire expanded. Many Armenians who had formerly been the subjects of Georgia or Persia were now placed under Romanoff rule. Their position as a minority group in a border province of Czarist Russia, although somewhat better than that of the Armenians who lived in Ottoman realms, was still much less than what they had hoped for. Armenians were now minority subjects of three competing Empires: Ottoman, Persian and Russian.

During the nineteenth century the Armenian subjects of the Turks observed the rising national aspirations of other Ottoman peoples. Some of the Greeks were able to break away from Ottoman rule in 1821 to form a small, independent Hellenic Kingdom. The Bulgarians and other Balkan groups were also agitating for autonomy. The Russo-Turkish War that ended in 1878 was another chain of disasters for the Ottomans, who believed that the Armenians had assisted the Czar's forces. Turkey was forced to cede more of its Armenian provinces to Russia. The Turks, however, never either forgot or forgave this military disgrace at their back door.

Armenian nationalists, facing the fact that their people were politically divided among Persia, Russia and Turkey, found it almost impossible to organize for effective rebellion. In the late nineteenth century Armenian political parties were formed to advance the national cause, but their headquarters were in Europe. Some demonstrations

118

were held in Istanbul and some of the provincial
capitals of the Ottoman Empire; however, they were
unlikely to change Turkish policies. Very few of
the Armenians in Turkey took part in these acts or
agitated for more freedom. Nevertheless, during
the First World War in 1915, the Young Turk junta
led by Enver and Talaat Pashas carried out an anti-
Armenian program that amounted to a genocide.
After the debacle of the First World War, a small
portion of traditional Armenian territory in eastern Anatolia and the Caucasus was proclaimed an
independent, democratic Armenian Republic, with
its capital located at Erevan. The new state faced
famine conditions with many of its normal human and
natural resources decimated. After bravely meeting
this crisis, it found itself caught between the
armies of the Kemalist Turks and the Russian Soviets. In 1920 the Soviets forcibly took over Armenia and annexed it into the Soviet Union as one of
its constituent republics.

On February 18, 1921 the Armenians successfully revolted against the Soviet regime and reinstated the free Republic of Armenia. This is the
first instance of successful resistance to Marxist
domination behind what became the "iron curtain."
The Armenians were able to hold out for seven
months, but in November and December of 1921 Communist rule was re-imposed on Armenia. The leaders
of the Armenian Republic were executed, jailed or
exiled. Sixty years have passed since these events
occurred, but there is still a cleavage among Armenian Americans regarding their attitude toward
Soviet Armenia. Some 2,400,000 of the 4,000,000
Armenians in the Soviet Union today live in the
Armenian Peoples' Republic. It is a major cultural
center for Armenians everywhere. Great pride is
expressed in the beautiful buildings and boulevards
of the capital city, and the new metro that is now
being constructed in Erevan. Each year some college age Armenian American young people go to study
at the University of Erevan. Tours to Armenia are
sponsored by many Armenian American organizations.
Yet there is great ambivalence, similar to that
which is felt by other peoples whose homeland have

Armenia and neighboring lands

"New" or Cilician Armenia and
Its Neighbors

120

become Soviet satellites. The different perspectives among Armenian Americans regarding the legitimacy of the Communist rule in Soviet Armenia partly explain some of the political and religious diversity among Armenian citizens of the United States.

Varieties of Armenian Christianity

All Armenians trace the origins of their historic national adherence to Christianity back to the work of Jesus' disciples, Bartholomew and Thaddeus. These two are believed to have been martyred attempting to evangelize Armenia. It is known that as early as 110 A. D. there were enough Armenian Christians for the pagan Kings of the country to persecute them. Other anti-Christian campaigns in Armenia took place in 238 and 280 A. D. In the year 301 A. D., however, St. Gregory (Krikor), who is designated as the "Loosavorich" or "The Illuminator" in Armenian history, was able to convert King Tiridates III. Christianity was adopted as the state religion of Armenia, making the Armenian Apostolic Church one of the oldest national ecclesiastical bodies in the world. St. Gregory went to Caesarea for consecration as the first primate or Catholicos of the Armenian Apostolic Holy Church, as this communion is officially known.

Since this early beginning, aside from some agnostic intellectuals and the atheism that is imposed on Armenian members of the Communist Party in the Soviet Union, most Armenians have been remarkably steadfast in their Christian adherence. Traditional Armenian fine arts are inseparable from Christianity. The Armenian alphabet was devised by a bishop, St. Mesrop. Most of the classical Armenian literature and music contained religious themes. The beautiful illuminated manuscripts and miniatures, for which Armenia is famed, were created by monks. The "khatchkar", an incised cross carved from massive, free standing blocks of basalt rock, was another famous Armenian art form. Armenian ecclesiastical architecture was a predecessor of three famous European styles: Romanesque,

121

Gothic and Moorish. After the Armenians lost their political autonomy in the fourteenth century their Church took on even greater importance for them as the preserver of their national ideals and values.

Over the centuries the seat of the Catholicos or spiritual head of the Armenian Apostolic Church has been at several sites. The traditional belief is that the Catholics first resided at Vagharshapat near Mount Ararat at the place that was called Etchmiadzin meaning "the place where the Only Begotten Son has descended." Here it was that St. Gregory had a vision directing him to build the cathedral on the spot. The present Catholicos of all Armenians, His Holiness Vasken I, is at Etchmiadzin, a town a short distance from Erevan in Soviet Armenia. At other times, however, the spiritual center of the Armenian Church was located in the city of Dvin, which was also the political capital of the nation. After the first Arab invasion of Armenia in 640 A. D. the catholicate was moved to Ani, the capital of the Bagratid Armenian Kingdom. When Ani was destroyed, the catholicate was eventually re-established at the Castle of Romkla on the banks of the Euphrates River, where it stayed for almost a hundred fifty years. In 1293 the catholicate came to Sis, the fortress capital of Cilician Armenia. After the city was conquered in 1375, however, it lost much of its former prestige and cultural vigor. The Catholicos at Sis refused to move his own headquarters, but in 1441 he agreed that a second Catholicos might be elected to take up residence at the traditional center of the Church, Holy Etchmiadzin. Since that time, there have been two catholicates of the Armenian Apostolic Church; the Catholicate of All Armenians in Etchmiadzin, and the Catholicate of the Great House of Cilicia. The Cilician Catholicate was originally at Sis but had to be moved to Antelias, a suburb of Beirut, Lebanon, where it functions today. For a period in history there was also a third catholicate at Aghtamar, an island in Lake Van in eastern Turkey, but it became extinct. In view of its troubled existence surrounded by many foes, it is not sur-

prising that Armenian Apostolic Christians found it
necessary to provide more than one center of leadership for their Church.

Although they adhere to identical doctrines
and practice the same polity, modern Armenian
Americans of the Loossavorchagan or "faith of the
Illuminator" persuasion are divided into two distinct eccesiastical bodies. The largest of these
is the Diocese of the Armenian Church of America,
established in 1898 and directly in communion with
the Catholicate at Etchmiadzin. Forty-two parishes
in fourteen states and Canada comprise its Eastern
Diocese, and there are fifteen churches in Arizona
and California in its Western Diocese. The present
head of the Armenian Church of America is the Most
Reverend Archbishop Torkom Manoogian. His seat is
at the St. Vartan Armenian Cathedral on Second
Avenue in New York City.

The other ecclesiastical body representing the
Armenian Mother Church in our country is the Prelacy of the Armenian Apostolic Church, established
in 1957 after controversies of more than twenty
years duration. Its thirty-four parishes in eleven
states, the District of Columbia and two Canadian
provinces are directly related to the Catholicate
of Cilicia at Antelias, Lebanon. The current Pre-
late of this communion in North America is His
Grace, Bishop Mesrob Ashjian. His seat is at St.
Illuminator's Armenian Apostolic Cathedral on East
Twenty-Seventh Street in New York City, within
walking distance of Second Avenue. The Cilician
group in the United States also has a Wester Diocese whose bishop resides in Los Angeles.

The physical separation of these two consti-
tuencies of the Armenian Mother Church dates back
to 1933 when political controversies were intense
among the Armenian diaspora. The Catholicos at
Etchmiadzin at that time had signed the Stockholm
Peace Pact, and in America it was believed that he
did so under Soviet pressure. As a result, some
Armenian Americans concluded that the head of their
Church was being manipulated in international poli-

123

tics by the Marxists. For a generation, Armenians in this country who thought this way were cut off from relations with any hierarchal See of their historic Church. Finally, their appeal to the See of Cilicia to take them in was accepted in 1957. They could then resume practicing their religion under its auspices.

Besides the many Armenian Americans who adhere to these two Loossavorchagan communions, there are also some members of the Armenian communities in North America who are Roman Catholics. Historically there were numerous efforts made by Latin Christians to absorb the Armenian Apostolic Church. The motive for church union was political and well as religious, because at times either the Armenians hoped to obtain the support of the Catholic powers of Europe, or the European Catholics wished to have the Armenians as their Middle Eastern allies. During the era when Cilician Armenia was extant, several Armenian Catholicoi favored merging with the Latin Church. The idea also appealed to the King of the time, who was actually of French extraction. The Armenian clergy and common people, however, so opposed this union that they were able to prevent its taking place.

Early in the eighteenth century an Armenian religious order was begun by the Abbot Mekhitar of Sivas with direct Roman Catholic patronage. Mekhitar first settled his community in Morea, the Greek Peloponnesus, but it soon moved to the island of San Lazzaro near Venice, Italy. Here a famous monastery was built as a center for scholarly studies of Armenian history, language and literature; as well as religious affairs. Always part of the Latin Church, the Monastery of San Lazzaro is still an important worldwide Armenian cultural center. In 1773 a separate Mekhitarite monastery was opened in Trieste. This group was forced to move to Vienna in 1811 during the Napoleonic invasion of Italy, and has also long been a center for preserving the Armenian heritage. Many schools and publications are sponsored by the Mekhitarite Order to serve Armenians wherever they are in the world.

124

It was not required that Armenians who entered into communion with Rome had to adopt the Latin mass, so in the eighteenth and early nineteenth centuries some Armenians did accept Roman Catholicism. Those who were Ottoman subjects and had accepted Papal supremacy obtained an officially recognized Roman Catholic Armenian Patriarchate in Cilicia in 1740. French and Italian diplomatic intervention with the Ottoman authorities also brought about the recognition by the Turkish government of a Roman Catholic Armenian Patriarch of Constantinople in 1830. In this way, the Armenians who adhered to the Latin Church became a recognized millet or religious community in the Ottoman Empire, distinct from the Armenian Mother Church. These Latin or Uniate Armenians were always a relatively small group drawn especially from the westernized and Europeanized classes. The same events that made other Armenians refugees from Turkey in the early decades of the twentieth century brought Roman Catholic Armenians as exiles to the United States. Today, several Armenian Rite Roman Catholic Churches function in our country, such as those in Belmont, Massachusetts and Philadelphia, Pennsylvania. Most of the Catholic Armenian immigrants, however, joined the existing parishes in the places where they settled.

The fourth main variety of modern Armenian Christianity dates back to 1846 when forty members of a reform minded group within the Armenian Apostolic Church in Ottoman Turkey organized the First Armenian Evangelical Church of Constantinople. They had accepted the Calvinist Protestant views advocated by American Congregationalists sent to the Ottoman Empire, beginning in 1820, by the American Board of Commissioners for Foreign Missions. The stated aim of these New England missionaries was to enlighten and revitalize the Armenian Mother Church. Their doctrines and practices, however, were vigorously rejected by the Armenian hierarchy, who had recently been confronted by the Roman Catholic challenge. All of the members of the little evangelical movement that had grown up within the Armenian Apostolic Church eventually were excommu-

nicated by the Patriarch of Constantinople. The
Protestant ideas had also earlier been banned by
the Roman Catholic Armenian Patriarch. Excluded
from both Armenian religious communities in the
Ottoman realm, the Protestant Armenians had to establish a new church body in order to receive civil
recognition as a millet. Without this arrangement
they wouldn't have been able to survive in Ottoman
Turkey. They were able to obtain the necessary
permission with the help of their American sponsors
who arranged for the British to intervene with the
Ottoman authorities.

The new Evangelical Movement spread very rapidly in Turkey after 1846, especially in the interior towns of Asia Minor. Soon associations or
unions of these Protestant Churches were being established on the pattern of the New England Congregationalists. The Kharpert Union began in 1856,
the Bithynia Union in 1864, the Central Union in
1868, and the Cilicia Union in 1872. By 1872
seventy-six Armenian Evangelical Churches were
functioning in Turkey. More than 4,600 people be-
longed to them and they served a total community
of about 20,000. Forty-five years later, in 1913,
the number of these churches had grown to 137.
They now had close to fourteen thousand members and
it was estimated that the Protestants in Turkey
were more than 50,000. An extensive network of
primary and secondary schools was managed by the
Armenian Evangelical Unions, as well as a half
dozen colleges jointly directed by local leaders
and American Board missionaries. Just before and
after the tragic events of 1915-1920, many graduates of these schools had to make their way to the
United States (Chopourian 1962, 1974:101. The most
thorough scholarly analysis of the Armenian Evangelical Movement is Giragos H. Chopourian's, The
Armenian Evangelical Reformation: Causes and
Effects. New York: Armenian Missionary Association of America, Inc., 1972).

Armenian Protestants in the United States today are these people and their descendents. They
usually affiliated with either Congregational or

Presbyterian Churches in their new communities.
The policy often was to absorb them into existing
churches. As a result, for instance, there are no
distinctly Armenian Evangelical Churches in Connecticut, although many Armenian Protestants settled
in that state. There are active Armenian Evangelical Churches, however, in both Massachusetts and
Rhode Island today. In all, there are over ten
thousand people in the United States who identify
themselves as Armenian Evangelicals. They either
belong to the twenty-six Armenian Evangelical Churches in our country, whose total membership is
about four thousand, or they are scattered among
other Protestant communions.

        The Armenian Evangelical Churches in America
are linked to the other Unions of Armenian Protestants in France and the Middle East. They
formed the Armenian Missionary Association of
America in 1918, which raises funds to assist with
financing building projects, providing scholarships for needy students, and doing relief work.
It also sponsors Haigazian College in Beirut, Lebanon which, until the Civil War there after 1976,
was a thriving institution of higher learning. An
Armenian Evangelical system of elementary and secondary schools in Lebanon and Syria serves the children and youths of these Protestant minorities. So,
although the Armenian Protestants are numerically
rather few, they make an extensive impact on Armenian affairs.

Armenian Political Parties

        Unless they have been thoroughly assimilated
into the dominant American civic and political organizations, Armenian Americans usually have strong
allegiances or preferences in the Armenian political arena. Depending on their basic political persuasion, Armenian Americans are likely to support
one or another charitable organization, subscribe
to a particular Armenian newspaper, or send their
children to an Armenian language school or summer
camp that is run by one or another politically

                        127

oriented group. To a large extent, political out-
look also determines whether to join a parish of
the Diocese (Etchmiadzin related) or Prelacy (Cilician related) wings of the Armenian Apostolic
Church. In other words, Armenian politics underlies many patterns of participation of Armenian
Americans in voluntary ethnic associations.

The origins of the Armenian political awakening in the nineteenth century are complex, but it
can be generalized that most of the early political
parties had to be organized outside of the Ottoman
Empire. The reason for this, of course, was the
opposition of the Ottoman regime to any national
movements among its subject peoples. As a result,
the first Armenian political party in modern times
evolved from a cultural and educational society.
A young Armenian school teacher from Constantinople
(Istanbul) by the name of Mekertitch Portugalian
worked first at the town of Tokat in central Anatolia and then at Van in eastern Turkey. He established new secondary schools for Armenians, set
up educational programs for adults, and organized
Armenian cultural societies. These activities made
him suspect in the eyes of the Sultan, so he was
banished from Turkey and had to live in Marseille,
France. There he began to publish a newspaper,
Armenia, which was planned to inform the world
about conditions in Turkish Armenia. Portugalian
hoped to attract assistance for the Armenians in
the Ottoman Empire from their compatriots in the
Diaspora overseas. In 1885 nine young men who had
been Portugalian's students at Van met in Marseille
to form a political party. Called the Armenakan
Party, its aim was to win through revolution the
right of the Armenians to rule themselves (Nalbandian 1967:97f). For the next decade the Armenakans
actively struggled to achieve their objective, but
even before the seige of Van in June, 1896, other
groups were doing more. The party members who survived the battle were forced to seek refuge in Persian territory where they were no longer influential.

128

Seven Russian Armenian students who were all convinced Marxists founded another political party in Geneva, Switzerland in 1887. They had also been inspired by Portugalian's _Armenia_, but the founders of the Hunchakian Revolutionary Party believed that class struggle was the only way to free the Armenians living under the despotism of the Czar and Sultan. They were themselves, however, the sons of middle class families and none of them had ever lived in the Ottoman Empire. Their activities established a leftist political network in Turkey and led to demonstrations by their followers among the Armenians there. There was an internal dissention within the Party in 1896 when one faction split off. Dormant for a period, the Hunchakian Party again became active after the 1920's. It is a factor in Lebanese and Syrian Armenian politics, and probably a few other Armenians in the Diaspora today side with this Marxist group.

Today, however, most of the Armenians living outside of the Soviet Union side with either the Armenian Revolutionary Federation (Dashnaksutiun) or the Armenian Liberal Democratic Party (Ramgavar) if they are politically active. The Armenian Revolutionary Federation was organized at Tiflis, Georgia in 1890 and was active in the Ottoman Empire during the next thirty years. This was the party that took the lead in establishing an independent, democratic Armenian Republic with its capital at Erevan in 1918. This free Armenian Republic was forcibly taken over by the Soviets in 1920 after they had reached an agreement with the Kemalist Turks. But on February 18, 1921 the members of the Armenian Revolutionary Federation led a successful revolt to oust the Marxist regime. The independent Republic of Armenian was reinstated and was able to maintain itself until November and December, 1921. Communist rule was then re-imposed on the country. This revolt was the first instance of the people in a Soviet satellite state trying to break Russian domination. The chief political objective of the Armenian Revolutionary Federation to this day is the establishment of a free and united Republic of Armenia outside of the Communist orbit on the soil that it claims as historic Armenia. The A. R. F. publishes periodicals in Armenian and several other languages, including English, to forward this cause. There is a large and active Armenian Youth Federation affiliated with this party, and the Armenian Relief Society is also its auxillary. The Armenian Revolutionary Federation's headquarters are in the Hairenik Building on Stuart Street in Boston, Massachusetts.

A Constitutional Democratic Party (Sahmanadrakan Ramgavar) was formed after the Young Turk Revolution in 1908 by bringing together three Armenian groups that had previously been active in Turkish Armenia. Contrary to the Armenian Revolutionary Federation which was and is prohibited in both Russia and Turkey, the Constitutional Democratic Party functioned legally in the Ottoman Empire until 1915. Its platform advocating constitutional reforms within Turkey brought it considerable support from the members of the Armenian commercial class in Cilicia, Constantinople, Egypt, France and America.

After World War One and the defeat of the Ottoman Empire, Constantinople was occupied by forces of the victorious European Allies. Their occupation made it possible for the surviving Armenians in the Turkish capital to again become politically active. Several groups of them who shared the Constitutional Democratic view brought into being the Armenian Liberal Democratic Party (Ramgavar Azatakan Kusaktsutiun) there in 1921. The victory of the Kemalists and the establishmen of the Republic of Turkey soon placed these Armenians in a different situation, but the party continues to work for the emancipation and well being of all Armenians through constitutional means.

The Armenian Liberal Democratic Party also publishes periodicals in the Middle East and the United States. Its American headquarters are located on Mt. Auburn Street in Watertown, Massachusetts. Armenian American young people from the families who back this political party are more likely to belong to the Armenian Youth Organization, although

130

it isn't directly an arm of the Party. Similarly, most adherents of the Armenian Liberal Democratic Party attend Diocese parishes and channel their philanthropic contributions through the Armenian General Benevolent Union (A. G. B. U.). This renowned organization, however, has a completely independent history and is also supported by many non-political Armenian Americans and people who have no connections with the Ramgavar Party. The A. G. B. U. sponsors publications, supports day schools and other community institutions for Armenians, gives scholarships to Armenian youths, and carries out relief work among needy Armenians.

Armenian Trouble Spots

At the present time there are five trouble spots or perplexities that are most critical from an Armenian American perspective. First among them is the continuing controversy with Turks regarding the Armenian Genocide, which officials of the Turkish Republic deny occured. Although the Armenians who were living in the Ottoman Empire incurred great loss of life and property between 1915 and 1923, their claims for reparations have never been considered, so this is a nagging problem. Since 1965 each year on April 24, the day when the massacres began with the Armenian community leaders in Constantinople taken from their homes and executed in 1915, demonstrations and memorial services have been held. Fourteen Turkish diplomats and members of their families have been assassinated in recent years by a radical Armenian group. A resolution was also introduced into the United States Congress to establish April 24 as an official annual American event. It is to be a day that draws attention to all instances of inhumanity in order to educate our citizens to prevent any more genocides. Needless to say, passage of this legislation is opposed by Turkish diplomats and representatives of Turkish American organizations.

A second perplexity for many Armenian Americans is their relationship to the Peoples' Republic

of Armenia, which is part of the Soviet Union. Today, about two and a half fellow Armenians live
there, by far the largest concentration in one spot.
Yet most Armenian Americans are staunchly anti-
Communist. The events of past history also cause
them to be ambivalent in their attitudes about this
nation occupied by the Soviets. Located in Soviet
Armenia, however, are their chief cultural and educational institutions. The seat of the Catholicos
of All Armenians is there. The situation is not a
comfortable one for many Armenian Americans.

Third, the on-going Civil War in Lebanon has
disrupted the large Armenian community there. As
a result of the conflict many Lebanese Armenians
have lost their property, are out of work, and
their communal institutions have suffered. Drives
to raise funds for relief and reconstruction in
Lebanon have been carried out by Armenian Americans
of all persuasions. Similar efforts were made to
assist the little Armenian community on Cyprus after turbulence there had caused them great damage.
The Armenian minority in Iran has also been very
vulnerable during the revolution there, and the
eyes of Armenian Americans also look toward their
compatriots in this part of the world.

The holy city, Jerusalem, is a fourth area
about which many Armenian Americans are concerned.
There has been an Armenian quarter in this ancient
city for centuries, and one of the historic Patri-
archates of the Armenian Church is there. A famous
Armenian theological seminary functions in Jerusalem, but the Armenian population of the city has
dwindled down to very few. The modern controversies between Arabs and Israelis have put this center of Armenian culture in jeopardy, so Armenians
especially long for a just and lasting peace in
this part of the Middle East.

A fifth basic perplexity is often expressed by
Armenian American parents and young people. Michael
J. Arlen powerfully portrayed it in a series of
articles called "Passage to Ararat" that first appeared in The New Yorker and were later published

132

as a book (Arlen 1975). An Americanized son of
British subjects whose mother was Greek and father
Armenian, Arlen eventually engaged in a quest to
discover his Armenian heritage. His experience
exemplifies the widespread fear that living comfortably in the United States is eroding the cultural
roots of Armenian Americans. Many assert that acceptance and toleration within an Anglo-dominant
pluralistic society produces a degree of assimilation unknown during all of those past centuries of
oppression under Byzantine, Ottoman, Persian or
Russian rule.

The recognition that Armenians have easily
been absorbed by the majority American milieu has
sparked a new interest in Armenian Studies. The
National Association for Armenian Studies and Research in Cambridge, Massachusetts was founded
over fifteen years ago to confront this problem.
Armenian Studies programs were established at institutions such as Harvard University, Columbia
University, The University of Pennsylvania, the
University of California at Los Angeles, and California State University, Fresno. An Armenian
American College has been opened at LaVerne, California and more than a dozen elementary and secondary level Armenian day schools are functioning
where ever there are good sized Armenian populations in the United States. An Armenian Library
and Museum of America has been established in
Belmont, Massachusetts and the Armenian Studies
Association has been organized as an affiliate of
the Middle East Studies Association. The Armenian
Assembly functions as a national lobby advocating
political policies on issues concerning Armenian
Americans.

The current Armenian American self image may
be best conveyed by these lines of poetry recently
written by the Rev. Vartan Hartunian (Hartunian
1976, Reprinted with permission).

I AM AN ARMENIAN

I am an Armenian
I belong to an ancient race
    whose roots are in the subsoil of history
    whose branches pierce the sky
    of man's hopes.
I have known ignorance
    and worshipped false gods,
    but once I saw the light
    I have never wavered from the
    path of truth.
My alphabet was not created for the
    babblings of earth but to proclaim the
    Word of God.
I am alive
    because I have died.
Nationals have conspired to dig my grave
    but I hold the scales of justice.
I own no territory
    but the earth is mine.
In the slavery of governments
    I am free
He who touches me
    touches God.
He who walks with me
    walks toward the light.
I am the silent voice
    that stills the thunder of the world.
I am primordial dust
    and will consume the world
    in the fire of love.

REFERENCES CITED

Arlen, Michael J.
1975 "Passage to Ararat," The New Yorker, February 3, pp. 32-74; February 10, pp. 36-73; February 17, pp. 34-83.

Chopourian, Giragos H.
1962 & 1974 Our Armenian Christian Heritage. Philadelphia: The Armenian Evangelical Union of Ameica, p. 101.

Hagopian, Richard
1952 Faraway the Spring. New York: Scribners.

Hartunian, Abraham A.
1968 Neither To Laugh Nor to Weep. Boston: Beacon Press.

Hartunian, Vartan
1976 I Am An Armenian. Belmont, Massachusetts: The Armenian Evangelical Union of North America, Inc.

Housepian, Marjorie
1957 A Houseful of Love. New York: Random House.

Malcolm, M. Vartan
1919 The Armenians in America. Boston: Pilgrim Press.

_____ 1976 Memoranda. New York: Prelacy of the Armenian Apostolic Church of America.

Nalbandian, Louise
1967 The Armenian Revolutionary Movement. Berkeley: University of California Press.

Saroyan, William
1940 My Name is Adam. New York: Harcourt.

Surmelian, Leon Z.
1945 I Ask You, Ladies and Gentlemen. New York: Dutton.

Tashjian, James H.
    1947 The Armenians of the United States and
        Canada. Boston: Armenian Youth Federation.

                OTHER SELECTED REFERENCES

Akgulian, Rose
    1974 "Sharpening Tradition for the Present,"
        The Armenian Church. 17(3), March, 5-10.

Antreassian, Jack (ed.)
    1969 Ararat: A Decade of Armenian-American
        Writing. New York: Armenian General Benevo-
        lent Union of America, Inc. See also current
        issues of Ararat.

    _____
    1937 The Armenians of Massachusetts. Boston:
        Armenian Historical Society.

Arzoumanian, Zaven
    1973 "Tradition in the Armenian Church," The
        Armenian Church, 16(9), November, 17-20.

Atamian, Sarkis
    1955 The Armenian Community: The Historical
        Development of a Social and Ideological Con-
        clict. New York: Philosophical Library.

Balakian, Nona
    1958 The Armenian-American Writer. New York:
        Armenian General Benevolent Union of America.

Boghosian, Armand
    1975 "Armenians and Ethnicity," The Armenian
        Reporter 8(37-38), July 24 and 31, 3f.

Grigorian, Siran
    1971 "Armenians in America: A Sociolinguistic
        Perspective," The Armenian Review 24 (3-95),
        Autumn, 37-55.

Haigentz, M.
1972 "A.G.B.U. Within the Armenian Reality,"
Hoosharar. 59(13), October 1, 3-6.

Hanessian, John, Jr. (ed.)
1973 Armenian Academic Personnel in the United
States: A Preliminary Survey. Bethesda,
Maryland: The Armenian Assembly.

Kherlopian, D. G.
1961 "Armenians Today," Middle East Forum 37(3),
March, 13-17.

Koenig, Samuel
1938 Immigrant Settlements in Connecticut:
Their Growth and Characteristics. Hartford:
Connecticut State Department of Education.

Kulhanjian, Gary A.
1975 An Abstract of the Historical and Sociological Aspects of Armenian Immigration to the
United States, 1890-1930. San Francisco:
R and E Research Associates.

Mahakian, Charles
1974 History of the Armenians in California.
San Francisco: R and E Research Associates.
This is a reprint of a 1935 thesis at the
University of California.

Malcolm, M. Vartan
1919 The Armenians of America. Boston: Pilgrim Press.

Minasian, Armen
1972 "Settlement Geography of Fresno Armenians,"
The Armenian Review, 25 (3-4, 99-100), Autumn
and Winter.

Mirak, Robert
1965 The Armenians of the United States, 1890-
1915. Unpublished Ph. D. dissertation, Harvard University.

Ricklefs, Roger
   1973   "A Sense of Identity: Small Groups Enjoy
          Revived Interest in Cultural Heritage," The
          Wall Street Journal. July 10, 1, 21.

Rustigian, Stella S.
   1979   "The Armenian Day School Movement in the
          United States," Unpublished Master of Arts
          Thesis, The University of Connecticut.

Samoniantz, Serge
   1973   "The Effects of Genocide on Armenians in
          the United States," Asbarez. Los Angeles,
          California 65 (5090), September 4, 3.

Sarafian, Kevork A.
   1963   From Immigrant to Educator. New York:
          Vantage Press.

Sarafian, Vahe A.
   1958   "Armenian Population Statistics and Arme-
          nian Political Realities Today," The Armenian
          Review. 11 (1-41), Spring, April, 78-84.

Sarkissian, Karekin
   1969   "The Armenian Church in Contemporary Times"
          in A. J. Arberry Religions in the Middle East:
          Three Religions in Concord and Conflict. Cam-
          bridge: Cambridge University Press, 482-520.

Stocker, Carol
   1980   "Families Recall Armenia Genocide," The
          Boston Globe, April 24, 61, 2.

Stone, Frank A.
   1975   Armenian Studies for Secondary Students.
          Storrs, Connecticut: World Education Project.

Tashjian, James H.
   1947   The Armenians of the United States and Can-
          ada. Boston: Armenian Youth Federation.

Yeretzian, Aram Serkis
1974 A History of Armenian Immigration to America with Special Reference to Conditions in Los Angeles. San Francisco: R and E Research Associates. This is a reprint of a 1923 thesis at the University of Southern California.

Yessian, Mark R.
1971 "The Political Assimilation of the First Generation Armenians in the United States," Armenian Digest. 2 (5 & 6), November-December.

THE ARABIC-SPEAKING COMMUNITIES IN RHODE ISLAND:

A Survey of the Syrian and Lebanese
Communities in Rhode Island

Marlene Koury Smith

Introduction

Within Rhode Island's panorama of ethnic groups, the Syrian and Lebanese communities are relatively small. The approximate known number, 3,500, is taken from records of their churches. This number could perhaps be doubled. However, it is impossible to determine the invisible minority number of non-church goers and the amount of leakage to local Latin rite churches due to inter-ritual marriages. (There is relatively little intermarriage outside of the Catholic church.) These marriages between Syrians or Lebanese who use Eastern forms of worship and any other nationality which uses the Latin form drain members from their churches, making positive numbers impossible to determine.

This tiny community of Arabic speaking people can be broken down according to their five churches, all of which use an Eastern form of liturgy. Three of the five give allegiance to Rome; the other two are Orthodox but independent of each other, one Greek Orthodox, one Syrian Orthodox, and have been separate from the Roman Church for more than a thousand years.

Table 1 lists the present churches and pertinent information relative to them.

I. Religious and Political Persecution -- The Main Cause for Migration

The story of why these people migrated from Syria and Lebanon is in some ways similar to other ethnic groups in the diversity of reasons for the migration, although religious and political perse-

TABLE 1

PRESENT SYRIAN AND LEBANESE CHURCHES

Church and Rite Used	Number of Families Registered	Nationality	Areas Served
St. Basil's Central Falls, R. I. Byzantine Melchite (Allegiance to Rome)	352	Syrian	Pawtucket Central Falls
St. Elias' Woonsocket, R. I. Byzantine Melchite (Allegiance to Rome)	60	Syrian	Woonsocket
St. Ephraim's Central Falls, R. I. Syrian Orthodox	100	Syrian	Pawtucket Central Falls Southeastern Massachusetts
St. George's Pawtucket, R. I. (as of 1977) Maronite Rite (Allegiance to Rome)	252	Lebanese	Providence, Pawtucket and suburban areas

| St. Mary's Pawtucket, R. I. Byzantine Orthodox | 170 | Predominently Syrian | Pawtucket, Central Falls Woonsocket Southeastern Massachusetts |

cution seem to be major causes. During the 18th and 19th centuries, Turks ruled the empire which began with the spread of Islam by the Arabs in the 7th century. Non-Muslims were organized in millets, religious minority communities with internal autonomy. However, young Christian boys were sometimes conscripted for palace administrative work or the Turkish cavalry, and Arab Christians were often treated in an inferior way, and subjected to "invidious laws of exception which operated to their detriment in taxation, justice and other rights of citizenship." (Antonius: 1965:32)

Arabs were still fiercely individualistic and sectarian despite the long centuries of Arabisation by which the Arabic language and race spread through the Middle East and Africa. The Turks as well as the British and French used religion as a divisive force among the Arabs. The 1860 Maronite-Druze conflict in Lebanon shows that even in the late 19th century, Arabs were more loyal to sect than to their common Arab heritage. The incident was used as a pretext for European interference which lasted well into the 20th century.

After 1908 when the Young Turk Movement gained restoration of the 1876 Midhat Constitution, the emphasis shifted from intro-Arab religious problems to Arab cultural and political persecution. Although political prisoners were released, and the 30,000 strong spy corps used by the Sultan to sow discord among his subjects was disbanded, Arab enthusiasm for the Constitution waned when it became evident that Arab cultural identity would be submerged in an Ottoman democracy with Turkish as the empire's language.

First-hand accounts of three Syrians, though not Rhode Islanders, afford interesting comparisons to Rhode Island migrants and the themes of religious and political persecution, as well as being personal and particular accounts rather than the usual impersonal and general accounts for migration.

Father Cyril J. Anid's settlement in New Jersey affords parallels to the arrivals in Rhode Island of an early priest of one Syrian community. Father Anid came to the United States in 1919 on a visit when he brought his sister here to live with relatives. While in America, he ministered to the spiritual needs of the Syrian and Lebanese people in the Paterson and Newark, New Jersey area. Father Anid states that the local priest was happy to see him since the Syrians "had been causing him some difficulties." (Anid 1967:13) After visiting the 350 families in the area and offering worship in an Eastern rite the people asked him to stay. Permissions were received from the local bishop, Rome, and the Melchite Patriarch, and Father Anid was here to stay.

In Rhode Island, the first Syrian Melchite parish, St. Basil The Great, in Central Falls also got its start when Father Ananias Boury was visiting the United States in 1908. (Visitor 1968:21) Although there is no record of the Syrians causing Bishop Harkins any difficulty, they did want a priest of their own rite and language, and petitioned the Bishop who allowed Father Boury to stay. Even later in the century, in 1947, another Syrian priest who was destined to become the first Melchite bishop in the United States, was visiting relatives here and was asked to remain as pastor of St. Basil's and St. Elias' when Father Jock, the previous pastor, passed away. Archimandrite Justin Najmy came to his post in much the same way as the original pastor. In the early years of the settlement, it seems that the Syrians commandeered visiting priests from the old country when it appeared they had a large enough community to support one.

Our second story concerns a young man, Salom Rizk, who was an American citizen, but who lived the first eighteen years of his life in Syria. His mother died in childbirth, and his grandmother, whose sons had all gone to America, kept the boy because she was lonely. After her death when he was about eight, he shifted for himself a great deal,

145

as was usual in the old country. He attended
school sporadically where his teacher finally became aware of his American citizenship and helped
him contact relatives in the United States. They
agreed to pay for his passage, a common practice
for immigrants. However, the quota system in the
1920's made it difficult for him to get here, and
it was not until 1927 that he arrived. In trying
to evaluate his motives for emigration, it was evident that he desired a better life, and education
was very important to him. However, his tales of
the religious animosity between the Christians and
the Druses, a Moslem sect, furnish evidence that
motives other than economics played part in the
emigration of Syrians and Lebanese. His tale would
be amusing if it were not an example of a tragic
aspect of Syrian and Lebanese history. He tells of
how a Christian man for whom he worked bought a
herd of pigs. He was hired as the pig herder.
Muslims consider pigs unclean, and when the herd
over-ran a Muslim's property, bloodshed almost resulted. Religious tensions (which resulted in a
massacre of approximately 14,000 Maronite Christians by the Druses in 1860) were far from dead
even in the 20th century.

Dr. Michael A. Shadid, who became a pioneer in
cooperative medicine in America, learned about
America in Beirut, at the American University
founded by Protestant missionaries, where he completed high school. Soon afterwards, a relative
from New York came and took him and his sister to
America. After a time earning money as a peddler --
as did Rizk and many Rhode Island Syrians -- he
went on to achieve his dream of becoming a doctor.
Shadid's account of his life in Syria is a story of
extreme poverty. His inability to afford a college
education could validate an economic motive for
migration. Yet, religious persecution again comes
to light as a cause when he speaks of his life in
Beirut as years of "fearful slinking through the
streets of a city teaming with hostile Moslems
where (he), a despised Christian, might be insulted,
beaten, or even murdered at any time." (Shadid
1939:26)

The problem of motivation for migration is a difficult one in the case of the Syrians and Lebanese. In all accounts dealing with the subject, the economic motive is given as a cause, and in the case of Professor Philip K. Hitti, the eminent historian of the Syrian and Lebanese, it is the major cause. (Hitti 1924:45) The economic factors were many: promitive agriculture, crop failures, heavy taxation by the Turks, loss of old trade routes due to the opening of the Suez Canal, and over-population. These things pushed the people out of the Old World, while at the same time America's industrial revolution and the comparative economic prosperity it offered pulled them here.

Yet, the fact remains that in the case of the Syrian-Lebanese community which emigrated as a whole, political and religious oppression played a larger role, and probably as great a role as the economic factor, which Hitti did not clearly emphasize. For instance, draft evasion was a cause for migration and was considered a form of oppression by the Syrians. In the mid-nineteenth century, the European powers began to take an increasingly active role in the Near East, and the Lebanese had obtained exemption from military service under the Turks because of a treaty negotiated by France after the slaughter of the Christian Maronites in 1860. By the early 1900's, however, both Syrian and Lebanese had to serve in the hated Turkish army. Rizk speaks of villagers hiding draft age men from the soldiers who came to get them, and even of men mutilating themselves to avoid service. In a conversation with a prominent Rhode Islander of Syrian descent, he spoke quite freely of relatives hiding from the authorities and he felt that draft evasion could be considered a cause for migration. (Nazarian 1972) Hitti states that the Syrians themselves felt a yearning for freedom was an important cause of their migration, although he feels that the economic motive was the real major cause. (Hitti 1924:51)

However, religious tension seems difficult to deny as a major cause of the emigration equal to

the economic cause. The stories of Rizk and Shadid
are only examples of how people actually felt.
Histories of Syria and Lebanon written after
Hitti's in 1924 place a heavier emphasis on religious persecution as a cause. A. H. Hourani
states that although there was no early persecution of Christians by Moslems, after 1860, the
date of the Druse massacre of Maronites, many
Christians wanted to leave a predominantly Moslem country where they were a persecuted minority.
(Hourani 1946:34) An article in the Providence
Journal confirms religious oppression and persecution as the cause for the emigration of the original Syrian community here in Rhode Island, stating
that they fled from religious strife only to enter
"a region of industrial struggle." Speaking of the
different Christian sects which emigrated, the paper notes that they shared "a long history of religious persecution by the Turks." Neither the city
dwellers from Damascus and Aleppo nor the peasant
herders from Lebanon had any intention of returning
to "a country where they were persecuted for their
Christianity." (Providence Journal 1929:8) In an
interview with Father Athanasius Saliba of St.
Mary's Orthodox Church, he stated that although
many of the people believed they would get rich in
America, political and religious oppression of the
Christian minority was an important cause of emigration. This can account for the fact that the
majority of those in Rhode Island who emigrated
were Christians, although they formed only a minority of the entire Syrian and Lebanese population
which might have emigrated. Father Saliba further
stated that some Christians felt more at home in
the Western, Christian world, since through the centuries, the Syrian and Lebanese Christians had
looked to their counterparts in the Western world
for protection. They were often made to feel like
strangers who didn't belong, he said, in the predominantly Moslem atmosphere of the Near East.
(Saliba 1973)

No attempt is here being made to discount the
economic motives for migration. However, in view
of the research done, it would seem that the eco-

nomic cause was not the sole major cause in the
case of the Syrians and Lebanese in general, nor
the Rhode Island Syrians and Lebanese in particular; and Maldwyn Allen Jones' statement that the
European Jews, the Armenians and the Syrians "who
were driven from their homes by persecution" were
exceptions to the rest of the post-Civil War groups
who were "uprooted by a common set of economic influences," (Jones 1960:205) seems correct.

II. Early Development of the Syrian and Lebanese
    Communities and Their Churches

        As soon as the Turkish ban on emigration was
lifted in 1895, Christians from Syria and Lebanon
began to arrive in large numbers and by 1899, the
number was sufficient to win them a separate
classification in government censuses from Turks --
although the label of "Turk" stuck to them far into
the 20th century, much to their chagrin. The number of Syrians and Lebanese who made up what could
be called the base of the community pyramid can be
gleaned from the following figures:

        Total Syrians to Rhode Island according
        to various Annual Reports (U. S. Dept.
        of Treasury 1899-1912) of the Commis-
        sioner General of Immigration 1899
        through 1912. 1,307

        Number of Syrians and Lebanese (Provi-
        dence Diocese 1912) according to Catho-
        lic church records, 1912:
                St. Basil. 400
                St. George 405
                Total   805

        The discrepancy between the two figures would
be accounted for by the Orthodox Syrians, for which
there were no accurate church figures. However, it
is obvious that by 1910, the time around which most
of the parishes were started, they must have been
here in sufficient numbers to form their own church
communities. The Melchites in the Pawtucket-Central

149

Falls area, and the Lebanese in the Providence
Federal Hill area had by 1910 and 1911 respectively, established their own churches. St. Mary's
Greek Orthodox was established in 1910, while St.
Ephraim's Syrian Orthodox came into being in 1913.
For the Melchites and the Maronites who were allied with Rome, there was a two-fold need for their
own national churches. The first was shared by
many other ethnic groups -- the language barrier
between them and the Latin rite clergy. However,
the second need was peculiar to them as Arabic-
speaking -- a difference in forms of worship.
They were not at home with the Western forms of
liturgy and when, as previously stated, Father
Boury was visiting here, the Melchites of the Blackstone Valley were able to form their own community
with him as their pastor. St. Basil's was dedicated in 1910, and St. George's, the Maronite church
led by Rev. Joseph Ganem, in 1911. Through their
churches, these people found a viable way of preserving their traditions. All of these churches
were small, and both St. Basil's and St. George's
had living quarters for their priests on the floor
above the main church. Compared to other churches
built in the diocese, the Syrian and Lebanese
churches were inconspicuous. The reasons for this
are probably that first, the communities were
smaller than others, and second, they were poor.

How did the majority of the early Syrians and
Lebanese earn their livings? Of the earliest migrants, those who had worked as weavers in Damascus
and Aleppo moved first into Olneyville and after
the textile strike of 1902 into the Blackstone Valley silk mills. Upon their arrival in Rhode Island,
they had worked and slept in the mills, not understanding anything of the nature of labor disputes.
Some of their leaders shared with the Franco-
American community in the Blackstone Valley a
knowledge of the French language, which was a help
to them in adjusting to their new lives. (Providence
Journal 1929:8) The French presence in the Near
East had consequences as far off as Rhode Island's
Blackstone Valley, and as late as 1965, French had
been used in a Syrian church in Woonsocket, a predominant French-Canadian city.

Others in the Blackstone Valley, especially
those in Woonsocket who emigrated from the small
village of Marrat, became peddlers. My childhood,
for instance, is filled with memories of days spent
on my grandfather's truck in which he peddled fresh
fruits and vegetables in Woonsocket, conversing
with his customers as well in French as he did in
Arabic and English.

The Maronites who settled in Providence in the
Federal Hill area were mountaineers and farmers who
came from small rural areas around Mount Lebanon.
These people became for the most part peddlers and
small shopkeepers in Federal Hill. (Providence Journal 1929:8. See also International Institute)

General characteristics of these people have
been stated as being their thrift, hospitality,
religious fervor, individualism, and clannishness.
Hitti claims that the topography of Syria and Lebanon produced isolated units of political and social
development which bred a sense of individualism
preventing cooperative effort (Hitti 1924). He
further says that of all the immigrant races, the
Syrians seem to be most jealous of those of their
group who aspire to leadership, and hence are
leaderless. His evaluation, made in the 20's when
the ethnic group feeling was perhaps stronger than
it is now contrasts with opinions expressed by two
people of Syrian and Lebanese descent interviewed
who have attained political success in the 70's
when one would think the sense of ethnic solidarity
would have been much watered down. Although it is
probably true that the early settlers were thrifty,
hospitable and religious, it would seem that these
traits could be attributed to almost any early ethnic group, more because of the social and economic
milieu than their ethnicity.

The reaction of other groups to the Syrians
and Lebanese is difficult to evaluate. There is
evidence that on occasions, a race prejudice
against them manifested itself. In Father Anid's
memoirs, he recalls an attempt by other parishes
in Paterson in 1934 to prevent his church group

from leading the annual religious parade because
the Syrians were not considered white. However,
when their turn came again fifteen years later,
no problem was encountered. Adele Younis in her
dissertation speaks of a court case in Charleston,
South Carolina in 1915 which was brought on by an
attempt to deny citizenship to Syrians because of
race questions (Younis 1961:285). Although no
written evidence was found in research of such a
problem in Rhode Island, oral evidence exists of
such feeling. On numerous occasions I have heard
mention made of the swarthy complexions and dark,
curly hair of these people, and would assume that
such feelings probably did exist especially in the
earliest years of their settlement. Perhaps the
worst slur, however, that could be made against a
Syrian or Lebanese was to be called a "Turk."

Only oral evidence exists in Rhode Island of
ethnic antagonisms with regard to the Syrian and
Lebanese. It has been suggested by a number of
people in conversations that such antagonism existed in Central Falls and Woonsocket between the
Syrians and the French.

Other ethnic groups did allow the Syrians and
Lebanese to hold religious services in the base-
ments of their churches. This does indicate a
positive attitude of acceptance on the part of
other church groups, although nothing was found to
indicate how the arrangements between the Syrians
and Lebanese and these other churches worked out.
Nevertheless, from the time St. Basil's was established as a parish around 1908 to the time the
church was built in 1910, services were held for
the Syrian community in the basement of the Polish
church, St. Joseph's in Central Falls. The Woonsocket Syrian community worshipped in the basement
of the French church, Precious Blood, until July
of 1930, "when . . . this procedure was no longer
satisfactory . . ." and Louis Salome, a parishioner,
donated a plot of land on which St. Elias was built
and dedicated in December of 1931 (Woonsocket Call
1931).

152

So little evidence is presented here with regard to ethnic antagonisms toward the Syrians and Lebanese that the only valid conclusions to be drawn must be termed loose generalizations arrived at intuitively, needing further research. Alliances between the Syrians and the Lebanese with other groups probably depended on the particular issues involved. Also, since they were such a small minority group and had no power economically or politically, they probably allied themselves with whatever group or groups were fighting the dominant group in power in the areas where they had settled. Surely, they were never a threat economically or politically to those in power since they were so few in numbers.

III. Evolution of Syrian and Lebanese Communities, 1920-1970, and the Churches' Role in Preserving Their Ethnic Identities

As the communities grew to maturity, their priests and churches played the major role in keeping them together, maintaining ties with the Old World and preserving old traditions. Table 2 indicates the country of birth of priests who have served the Syrian and Lebanese communities since around 1908 and how the churches, through their priests, have linked the Syrian and Lebanese Americans to the old countries.

What becomes evident from Table 2 is that the communities have been able to keep in touch with the Old World through priests of all denominations, since with the exception of the most recent priests, all of them have come from Syria, Lebanon or Turkey. This would seem to have been a force in keeping alive a feeling for the old traditions more than if these communities had been served by American-born priests for the past two generations, before the dioceses were established in the 70's.

TABLE 2

COUNTRY OF BIRTH OF PRIESTS WHO HAVE SERVED THE SYRIAN AND LEBANESE[a]
COMMUNITIES SINCE 1908 IN CHRONOLOGICAL ORDER

Years Served[b]	Country of Birth	Church	Priest
1908-1919	Syria	St. Basil	Rev. Ananias Boury
1911-1922	Lebanon	St. George	Rev. Joseph Ganem
1919-1948	Syria	St. Basil	Rev. Timothy Jock
1931-1948	Syria	St. Elias	Rev. Timothy Jock
1922-1949	Lebanon	St. George	Rev. Nemetallah Gedeon
1924-1927	Lebanon	St. Ephraim	Rev. Michael Murad
1927-1933	Syria	St. Ephraim	Rev. Peter Barsoum
1933-1939	Turkey	St. Ephraim	Rev. Paul Samuel
1949-1966	Syria	St. Basil	Archimandrite Justin Najmy
1949-1966	Syria	St. Elias	Archimandrite Justin Najmy
1949-present	Lebanon	St. George	Rev. Peter Hobeika
1951-1980	Syria	St. Mary	Rev. Athanasius E. Saliba
1952-present	Syria	St. Ephraim	Rev. Abdoulahad Doumato
1966-1973	Syria	St. Basil	Rev. Peter Capucci
1966-1973	Syria	St. Elias	Rev. Peter Capucci
1966-present	United States	St. Basil	Rev. Joseph Haggar
1966-1973	United States	St. Elias	Rev. Joseph Haggar
1973-1980	United States	St. Elias	Rev. James King
1980-present	United States	St. Elias	Rev. Joseph Haggar
1980-present	United States	St. Elias	Rev. Kenneth Sherman (Asst.)
1980-present	United States	St. Mary	Rev. Timothy Ferguson

[a] Rev. Saliba, St. Mary's, reported in 1973 that all thirteen priests who have served the community since its inception have come from Syria and Lebanon. Now Bishop Saliba works administratively in the Patriarchy in Antioch.

[b] St. Ephraim's destroyed by fire, 1939. Parish inactive until 1950.

154

The Patriarchal system used by the Eastern rite churches has also served to preserve ties with the Old World. Although until recently, the local Eastern rite Catholic parishes came under the the discipline of the Latin diocese in which they were located, their bishops and Patriarchs were all in the old countries. Visits from these church dignitaries provided occasions for great celebrations by the tiny communities and increased the feeling of closeness between the Syrian and Lebanese Americans and the land of their forefathers.

Newspaper research brought to light an interesting fact about most of the Syrian and Lebanese priests. Their knowledge of languages would seem hard to match by any other ethnic group's priests. Where the Syrians and Lebanese needed a priest of their own due to the language barrier, their priests could have ministered to the French parishes in the Blackstone Valley, for the priests were multi-lingual and all knew the French language quite well. Newspaper accounts of the dedication of St. Elias noted that the priest "will read the Gospel and epistle in Syrian, French and English" (Woonsocket Call 1931). I can remember wondering, as a child, why I had to listen to good Father Najmy give the same sermon in French, Arabic and English.

At St. George's parish, where the liturgy is said in the ancient Aramaic language spoken by Christ, the present pastor, Father Hobeika, is also multi-lingual, and has written a number of works in French on St. Ephraim, and on the Holy Eucharist (Providence Journal 1966 (B). Visiting clergymen share this multi-lingual ability: Archibishop Chami who visited the Melchite community in 1955 was versed in English, French, Arabic, Latin and Greek; Bishop Francis Zayek who visited the Lebanese Maronites in 1966, spoke to them in English, Arabic, Portugese, Italian and French, and also speaks Latin, Spanish and Aramaic (Providence Journal 1966 (B); and Archbishop Edelby visiting as recently as 1965 still preached his sermon at St. Elias in French, English and Arabic (Woonsocket Call 1965).

155

A pioneering effort by one of the Syrian priests to preserve the language of the Syrians was an eventual failure. Father Jock of St. Basil's, established the first Melchite parochial school in the United States in 1921. The school lasted for thirteen years, and at its peak enrolled 156 students who learned Arabic for two hours each day in addition to the regular classroom subjects (Visitor 1968:21). However, by 1934 the Great Depression claimed among its victims the pioneer Arabic school -- it closed its doors and with its passing, an era in ethnic history passed for the Syrian community. Never again was such an attempt made to organize a parochial school to preserve the Arabic language. However, as recently as 1950-51 and then again in 1958-59, Father Hobeika organized classes for the teaching of Arabic and Aramaic. He stated that he felt it was a "novelty" which did not sustain the attention of the younger people (Hobeika 1973). Father Haggar of St. Basil's has inaugurated an extensive Sunday school program, however, where the youngsters of St. Basil's are given an appreciation of the religious heritage of the Melchite rite. In 1976, the Arab-American Ethnic Heritage subcommittee of Rhode Island '76 sponsored Arabic classes at Pawtucket High School. Abdoulahad Abdulky taught 100 students enrolled in the program. Arab-Americans have remained part of the governor's Ethnic Heritage Committee formed in 1977.

In the decades following the early years, the shift in needs and interests of the Syrians and Lebanese can be traced by observing the formation of different organizations. Naturally, in the early years help for new arrivals in adjusting to life in America took precedence, and the Aleppian Aid Society located in Central Falls was an organization whose primary purpose was of a social welfare nature. However, by the 40's, the second generation was showing its desire to be a part of the American scene. In November of 1949, the Syrian-American club was formed in Woonsocket, having the dual purpose of closer unity among persons of Syrian descent, and a desire to take part in all civic

156

activities (Woonsocket Call 1949). Small as the
ethnic group was, the stirrings of political involvement had begun, and the beginning of an economic middle class was making its first appearance.
In 1951, a group from St. Ephraim's heard a teacher
speak on the need for voting (Providence Evening
Bulletin 1951). In 1960, Mayor Morrisette of Central Falls spoke at the 50th anniversary of the
founding of St. Basil's, remarking how the church
had kept the ethnic group together (Providence
Journal 1960). In 1962, Congressman Fernand J.
St. Germain spoke at a drive opened for the building of a new church for St. Ephraim's, and even
donated $100 toward the building fund (Providence
Evening Bulletin 1962). As small as the Syrian
voting bloc was the ethnic politics of Rhode Island demanded that politicians court its favor.
By 1964, the groups were hearing speakers on how
to gain public office, and it is during this decade
that political success began to come to the small
ethnic minority.

A further indication of efforts to preserve
ethnic identity is shown in the manner in which
the communities attempt to keep the youth of the
group, some of whom are by now fourth generation,
involved in the ethnic community. A popular method
of retaining the interest of the young who perhaps
would have little attachment to the heritage of
their ancestors, is the feting of deserving ath-
letes and scholars of the community at annual
awards banquets. During the 60's, this type of
activity began, and one such group, the Arabic
Educational Foundation, of Blackstone Valley,
founded in 1966, awards scholarships to deserving
youngsters who are at least one-fourth Arabic.

As the community developed into the 70's
socially along these lines, the religious aspect
of the Maronite and Melchite communities received
a boost when in 1966, both rites received their
own bishops in the United States to head their
churches here. The importance of these events to
the groups lies in the fact that previously these
communities were under the discipline of the Latin

diocese in which they were located although liturgically they usually followed the Patriarchs of their Eastern rite. The Maronites became a diocese in November 1971, and their bishop, Francis M. Zayek was installed as Bishop of the diocese in June 1972. The Melchites were not a diocese until July of 1976 although they had a bishop since 1966 also. Now the line of authority is more like the diagram shown below--

Diagram of Authority

Local Maronite Church	Local Melchite Churches
(St. George)	(St. Basil, St. Elias)

Maronite Bishop:	Melchite Bishop:
Bishop Francis Zayek	Bishop Joseph Tawil
See in Brooklyn, New York	See in West Newton, Mass.
(for all U. S. Maronites)	(for all U. S. Melchites)

Maronite Patriarch	Melchite Patriarch

Pope

Of course, the appointment of Bishop Zayek was a cause of great celebration among the Lebanese Maronites of Rhode Island, but the elevation of Archimandrite Justin Najmy from pastor of St. Basil's and St. Elias' to become the first Melchite bishop in the United States was a cause for a double celebration -- first to at last have their own bishop, and second, to have as their bishop the man who had been their pastor and friend for the past eighteen years in Rhode Island. Father Najmy, as previously mentioned, had become pastor of the two parishes upon the death of Father Jock in 1949, and "had it in (his) mind to stay in Central Falls the rest of (his) life to serve the souls of (his) parish" (Providence Journal 1966 A). He was consecrated in a two and one-half hour ceremony on May 29, 1966, by his former seminary classmate, Archbishop Athanasius Toutoundji, in an Oriental ceremony conducted primarily in Arabic, with some English, at

158

the Cathedral of the Holy Cross in Boston, Massachusetts (Woonsocket Call 1966). Richard Cardinal
Cushing, robed in Byzantine dress delivered the
sermon. Bishop Najmy's death on June 11, 1968 was
an occasion of deep sorrow for all United States
Melchites, but especially so for the families of
St. Basil's and St. Elias' who had grown to know
and love him during his eighteen years of service
to them (Boston Herald Traveler 1968).

IV. <u>Present Role of the Syrian and Lebanese Communities and Their Churches</u>

Today, the Maronite diocese in the United States
has 48 parishes, 5 missions and a population of
30,887, while the Melchites have 26 parishes, 7 missions and a population of 22,358 (Catholic Directory 1980:582, 817). In 1924, Hitti concluded that
the process of evolution would make Maronites and
Melchites become "American Catholics" unless they
obtained their own bishops, while the Orthodox
Syrians would move closer to the Episcopal Church.
As part of the Russian Orthodox Church under the
protection of Russia since 1774, St. Mary's Orthodox Church was a mission and had been sent an Arab
bishop around 1908 (Ferguson 1981), and despite the
fact that for more than forty years after that pre-
diction, the Melchite Syrians and the Maronite
Lebanese were without their own bishops, their
parishes survived. The practicing Melchites have
indeed grown, since in 1924 there were only approximately 10,000 of them in the country (Hitti 1924)
compared to 22,358 today. As for being absorbed by
Latin rite or American churches -- there has definitely been a leakage to the Latin churches due to
inter-ritual marriages, especially when the groom
is not of an Eastern rite since canon law demands
that the rite of the male partner be followed.

Although the difference between Eastern rite
Catholics and Latin rite Catholics is only a matter
of form and not substance -- a difference in <u>ways</u>
to worship God and not the <u>nature</u> of God who is

159

worshipped -- there is a difference in what could be called atmosphere between the two. The Eastern liturgy is more solemn and mysterious. For instance, the priest still faces the sanctuary rather than the people and in theory a screen should hide the altar, sanctuary and priest from the people during the early parts of the liturgy. The Maronites who use the rite of St. James in ancient Aramaic have been in communion with Rome since the early days of the Church, while the Melchites had an interrupted communion from about the 11th to the 18th centuries. The Melchites have followed the Byzantine Rite mainly in the Arabic language since the 12th century (Catholic Dictionary 1980).

Another difference from the Latin rite is the manner of dispensing the sacraments. Melchites traditionally received communion under both species, standing; at Baptism, the child is immersed in the fount and also receives the sacraments of Holy Eucharist and Confirmation at that time. The Maronites combine Baptism and Confirmation. These traditions are similar to the Orthodox with whom both the Melchites and Maronites share common religious backgrounds.

The Melchites also share with the Orthodox a Patriarchal system. The Patriarch and Synold of bishops govern the Melchite church and "constitute the superior authority for all affairs of the Patriarchate, including the right to . . . nominate bishops of their rite" (Abbott 1966:378). While the Council of Vatican II seems to uphold the semi-independence of many Eastern rites and give their Patriarchs the right to nominate their bishops as previously mentioned, the Pontiff still has the inalienable right "to intervene in individual cases" (Abbott 1966:378). After Bishop Najmy died in June of 1968, a controversy arose between Rome and Patriarch Maximos V. Hakim about this right, since Rome claimed the right to appoint was not law until the new code of canon law was published. A discussion between Rome and Antioch lasted more than a year. Finally, the Patriarch and Synod sent a list of three names to the Pope from which he chose the new bishop, Joseph Tawil, in November of 1969. Although it would seem that according to Vatican II, Melchites can nominate their own bishops, the matter does not seem to have had a final interpretation (Sherman 1981).

The relationship between the Catholic Church and the Orthodox Church is much closer, according to Rev. Allen Maloof, a Melchite author, than that between the Catholic Church and the Episcopal Church (Maloof, p. 12). The Episcopal or Anglican similarities to the Catholic faith are merely exterior -- a ritual similarity to the Latin rite -- while the Orthodox has an interior, spiritual closeness in much of their basic dogmas and sacramental system. However, the matters separating them are important of course. For instance, the greatest difference is the question of papal infallibility which is denied by the Orthodox. The Orthodox recognize divorce, although the process for obtaining one is complicated, while Catholics do not. Another major difference is that the Eastern Orthodox church has maintained the traditional view which admits married men to ordination. Once ordained, however, the ban on marriage is the same as in the Catholic Church.

It seems that the Syrian and Lebanese churches have remained fairly stable after reaching their peaks in the 20's, despite leakage to the Latin churches from inter-ritual marriages. Table 3 which compares the number of families in the parishes when they began to the present active number indicates some growth. These figures were received from the present pastors, who indicated that the number of families has remained fairly stable in recent years.

TABLE 3

NUMBER OF FAMILIES IN PARISHES WHEN INCORPORATED AND AT PRESENT

Parish	Early Number	Present Number
St. Basil's	100	352
St. Elias'	25	60
St. George's	100	252
St. Mary's	100	170
St. Ephraim's	40	100

A fair assessment would be that these churches will not be assimilated into the Protestant or Latin churches despite the leakage through inter-ritual marriages, and with the leadership of their own bishops, should become revitalized. As for the merger of the Orthodox with the Protestant churches as Hitti suggests (Hitti 1924:119), it would seem more likely that a closer affiliation between the Orthodox and the Melchite church would occur, although it is a far-distant possibility. The collegiality of bishops spoken of in Vatican II is an indication of the possible areas of agreement which might be pursued in future years. Father Maloof sees the ecumenical spirit trying to deal with the problems which separate the two groups. This forms a great "reunion endeavor of the Twentieth Century" (Maloof p. 23), in which the Eastern rites of the Catholic church can play a large role.

Here in Rhode Island, there is a tangible example of a cooperative spirit being shown between the two Orthodox churches and the Melchite church, and that is the formation in 1966 of the Arabic Interfaith and Educational Council of the Blackstone Valley. This group has as its aim the promotion of friendship between the Arabic peoples of the area and the preservation of their cultural heritage and traditions. It is made up of three Syrian churches, St. Basil, St. Mary, and St. Ephraim, and the Arabic Educational Foundation. Through this council, a degree of unity by virtue of common heritage has been achieved. The clannishness Hitti speaks of has been somewhat overcome in this group. However, the absence of the other two churches -- St. Elias and St. George -- makes one wonder why in such a small minority they have not all banded together in one large group. The Lebanese have their own club which does award scholarships, the Lebanese-American Club located in North Providence.

Naturally, since the Syrians and Lebanese have been here since the turn of the century, they have moved upward economically. Evidence of this can be seen by comparing the vocations of the group in the

early years to the present time. In the early
years, most were peddlers, laborers, and none were
professionals in this country (International Institute 1928 & 1935). Today, there are Syrians and
Lebanese in almost all walks of life -- doctors,
dentists, lawyers, teachers and small businessmen.
Further evidence of the upward economic mobility
of the group can be gleaned from the fact that
they are now awarding scholarships to deserving
young people of their communities. In 1966, the
first year the Arabic Educational Foundation was
in existence, it awarded $500 in scholarships.
As of 1981, the Foundation had awarded more than
250 scholarships in the amount of $62,500.

Along with upward economic mobility comes
political involvement. Leo E. Carroll in "Irish
and Italians in Providence, Rhode Island, 1880-
1960" refers to a theory linking upward economic
mobility with political involvement which has been
advanced by Samuel Lubell and refined by Robert A.
Dahl and Raymond E. Wolfinger (Carroll 1969:67-74).
Basically, the theory proposes that before members
of any ethnic group attains political success, the
group must reach an economic plateau of middle
class from which both economic support can come
and political leaders can emerge. In the case of
the Syrians and Lebanese, this appears to have been
the case. Political success has come in the 60's
and 70's for these groups. The following persons
of Syrian and Lebanese descent have attained elected office in the State of Rhode Island in the last
two decades:

James Allam   - City Councilman in Woon-
                       socket (now president
                       of the City Council)
                     - Feb. 1981 named Executive
                       Director of the Rhode
                       Island Public Buildings
                       Authority.

Morphis Jamiel   - State Representative from
                       Bristol

Daniel Issa   - Chairman of the School
                         Committee in Central
                         Falls

James Marons   - School Committeeman in
                         North Providence

Maureen Massiwer   - School Committeewoman in
                         Pawtucket
                       - now an aide to Governor
                         J. Joseph Garrahy

Anthony Solomon   - General Treasurer of Rhode
                         Island
                         (Former State Representative
                         of Providence)

In interviews with both Mr. Allam and Mr. Solomon, it was their feeling that the ethnic group supported them quite solidly. Mr. Allam contended that despite the fact that three other members of the small Woonsocket Syrian community ran in opposition to the group with which he ran, the clannishness and factionalism spoken of by Hitti did not affect the voting of that small group. Allam felt that the community possibly voted for all the members of the community who ran, since this was possible in the seven man council race. Pride in the group transcended political differences, he felt, especially in older members of the community who had probably long awaited political success for one of their own (Allam 1973).

Mr. Solomon, who ran unendorsed in a primary for State Representative, spoke of the members of the Lebanese group working untiringly for him, especially on election day, although Mr. Solomon also noted that the district he represented was one in which the Lebanese were only a tiny minority (Solomon 1973). The ethnic community gave him strong support in his successful statewide bid for General Treasurer.

Both Mr. Solomon and Mr. Allam believe they received strong support from their groups, although

165

neither group is large enough to bring political success without support from other ethnic groups.

The degree to which social assimilation has taken place in the group can be somewhat measured by comparing two factors -- the number of inter-ritual marriages from the early years to the present. It was found, not surprisingly, that in the early years the communities remained quite insulated from other ethnic groups and inter-ritual marriages and families of mixed nationalities in the parishes from the early years to the present. It was found, not surprisingly, that in the early years the communities remained quite insulated from other ethnic groups and inter-ritual marriages and families of mixed nationalities were few. Bessie Bloom Wessel's study of ethnicity in Woonsocket in the late 1920's notes that out of twenty-five children of Syrian descent, all twenty-five had Syrian mothers and fathers (Wessel 1931:76). A corollary of this would be that the number of families of mixed nationality in the parish was non-existent or very small.

As the years progressed, marriages between two nationalities increased, a fact noted by Alice M. Towsley in the study she did on intermarriages in Stanford, Connecticut and Woonsocket, Rhode Island (Towsley 1928:59). All of the pastors interviewed agreed that in the earliest years of the settlement of the Syrians and Lebanese, there were no such marriages and consequently no families of mixed nationality in the parishes. However, Table 4 indicates the percentages of families of mixed nationality now present in the parishes:

TABLE 4

PERCENTAGE OF FAMILIES OF MIXED NATIONALITY[a]
IN THE SYRIAN AND LEBANESE CHURCHES
IN RHODE ISLAND

Parish	Percentage
St. Basil's	70%
St. Elias'	33%
St. Ephraim's	50%
St. George's	33%
St. Mary's	25%

(a) These figures are based on either the man or
woman being of a nationality other than Syrian
or Lebanese, although in most cases, when the
woman marries outside the nationality, the new
family does not continue in attendance at the
national church.

Table 5 indicates the progression of assimilation from the earliest records of St. Basil's and
St. Elias' on the numbers of inter-ritual marriages
to the present. It will be noted that marriages
within the group outnumbered those between nationalities for almost fifty years until 1949, and that
the following year, 1950, was the last year that
marriages within the group outnumbered those between
nationalities. Although only sample years are
listed, the parish records for all years were
checked and indicate that the conclusions drawn are
valid.

167

TABLE 5

NUMBER OF MARRIAGES BETWEEN TWO SYRIANS AND
BETWEEN ONE SYRIAN AND ANOTHER NATIONALITY
FROM RECORDS OF ST. BASIL'S AND ST. ELIAS'
IN SAMPLE YEARS

Year	Homogeneous	Mixed
1920	8	none
1921	12	1
1937	4	1
1938	3	3
1948	12	6
1949	8	10
1950	8	4
1959	2	18
1969	none	7
1972	1	9

The degree of Americanization of Americans of "new" immigrant stock is complex and difficult to measure. However, if loyalty to the United States and willingness to serve in her armed forces is any indication of such Americanization, one would have to rate the Syrian community of Woonsocket highly. It is interesting to note the degree to which second generation Syrians supported their country during World War II in comparison to the rampant draft evasion prevalent among Syrians in the old country under the Turkish empire. In World War II,

Woonsocket's "smallest Catholic parish . . . probably (had) the largest proportion of its men in the
nation's armed services" (Woonsocket Call 1942).
Of the twenty-five Syrian families in the parish,
twenty-nine men served, including nine sets of
brothers.

Future accelerated Americanization and perhaps
disintegration could result from the fact that
Eastern rite priests are now being trained in America. St. Basil's Seminary in Methuen, Massachusetts
was founded in 1953, and has been training American-
born men to the priesthood. Three men of Italian-
American descent have been so trained, and Father
James King, an Irish-American who trained there was
the first to serve that parish. Presently Rev.
Joseph Haggar is pastor of both St. Basil and St.
Elias churches, with Rev. Kenneth Sherman as assistant. Both are American born and trained.

The present communities have lost some ethnic
unity due to the increasing number of inter-ritual
marriages and the leakage this causes to Latin rite
churches. This invisible minority made up of
people like myself of Arabic descent who attend
neighborhood rather than ethnic churches, would
probably double the number of church-going Arabic
families. Another cause of the loss of ethnic
insularity and unity that tends to accelerate
assimilation lies in the fact that very few immigrants now arrive from the old countries. If one
compares the total number of Syrians arriving in
the entire country in 1972 which was 1,012 immigrants (U. S. Dept. of Justice 1972) to the number
of Syrians who settled here in Rhode Island in 1913
(the peak year of immigration) which was 296 immigrants (U. S. Dept. of Treasury 1913), one can see
the drop in immigration of the Syrians to this
country. The number of immigrants who came to
Rhode Island only in 1913 represents approximately
33% of the total figure for the entire country in
1972. More detailed figures would be necessary to
properly correlate the information, but it is evident that immigration has slowed down.

What conclusions can be drawn about the Syrians
and the Lebanese and their history in the State of
Rhode Island? How have they progressed economically,
politically and socially? How have they retained
their religious and cultural heritage and what pre-
dictions can be made about future generations keeping alive this heritage?

Economically, the Syrians and Lebanese of the
state have moved up the ladder fairly well and have
moved into all types of vocations and professions,
providing a middle class within the group. This
led to political involvement beginning in the decade
of the 50's with interest, and leading to success
in the 60's and 70's. Socially, they have assimilated through marriage with many other groups compared to their early insularity. This, however,
has caused some loss of ethnic identity. These
findings could perhaps apply to every ethnic group
in the state. However, the one factor which seems
to differentiate the Syrians and Lebanese from most
of the other groups is their Eastern form of worship, and consequently their churches have been
very instrumental in keeping the groups, which are
very small and could easily be totally assimilated,
from disintegrating. Social affairs of an ethnic
nature are promoted through the churches and even
fourth generation Syrians and Lebanese enjoy "hafla"
(social gatherings) and "mahrajans," (festival).
The recent appointment of Maronite and Melchite
bishops and the establishment of dioceses in the
United States will be a help in preserving these
churches. The Catholics of Eastern rites are a
link to the Orthodox churches of the same ethnic
groups and can promote ecumenism and provide hope
for a future rapproachment. As both the Roman and
Orthodox churches continue evolving, perhaps in
future generations this re-unification might be
more possible. In December 1972, Roman Catholics
participated in the Orthodox Liturgy of St. James
"for what may (have been) the first time in America" when Father Doumato, pastor of St. Ephraim's
invited the class he had been lecturing on the beliefs and forms of his church for the School of

Ecumenical Theology sponsored by Our Lady of Con-
solation Church in Pawtucket, to join the Orthodox
celebration. There were Roman Catholic nuns in
attendance who received Holy Communion, and this
can be seen as a step in the direction of greater
understanding (Providence Journal 1972).

In recent years, the degree of Arab consciousness has risen, evidenced by the formation of various national organizations such as the Association
of Arab-American University Graduates (1967), the
National Association of Arab Americans (1972), and
the American Arab Anti-Discrimination Committee
(1980) of which former U. S. Senator James G.
Abourezk is a founder.

However, it would seem that the preservation
of ethnic identity for the vast majority of Arab-
Americans in Rhode Island will continue more
through identification with the Syrian and Lebanese churches than with national Arab organizations. The churches will continue to be the vehi-
cle which will prevent assimilation, at least during this century.

REFERENCES CITED

Allam, James
    1973 Personal interview. February (primary
        source, unpublished).

Anid, Cyril J.
    1967 I Grew With Them. Jounieh, Lebanon: The
        Paulis Press. (primary source, published)

Antonius, George
    1965 The Arab Awakening (1946) G. P. Putnam's
        Sons, Capricorn Books: New York.

Bethmann, Erich W.
    1950 Bridges to Islam: A Study of the Reli-
        gious Forces of Islam and Christianity in
        the Near East. Nashville: Southern Publish-
        ing Association.

Boston Herald Traveler
    1968 Bishop Justin Najmy of Melkite Catholics.
        12 June, obituary page (primary source, pub-
        lished).

Carroll, Leo E.
    1959 Irish and Italians in Providence, Rhode Is-
        land, 1880-1960. Rhode Island History, Sum-
        mer XXVIII: 67-74.

Catholic Dictionary, The Modern
    1980 John A. Hardon, S. J., editor. Doubleday
        and Company, Inc.: Garden City, N. Y.

Catholic Directory, The Official for the Year of Our
    Lord 1980
    1980 P. J. Kenedy & Sons: N. Y. Editor A. J.
        Corbo

Doumato, Rev. Abdoulahad
    1973 Telephone interview. April.
    1981 Telephone interview. March. (primary
        source, unpublished)

Ellis, John Tracy
    1969 American Catholicism 2nd ed. The Chicago
    History of American Civilization. Chicago:
    University of Chicago Press.

Ferguson, Rev. Timothy
    1981 Telephone interview. March. (Pastor at
    St. Mary's Orthodox) (primary source, unpub-
    lished).

Haggar, Rev. Joseph
    1973 Personal and Telephone Interviews. Febru-
    ary and March.
    1981 Telephone interview. March. (primary
    source, unpublished).

Hitti, Philip K.
    1924 The Syrians in America. New York: Doran
    Publishing Company.
    1965 A Short History of Lebanon. New York: St.
    Martin's Press.

Hobeika, Rev. Peter
    1973 Personal and telephone interviews. March.
    1981 Telephone interview. March

Hourani, A. H.
    1946 Syria & Lebanon: A Political Essay. New
    York: Oxford University Press.

International Institute
    1922 & 1935 (bound together -- Providence Public
    Library) Survey of Foreign Communities of
    Providence. Providence, Rhode Island: By
    the Author.

Itzkowitz, Norman
    1972 Ottoman Empire & Islamic Tradition. Al-
    fred A. Knopf: New York.

Jones, Maldwyn Allen
    1960 American Immigration. The Chicago History
    of American Civilization. Chicago: Univer-
    sity of Chicago Press.

King, Rev. James
    1973 Telephone interviews. April & May. (primary source, unpublished).

Maloof, Rev. Allen.
    N. D. Eastern Rites of the Catholic Church (Pamphlet No. 290) Huntington, Indiana: Our Sunday Visitor, Inc.

Mansfield, Peter
    1976 The Ottoman Empire and its Successors. (1973) St. Martin's Press: New York.

Nazarian, Dr. John
    1972 Telephone interview (primary source, unpublished).

Pawtucket Times
    1954-1972 Various articles 1 Dec. through 6 Oct.

Providence, Diocese of
    1912 Archives: Parish Records Books

Providence Journal/Evening Bulletin
    1929 Early Settlers Slept and Ate in Mills on First Arrival Here in 1902 -- Maronites, Peasant Herders, Take to Peddling, Old Customs Cherished. 24 April, p. 8 (Journal).
    1951 Young Men's Group Hears Teachers Speak on Need for Voting. 9 April (Bulletin).
    1960 2 April (Bulletin).
    1966a By A New Bishop: Humble Aspiration Must Be Set Aside. 10 March (Journal).
    1966b 12 November (Journal).
    1972 Catholics Attend Syrian Service. 2 Dec.
    1981 Arab Foundation.

Rizk, Salom
    1949 Syrian Yankee. Garden City, N. Y.: Doubleday & Company, Inc.

Shadid, Michael A.
    1939 A Doctor For the People. New York: The Vanguard Press.

Saliba, Rev. Athanasius E.
    1973 Telephone interview. April. (primary
        source, unpublished).

Sherman, Rev. Kenneth
    1981 Telephone interview. March 21. (Assis-
        tant: St. Basil's, Central Falls, and St.
        Elias Mission, Woonsocket, Melkite Churches)
        (primary source, unpublished).

Solomon, Anthony
    1973 Telephone interview. April. (primary
        source, unpublished).

Visitor (formerly Providence Visitor)
    1935 26 September
    1960 30 September
    1968 St. Basil's Parish, Central Falls and St.
        Elias' Parish, Woonsocket, 26 April, p. 21.

Woonsocket Call
    1931-1971 Various articles 19 December through
        1 March.

NOTES

I wish to acknowledge the invaluable help of
Dr. Robert Laffey, visiting lecturer in Middle East
history at the Providence College School of Continuing Education who read the manuscript and offered suggestions dealing with political history,
immigration factors and the development of the
Rhode Island Arab community. Any conclusions
drawn in these areas, however, are of course, my
responsibility.

AZOREANS IN AMERICA:
MIGRATION AND CHANGE RECONSIDERED

Mark J. Handler

The study of immigration has a venerable tradition in American social science -- a long-term
interest that has been motivated by a perception of
the immigrant as a social problem. But beyond such
applied interest, the study of immigration has two,
more fundamental, theoretical contributions to
make. First, migration provides a special labora-
tory for examining the relative importance of social and cultural factors in anthropological explanation. In most research settings it is difficult
to distinguish the effects of situational constraints from the effects of taken-for-granted
ideas. It is only when ongoing social relations
are broken that we can investigate the interplay of
belief and context, or of conformity and practical
interest in shaping behavior. Migration provides
such occasions for study. The immigrants' new society differs from their old both culturally and
structurally and the study of immigrant adaptations
contributes to our understanding of these two types
of factors.

Second, the study of immigration is, in a
sense, the study of American society. Advocacy
of cultural pluralism is becoming an official
ideology in the United States, but this new legitimacy should not lead us to think that ethnicity
itself is new in America. Structural pluralism,
ethnic enclaves, and differential access to "common" institutions are historically normal to American social structure -- they appear as temporary,
aberrant, or pathological only from the perspective
of ideologies (e.g., Anglo-conformity) which justify the privilege of an elite which is itself, in
part, ethnicly defined.

Written at the midpoint of ongoing research
on Azorean immigration in New England, the present
paper is a critical discussion of accepted models

of migration and ethnicity, set within a general
description of Azorean immigration and Portuguese-
American culture.

Part of the preparation of the present work
and fieldwork in the Azores, from November 1973 to
July 1975, was supported by NIH Grant IT 32 MH14249.
My research in the Azores and New England is part
of a larger project on Portuguese culture and migration conducted under the auspices of the Department of Anthropology, Brown University. The other
project members and their research sites are:
Z. Caroline Brettell (Northern Portugal, Paris, and
Toronto), Stephen Cabral (New England, Sao Miguel,
and Madeira), George L. Hicks (Azores, principally
Sao Miguel, and New England), Philip Leis (New
England and the Algarve), and Deirdre Meintel
Machado (Cabo Verde and New England). The theoretical perspective of this paper owes much to my
long-term and continuing dialogue with Professor
George Hicks. The paper has benefited from a critical reading by Dr. Linda Stone. I am, of course,
responsible for any errors.

Portuguese in the United States: Settlement History

Of nationalities immigrating to the United
States, the Portuguese are one of the least known.
This is not surprising for they constituted only
0.86% of all immigrants to the United States from
1820 to 1974, ranking 14th among European countries. Estimates put the current number of persons
born in Portugal or of Portuguese-descent in the
United States at 1,000,000 (Ussach 1975:48; Rogers
1974:37). However, while the Portuguese have little nation-wide recognition, they are heavily concentrated in a few areas where they are far from
invisible. Most Portuguese migration has been to
south-eastern New England and central California.

Portugal has long had a very high rate of emigration, but the majority has been to Brazil and,
after the mid 1950's, to France. The United States
has been the destination of only perhaps 10% of all

Portuguese migrants. But in emigration, too, there is geographic concentration -- a few districts account for almost all of the migration to America. From the Azores (the region of origin of most Portuguese in the United States) over 90% of the outmigration is to North America, slightly more than half destined for the United States (see Tables 3 and 4).

Portugal, though small in area and population, consists of regions whose social, cultural, and ecological differences and the distinct social identities of their inhabitants make it important that we distinguish Portuguese immigrants by their communities of origin. There are, of course, elements common to all the regions and the majority of immigrants do share similar occupational and educational backgrounds. While these differences and similarities cannot be examined here in any detail (and as yet have not been fully investigated), in outlining Portuguese migration to America, major areas of emigration will be indicated. In order of their importance to Portuguese-American immigration (see Tables 5 and 6), the broad donor areas are:

Azores: an archipelago of nine islands in the North Atlantic, 800 miles west of continental Portugal, 2100 miles from New York. Population in 1970 was 291,028. The nine islands are administratively grouped in three districts: Ponta Delgada (Sao Miguel and Santa Maria), Angra do Heroismo (Terceira, Sao Jorge, and Graciosa), and Horta (Faial, Pico, Flores, and Corvo). This organization was in effect until the 1976 Constitution provided partial decentralization, establishing the archipelago as an autonomous region. Sao Miguel and Santa Maria are the easternmost, Corvo and Flores are in the extreme west of the archipelago, and the rest are clustered in the center. Economically and politically the most important island are Sao Miguel, Terceira, and Faial, with Sao Miguel the largest in population and area of all the islands. The Azores were uninhabited until colonized by the Portuguese in the fifteenth century. Migration to the United States from Sao Miguel and Santa Maria tends to be to New England, that from Terceira to California.

Cape Verde: (before 1975 part of "Overseas Portugal" -- the official euphemism for colonial territories -- now independent) an archipelago of 14 islands (9 inhabited) about 400 miles off the coast of Senegal. The 1970 population was 199,661. Cape Verdeans are of Afro-Portuguese descent and in the United States are sometimes referred to as "Black Portuguese". Cape Verdeans have emigrated to both California and New England.

Madeira: Six islands, two inhabited, in the North Atlantic north of the Canaries. 1970 population was 253,220. Madeiran emigration has been principally to South not North America.

Continental Portugal: had a 1970 population of almost 8,124,019. Twelve regions (provinces) are recognized, divided in 18 administrative districts. Though the continent as a whole is second to the Azores in number of emigrants to the United States, no single district (except Lisbon and, perhaps, Aveiro) makes a sizeable contribution to Portuguese-American immigration. Following general patterns of Portuguese out-migration, the districts of Northern Portugal account for most of the continental emigration to North America, with almost no migrants originating in the southern province of Alentejo.

This paper concentrates on the Azores because it is the most important single region of origin of Portuguese in America. The other important group, the Cape Verdeans, are the subject of Machado's paper in this volume.

This historical outline is drawn from several secondary sources (Antunes 1973; Bohme 1956; Ferst 1972; Pap 1949; Rogers 1974; Serrao 1974; Taft 1923; Ussach 1975). Cited statistics should be taken as only suggestive of actual magnitudes of migration. The reliability of these figures is questionable for several reasons: (a) accuracy of counts and records, (b) variability of categories enumerated (e.g. "Portuguese", "Azorean") from period to period and between sources, (c) unrecorded migration (particularly clandestine emigration).

Three periods of Portuguese immigration can be distinguished: small-scale migration from the 16th century to 1870; a first wave of mass-migration, 1871-1926; a second wave of mass-migration, 1966-present.

16th century-1870: There were Portuguese among the early explorers of North America but no permanent settlements in the 16th century. Sporadic and numerically unimportant immigration occurred in the 17th century. This migration was mainly individual, though groups of Portuguese Jews (arriving via Brazil) established settlements in New Amsterdam and in Newport, Rhode Island in the latter part of the century. This was not, however, a continuing migration.

The arrival of Yankee whalers in the Azores in the late 18th century initiated continuous Portuguese migration to the United States. Prevailing winds and the need to replenish supplies and crews made the Azorean ports (principally Horta, Faial), and also the Cape Verdes, regular way-stations for Atlantic whalers. In the 19th century New Bedford, Massachusetts was the center of New England whaling and consequently the focus of Portuguese (Azorean and Cape Verdean) settlement during the first two-thirds of the century. Early in the century other settlements were established along the New England coast (e.g., at Martha's Vineyard, Cape Cod, Gloucester, Boston, and Providence) and, soon after, smaller settlements formed in Fall River, New London, and New York City.

California was, and continues to be, the second major area of Portuguese settlement. Here, too, continuous immigration was stimulated by the whaling industry. New England whalers bound for the Arctic used San Francisco as a way-station and some of their Azorean crewmen settled there. The gold rush attracted more Portuguese, from New England and directly from Portugal. From 1850 to 1880 shore-whaling flourished along the California coast and was dominated by Portuguese (Bohme 1956).

Third in importance as an area of settlement was Hawaii. The earliest immigrants were again sailors. Between 1830 and 1878 about 400 arrived, half from Cape Verde, the rest from the Azores (Pap 1949:6).

Singular instances of group migrations to other areas occurred -- to Louisiana in 1840 and to Illinois in 1849. No continuous migration was established in either of these areas.

Mass-Migration (1), 1871-1926: According to the U. S. Census there were 8,976 persons of Portuguese birth in the continental United States in 1870. While 2,658 Portuguese had immigrated between 1861 and 1870, five times as many (14,082) arrived in the following decade (Pap 1949:6). From 1821 to 1870 an average of 105 Portuguese entered the United States annually. In the period of mass-migration 1871-1930, the average was almost forty-fold greater: 4,224 per year (see Table 1).

The majority of the early migrants had been from the Western Azores (Faial and Pico) but during the last quarter of the 19th century an ever increasing number came from Sao Miguel. The smaller Cape Verdean stream continued through this period and, from the end of the 19th century, Madeira was also an important donar area. Migration from continental Portugal was not appreciable until after 1910 (Pap 1949:7).

In the years 1913-1917 out-migration from Portugal to all countries totaled 163,411 of which 25% was to North America. The Azores provided 13% of the migrants in those years, with 95% destined for North America. Fifty percent of the Portuguese migrants to North America were Azorean, 32.5% from Sao Miguel (computed from figures in Taft 1923:88, Table 10.).

From the beginning of this period to the present, two motives for migration stand out. The principal consideration has been economic: poverty and limited opportunity for economic mobility in Portugal, while in the United States expansion of industry and growing organization and militancy of native workers created a demand for immigrant labor. Even entering as an unskilled laborer (as most did), an Azorean immigrant experienced an appreciable rise in standard of living. The intent of many was to earn money in America with which to buy land in the Azores, but most migration was in fact permanent (return migration was perhaps 1/4 or 1/5 the magnitude of immigration). (Estimated from Taft 1923: 101, Table 12.) A secondary motive was escape from military service. Strictly enforced universal conscription created a steady stream of clandestine migration to Europe and North America.

From Table 2 we see that throughout this period, California and southern New England were the major centers of Portuguese immigration. In 1880 slightly over half the Portuguese immigrants were residing in California; Massachusetts was second in importance with 22.9%. By 1920 the East Coast had gained preeminence with only 31% then resident in California and over 62% in New England (50% in Massachusetts alone). Migration to Hawaii was mainly between 1878 and 1899, mostly contract laborers from Sao Miguel and Madeira. There was little subsequent migration, and many of the immigrants later left Hawaii for California (Pap 1949: 8).

At the end of the 19th century petroleum replaced sperm oil and the whaling industry declined rapidly. New Bedford, followed by Fall River, shifted to textile manufacturing and most of the Portuguese in these and other New England communities shifted from the sea to industrial labor (though some remained in fishing and farming). (Pap 1949:7). Factory owners favored hiring immigrant labor as a means of combating the growing strength of domestic labor unions. In 1904, following strikes in Fall River mills, there was

183

direct labor recruitment in Sao Miguel. By 1909
25% of the foreign-born workers in New Bedford
mills and 20% in Fall River were Portuguese (Pap
1949:14).

Whaling in California also declined in the
1880's but a number of Portuguese had already shifted to fishing. In the 1880's most of the fisher-
ies and markets were controlled by Italians and
Portuguese. In 1888 about 20% of the foreign-born
fishermen in California were Portuguese (Bohme
1956:239). Commercial fishing greatly expanded
after the turn of the century and Portuguese immigrants were sixth in numbers in the industry
(native-born Americans and Italian immigrants were
1st and 2nd). However, the majority of Portuguese
in California took up farming. From the 1850's
through the 1880's Portuguese settled and bought
land in all the major agricultural areas of the
state. They engaged in vegetable truck farming,
sheep raising, vineyard keeping and large field
crops. In 1920, first generation Portuguese had
10% of the farms owned by foreign-born (Bohme 1956:
241-242). The Portuguese were especially prominent
in the dairy industry. State-wide, early in the
century, they were the largest group in terms of
herds owned. After World War II they were second.
In some areas, e.g., the lower San Joaquin Valley,
70-75% of the dairy herds are said to be Portuguese
owned (Bohme 1956:243).

The first wave of mass migration was brought
to an end by the reversal of 'open door' immigration
policy. The first attempt at restriction was the
introduction of a literacy requirement in 1917.
After an initial drop (probably due as much to the
World War) the law caused little if any reduction
in the magnitude of immigration, though it did
select for immigrants with higher levels of education. But in the mid-1920's, half a century of
nativist agitation (now combined with opposition
from organized labor) succeeded in severely re-
stricting immigration to the United States. Guided
by racial nativists and eugenicists, nationality
quotas were established in 1921 and tightened in

1924. The quotas reduced the volume of immigration by 76%, to an annual limit of 150,000 with the greatest restrictions aimed at Southern and Eastern Europeans. Portuguese immigration was reduced from the 1911-1920 annual average of almost 9,000 (19,195 in the peak year of Portuguese immigration, 1921) to an annual quota of 440. In the twenty years from 1931-1950 a total of only 10,752 Portuguese immigrants came to the United States (US 1974: Table 13). Volcanic eruptions in Faial in 1957 led to special quota exemptions (the Azorean Refugee Act of 1958) under which an additional 4,811 Portuguese entered (US 1974: Table 6E).

Mass-Migration (2), 1966-present: The passage of the Immigration Act of 1965, ending forty years of restrictive and discriminatory quotas, initiated a new period of mass immigration in the United States. The new law provides for admission of immediate family of U. S. citizens without numerical limitation, and a further maximum of 20,000 visas to each Eastern Hemisphere country (with preference given to relatives of citizens and resident aliens).

Portuguese immigration since 1966 has averaged almost 12,000 per year -- higher than the annual average in the first period of mass-migration (see Table 1). Whereas in all previous periods Portuguese have accounted for less than 1% of total immigration, they have constituted 3% of all immigration since 1966. In southeastern New England they are currently the largest immigrant group. In Massachusetts twice as many Portuguese as Italians are now immigrating (Ussach 1975:48; Rogers 1974:37).

Comparing Table 3 and Table 4 we see that the percentage of total Portuguese emigration destined for the United States in the years 1970-1972 is almost double that for the preceding twenty years. These tables also reveal a growing shift in Azorean emigration to Canada in preference to the United States. As Table 6 indicates, Azoreans continue to constitute the majority of Portuguese immigrants to the United States (53%), most of the rest are from Continental Portugal, with only 0.7% arriving from

185

Madeira. Approximately 400 Cape Verdean immigrants
are reported for 1968 (Rogers 1974:36). At this
rate they would account for 3-4% of Portuguese immigration. A fair estimate would be that before
the 1926 cut-off, 6% of Portuguese immigration to
the United States was from the Cape Verdes.

Table 2 shows the distribution of first generation Portuguese in the United States in 1974.
Almost 60% resided in New England while California
had only 18%. The increased importance of New Jersey as a center of Portuguese settlement is also
apparent. In the older areas of settlement in
Massachusetts, persons of Portuguese descent presently constitute the majority (in, for example,
Fall River and New Bedford). Recent years have
also seen the growth of new Portuguese communities
in smaller towns of New England.

General characteristics of current Portuguese
immigrants are suggested by the following 1974 immigration statistics: of a total of 11,302 immigrants to the United States from Portugal, 50.2%
were female and 38% were between the ages of 20-39
(computed from U. S. 1974: table 9). Of 4,544
Portuguese immigrants reporting occupations only
5.3% were professional, technical, or managerial;
21.7% were craftsmen; 12.2% operatives; 22.4% non-
farm laborers; 11.8 % far laborers and foremen; and
14.4% were private household workers (see Table 7
for comparisons with "All Europe" and Italians).

From this general review of Portuguese immigration we now proceed to a discussion of the nature of migration and its effects.

TABLE 1: IMMIGRANTS TO THE UNITED STATES

| | All Countries | | Italy | | Portugal | |
	total	/year	total	/year	total	/year
1821-1870	7,368,853	147,377	25,488	510	5,237	105
1871-1930	30,384,774	506,413	4,625,667	77,095	247,443	4,124
1931-1965	5,529,261	157,979	390,073	11,145	44,648	1,276
1966-1974	3,421,452	380,161	216,817	24,091	105,845	11,761
1820-1974	46,712,725	301,372	5,159,026	33,929	399,845	2,580

SOURCE: U. S. Immigration and Naturalization Service Annual Report 1974,
compiled from Tables 13 and 14 (pp. 56-59).

(figures on Italian immigration are included for comparison because
Italians are well known in the literature on migration and because
they are prominent in the areas of Portuguese concentration in New
England).

TABLE 2: DISTRIBUTION OF 1ST GENERATION PORTUGUESE IMMIGRANTS
IN THE UNITED STATES

	1860[1]		1880[1]		1900[1]		1920[1]		1940[2]		1974[3]	
	#	%	#	%	#	%	#	%	#	%	#	%
U. S.	5,477		15,650		48,099		106,437		88,098		110,859	
Calif.	1,580	28.8	8,061	51.5	15,583	32.4	33,409	31.4	29,628	33.6	20,131	18.2
Conn.	265	4.8	244	15.6	655	1.4	1,410	1.3	2,252	2.6	8,383	7.6
Hawaii					7,668	15.9					104	.1
Mass.	1,421	25.9	3,582	22.9	17,885	37.2	53,545	50.3	36,450	41.4	42,756	38.6
N. J.					151	.3	825	.8	2,643	3.0	12,977	11.7
N. Y.	449	8.2	422	2.7	823	1.7	1,973	1.9	4,580	5.2	6,921	6.2
Pa.	117	2.1	210	1.3	191	.4	885	.8	926	1.1	1,625	1.5
R. I.	110	2.0	395	2.5	2,865	6.0	11,615	10.9	9,776	11.1	14,766	13.3

[1]Compiled from Taft (1923) Table 26 (p. 119); original source U. S. Censuses 1860, 1880, 1900, and 1920. Portuguese = "Portugal" and "Atlantic Islands" (does not include Cape Verde). Figures provided only for states reporting 100+ Portuguese. 1920 figure for Hawaii not available in Taft.

[2]Compiled from Pap (1949) p. 10; original source 1940 U. S. Census. Portuguese = "whites born in Continental Portugal or Azores" (excludes Madeira and Cape Verde).

[3]Compiled from U. S. Immigration and Naturalization Service Annual Report 1974, Table 35 "Aliens who reported under the Alien Address Program by selected nationalities and state of residence".

TABLE 3: DISTRIBUTION OF PORTUGUESE EMIGRATION FROM VARIOUS DISTRICTS OF ORIGIN BY COUNTRY OF DESTINATION, IN PERCENTAGES, 1950-1969.

% of emigrants from	Canada	U.S.A.	Destined for Brazil	Venezuela	France	Other
Angra do Heroismo	23.0	69.8	6.3	0.3	0.1	0.5
Horta	24.9	73.6	1.0	0.1	.0	0.4
Ponta Delgada	48.5	42.6	3.9	0.2	0.1	4.7
Funchal	0.8	0.7	35.6	46.5	.0	16.4
Lisboa	9.5	9.5	15.1	1.4	31.0	33.5
Viana do Castelo	4.1	3.3	26.5	1.3	59.6	5.2
All Portugal	6.2	8.4	31.4	7.4	34.7	11.9

Source: adapted from Antunes (1973) Table 9 (p. 27). (based on "official emigration" only -- does not include clandestine migration, which if considered would increase France's share by almost 10%).

(In this and tables 4-6, Viana do Castelo appears, somewhat arbitrarily, to illustrate patterns of migration from Northern Portugal).

189

TABLE 4: DISTRIBUTION OF PORTUGUESE EMIGRATION FROM VARIOUS DISTRICTS OF ORIGIN BY COUNTRY OF DESTINATION, IN PERCENTAGES, 1970-1972.

% of emigrants from	Canada	U.S.A.	Brazil	Venezuela	France	Other
Angra do Heroismo	34.3	65.1	———	0.4	0	0.2
Horta	37.1	62.8	———	0	—	0.1
Ponta Delgada	56.0	41.6	2.5	0.1	0	2.3
Funchal	0.9	1.4	2.5	88.8	0.1	6.3
Lisboa	8.1	12.2	2.1	0.8	17.5	59.3
Viana do Castelo	12.0	16.1	3.4	0.6	55.3	12.6
All Portugal	11.9	15.3	2.4	5.9	29.1	35.4

Source: adapted from Antunes (1973) Table A-6 (p. 95).

TABLE 5: COMPOSITION OF PORTUGUESE EMIGRATION TO VARIOUS COUNTRIES
BY DISTRICT OF ORIGIN, IN PERCENTAGES, 1950-1969.

% of emigrants to	Originating in					
	Angra[a]	Horta	P.D.[b]	Funchal	Lisbon	Viana[c]
U. S. A.	14.4	13.0	31.6	0.7	6.8	2.1
Canada	6.3	5.9	48.1	1.1	9.2	3.5
Brazil	0.3	0	0.8	9.6	2.9	4.5
Venezuela	0.1	0	0.2	52.7	1.1	1.0
France	0	0	0	0	5.4	9.1
All Countries	1.7	1.5	6.2	8.4	6.0	5.3

Source: adapted from Antunes (1973) Table 9A (p. 28). (based on
"official emigration" only -- does not include clandestine
migration).

(a) Angra do Heroismo; (b) Ponta Delgada; (c) Viana do Castelo

TABLE 6: COMPOSITION OF PORTUGUESE EMIGRATION TO VARIOUS COUNTRIES BY DISTRICT OF ORIGIN, IN PERCENTAGES, 1970-1972.

% of emigrants to	Originating in					
	Angra	Horta	P. D.	Funchal	Lisbon	Viana
U. S. A.	15.6	8.3	28.9	0.4	8.8	3.2
Canada	10.5	6.3	49.9	0.3	7.5	3.1
Brazil	—	—	0.2	0.4	9.7	4.5
Venezuela	0.2	0	0	64.8	0	0.3
France	0	—	0	0	6.7	5.8
All Countries	3.6	2.0	10.6	4.3	11.1	3.1

Source: adapted from Antunes (1973) Table A-7 (p. 96)

TABLE 7: OCCUPATIONS OF IMMIGRANTS FROM PORTUGAL, ITALY, AND ALL EUROPE
YEAR ENDING JUNE 30, 1974

| | immigrants (reporting occupation) by major occupation group, in % | | | | | | | | | | | |
	A	B	C	D	E	F	G	H	I	J	K	L
Portugal	2.2	3.1	0.8	4.4	21.7	10.6	2.6	22.4	0.2	11.8	5.8	14.4
Italy	6.9	3.7	1.2	2.9	29.8	15.0	2.0	15.8	0.3	10.0	8.6	3.7
All Europe	18.0	5.9	2.2	7.7	20.3	10.5	2.0	9.1	0.3	8.7	10.2	5.2

A. Professional, technical and kindred workers
B. Managers and administrators, except farm
C. Sales workers
D. Clerical and kindred workers
E. Craftsmen and kindred workers
F. Operatives, except transport
G. Transport equipment operatives
H. Laborers, except farm
I. Farmers and farm managers
J. Farm laborers and farm foremen
K. Service workers, except private household
L. Private household workers

Source: computed from U. S. Immigration and Naturalization Service Annual
Report (1974) Table 8.

193

Images of Immigration

Perhaps the most widely accepted description of the immigrant experience is Oscar Handlin's:

> Emigration took these people out of traditional, accustomed environments and replanted them in strange ground, among strangers, where strange manners prevailed. The customary modes of behavior were no longer adequate, for the problems of life were new and different. With old ties snapped, men faced the enormous compulsion of working out new relationships, new meanings to their lives, often under harsh and hostile circumstances.
> (Handlin 1951:5)

> The immigrants lived in crisis because they were uprooted. In transplantation, while the old roots were sundered, before the new were established, the immigrants existed in an extreme situation. The shock, and the effects of the shock, persisted for many years; and their influence reached down to generations which themselves never paid the cost of crossing.
> (Handlin 1951:6)

Since immigrants are objects of study largely because they are defined as social problems, it is not surprising that the stress of migration is so emphasized. This view provides a sympathetic and liberal explanation for the perceived problems and pathologies of the immigrants. It is an explanation that argues environment over innate cause. Further, by placing the blame for the immigrants' difficulties on the process of migration it frees American institutions and elites of responsibility. This variation of "blaming the victim" has many parallels in American social science. The poor have problems because they have a pathological subculture (the "culture of poverty"), though historical factors beyond their control were originally responsible for the development of this culture.

194

The American Negro has problems because he has no culture, it having been stripped away by the brutality of slavery (an alternative view finds a pathological black sub-culture). The culture concept can be used to 'explain away' as well as to explain. See Szwed (1969) and Valentine (1968) for critiques of these theories.

Explanations of immigrant problems as inherent in the process of migration have in common a focus on culture: conflict of old and new cultures, inadequacy of native culture, deculturation, etc. Yet these explanations have been developed without ethnographic knowledge of the migrants' communities of origin. They are further flawed by a mistaken assumption of cultural homogeneity as the natural condition of American society. The following discussion reexamines two of these explanations in the light of ethnographic knowledge from the Azores and of a pluralistic model of American society.

(1) In descriptions like Handlin's, emigration is portrayed as a leap into the unknown, an uprooting which causes personal and social disorganization. But such characterizations do not apply to Azorean emigration and, on demographic grounds alone, it can be doubted that they apply, except in rare cases, to any migrations (one exception is the forced migration of refugees). There is little "crisis" and "shock" of uprooting because migration is normally a large-scale, institutionalized phenomenon.

The scale of Azorean emigration can be illustrated by figures from the District of Ponta Delgada. In the decade 1910-1920 emigration from the District totalled 28,000 in a population of 146,000 and in 1960-1970 59,000 in 218,000 (Distrito 1973). Currently, emigration is exceeding natural increase -- from 1968 to 1972 total population declined by 17% (computed from Portugal 1974:15). Within districts, out-migration is not uniform, so the real magnitude and impact of emigration is better realized by observing that there are villages which have lost 75% of their population in the last

15 years. Such large-scale emigration is already
a century old.

Emigration is institutionalized in the Azores:
there is a body of knowledge and standardized expectations associated with it; the "emigrant" exists
as a social role. Azoreans have maintained an explicit public awareness of migration. Stories about
emigration to America were published in Faial as
early as 1884. The stereo-typical emigrant, the
Califona, is featured in jokes and popular theater.
The situation of Azoreans in the United States and
the effects of emigration on the islands is a topic
of church sermons. Knowledge of America, of the
communities of destination, is extensive and generally accurate. There are few Azoreans who do
not have relatives in the United States or Canada;
and common sights in many Azorean homes are calen-
dars and pictures bearing the names of American
towns and businesses. The bulk of personal mail is
to and from North America. A quarter of the films
shown and music broadcast in the Azores are American. And in May and June daily flights are filled
with emigrants and their descendants returning for
vacations in their communities of origin. Given
such communication it is not surprising that men
who have never left the islands can discuss wages
for various jobs in the United States, know the
names of towns and streets in Massachusetts and
Rhode Island, have heard of Watergate, and have
opinions about racial conflict in American cities.
Normally, by the time a visa is obtained, an emigrant has already arranged a temporary place to
live and a job in America. And in the new home and
at the new job the migrant is surrounded by Portuguese-speakers: fellow islanders, former village
neighbors, relatives, and others.

Thus, with the exception of the pioneers of
mid-19th century and earlier, an Azorean migrating
to New England or California neither followed an
unchartered course nor travelled alone. Vecoli,
writing of Italian migrants (contadini) in Chicago,
similarly criticizes the Handlin view:

196

While there is no desire to belittle
the hardships, fears and anxieties to which
the immigrant was subject, there are good
reasons for contending that Handlin over-
states the disorganizing effects of emigration . . . . Handlin . . . dramatically
pictures the immigrant ceasing to be a member of a solidary community and being cast
upon his own resources as an individual.
But this description does not apply to the
contadini who customarily emigrated as a
group from a particular town, and, once in
America, stuck together . . .
(Vecoli 1964:407-408)

Evidence of patterns of extensive communication and
chain-migration make it likely that, like the Portuguese and the Italians, other nationalities did not
experience migration as a leap into the unknown.

(2) A second formulation of the immigrant problem is perhaps dated now that the "melting pot" is
out of fashion. In this view, the natural and inevitable result of migration is the acculturation
of the minority group: over time the values, beliefs, and norms of the immigrants are replaced by
those of the dominant host society. Cultural homogeneity is held to be the normal state of society
and the basis for successful integration within it.
Measured against this normal career of acculturation, some ethnic groups are seen to be "retarded".
Responsibility for this failure to acculturate is
assigned to the immigrants themselves. For example,
in the debate over immigration restriction during
the first quarter of the century, the exclusionists
argued that Southern and Eastern Europeans were in-
capable of "Americanization" because the cultural
abyss was too great for them to bridge. In other
theories, ethnic enclaves were seen as harmful to
immigrants and their descendants because they insulated them from the larger society and thus
slowed acculturation.

If there is now a tendency to applaud cultural
difference rather than condemn it, there is also a

tendency to take ethnicity as a natural given, just as acculturation was once assumed to be inevitable. The 'leap into the unknown' is a faulty view of migration. But here the problem is a faulty view of American society and requires a reconsideration of the nature of adaptation in a plural society.

That immigrants organized along ethnic lines was neither aberrant nor undertaken wholly at their own initiative. It was not the power of primordial ethnicity that kept immigrants from "melting". Rather, the migrants found themselves in a society where many institutions were ethnically structured, where resources were available to individuals as members of ethnic groups (Schiller 1977). Examples come readily to mind -- though they are often forgotten in discussions of acculturation. By the beginning of the century, the Catholic Church was establishing "national" parishes. Ethnic monopolies of crafts and occupations were widespread. In politics, ethnicity played an important role long before the recent recognition of the "ethnic vote". Cornwell (1970) links the development of the classic political machines of the turn of the century to immigration: the machines were organized along ethnic lines, with successive waves of immigrants furnishing the clienteles for the bosses' and ward heelers' patronage and exploitation. Political machines based on Protestant "old stock" clienteles were equally ethnic organizations despite their self-designation as "American". These examples appear to reflect primordial ethnic bonds until, as will be shown for the Portuguese, it is understood that American ethnic categories do not correspond to immigrants' pre-migration social identities.

At the same time that immigrant aid societies, social workers and others were telling immigrants they must 'Americanize to get ahead', experience was teaching them that their place in America was as members of an ethnic group. As Gordon writes in this regard:

Those who had for a time ventured out
/of the ethnic enclaves/ . . . had been
lured by the vision of an "American" social
structure that was somehow larger than all
subgroups and ethnically neutral. And were
they, too, not Americans? But they found
to their dismay that at the primary group
level a neutral American social structure
was a myth -- a mirage. What at a distance
seemed to be a quasi-public edifice flying
only the all-inclusive flag of American
nationality turned out, on closer inspection, to be the clubhouse of a particular
ethnic group -- the white Anglo-Saxon Protestants, its operation shot through with
the premises and expectations of its parental ethnicity.

(Gordon 1964:113)

In actuality, then, the ethnic organization of immigrants was not a non-adaptive, conservative resistence to acculturation but a necessary adaptation to a society in which ethnicity was a major
organizing principle. Immigrants were taught to be
ethnic -- with major American institutions serving
as the agents of this acculturation'. See Schiller's (1977) detailed analysis of the role of the
Democratic Party in creating Haitian ethnic identity in N. Y. City. Also important in the creation
and maintenance of ethnic boundaries are "ethnic
brokers": individuals who function as intermedi-
aries between an ethnic group and other groups and
institutions (see Brettell 1977; Trueblood 1977).

Adapting to What: Looking for America

If not disorganization or Americanization,
then what type of change does migration entail?
What happens to Azoreans when they come to the
United States? As a shorthand answer we can say
that they become Portuguese-American. That is,
they neither become "American" (as depicted in the
Melting Pot or Anglo-Conformity models) nor do they
remain Portuguese (as in the Pluralist model).

As a result of chain-migration the immigrant's
new community in America is normally an ethnic enclave composed of other immigrant compatriots and
longer established co-ethnics. From these predeces-
sors the immigrant does not learn of America -- as
accounts of ethnic enclaves as half-way houses
would have it -- but, rather, learns their conception of America. An immigrant does not adjust to
the American way of life -- he or she adjusts to an
American way of life. In so adjusting and acculturating the Azorean immigrant becomes Portuguese-
American.

Becoming Portuguese-American involves learning
the beliefs and acting in accord with the norms of
Portuguese-American culture. Several points must
be made about such ethnic cultures. The usual view
of ethnic "subcultures" is that they result from
the maintenance of old-world customs. In the light
of ethnographic knowledge of migrant donor communities, this view is easily shown to be erroneous:
Portuguese-American culture is not Portuguese culture. But the change that creates ethnic cultures
is not the simple borrowing from a dominant host
culture depicted in acculturation theory. The new
norms and ideas may originate in the United States
or they may represent a selection, a new valuation,
from pre-existing patterns in the donor community.
A new structure of opportunity can stimulate original adaptations or permit the expression of ideas
present, but suppressed before migration.

Within a framework of inter-ethnic relations,
'custom' has a symbolic function. Where social
categories are defined by putative cultural differences, customs serve as boundary markers (Barth
1969; Cohen 1969). Thus some traits are publicly
recognized in New England as "Portuguese" and their
traditionality is emphasized. Such ethnic markers
do not always have the historical significance
claimed for them.

The following anecdotal material illustrates
these points for Portuguese-American culture:

(1) <u>Speaking of silverware</u>. Leo Pap (1949), in his study of Portuguese-American speech, found two major developments: a moderate leveling out of some native regional speech differences and a considerable amount of Anglicization, chiefly in vocabulary. In the present context it is important to emphasize that this English influence is a separate process from the use of English by bilingual speakers. While some immigrants -- and certainly most second and later generation -- use English in many situations, the point here is that the Portuguese they speak is not identical to that used in their communities of origin.

Even if, as Pap (1949:145) asserts, this speech variation does not scientifically qualify as a dialect, it is treated as such by Azoreans and Continentals who have not emigrated. Not only do Portuguese visitors comment on the "accent" with which Portuguese is spoken in, for example, Fall River, but in the Islands this speech has been stereotyped for depicting emigrants in jokes and theater. It should also be noted that some of the Anglicizations found in Portuguese-American communities have entered popular Azorean speech. Such borrowing are known as "califonismos" or "americanismos" (see Borges 1960).

As would be expected, this speech variation is standard among the second generation and long-term immigrants. However, in contacting immigrants I had known in the Azores, it was striking to observe the rapidity of linguistic change. After less than a year in Massachusetts one woman had already acquired an "accent" and an altered vocabulary -- a source of some humor for friends visiting from the islands.

According to Pap (1949:83-123), some borrowings from English are "necessary": where a new concept is encountered in America for which there is no ready Portuguese term. Other borrowings are due simply to linguistic intimacy with English speakers. In both cases there are instances of "semantic borrowing" (where a Portuguese word takes on a meaning

201

of an English word which resembles it either in sound or partial synonymity) and of "morphological borrowing" (loan-words from English are adapted to Portuguese phonology). Examples of semantic borrowings: _cela_ (in standard Portuguese "cell") to 'cellar'; _papel_ (in standard Portuguese "paper", the material in general) to mean 'newspaper' (_jornal_ in standard Portuguese); _correr uma estoa_ (_correr_ in standard Portuguese "to go fast", "to run after", etc.; _estoa_ is an adapted loan word from 'store') to mean 'to run a store' (_dirigir uma loja_ in standard Portuguese); _escola alta_ (in standard Portuguese "tall school building") to mean 'high school' (_colegio_ or _escola superior_ in standard Portuguese). Adapted loan words: _a cana_ from 'tin can' (in standard Portuguese _a lata_); _o traque_ from 'truck' (in standard Portuguese _o camiao_ or _a camioneta_); _as Crismas_ from 'Christmas" (in standard Portuguese _o natal_). These examples are taken from Pap (1949) Chapter 4.

A case not elaborated by Pap is that of English substitutions guided by what the immigrants take to be "American" norms of propriety. Pap does cite the contrary case, where an English borrowing sounds like an obscene Portuguese expression but is used freely. For example, the Portuguese word for 'corner' _canto_ has been replaced by the English borrowing: _cona_ which is a homonym for an obscene term for 'female genitals.' Pap concludes that ". . . many Portuguese immigrants (not only men) seem to be well aware of the existence of those obscene homonyms. Yet the corresponding loanwords are employed very frequently in Portuguese immigrant speech, without any embarrassment, i.e., the speakers do not seem to be disturbed by unpleasant associations." (Pap 1949:93)

In correspondence in 1978, Professor Pap informed me that he has not heard the _naifa_ usage though he has seen it reported. As "playful speculation", he suggested a further consideration that had not occurred to me: that the same motivation for the adoption of _naifa_ may have blocked use of the Anglicism foca (from 'fork'). Foca would be a taboo homonym with the English 'fuck' and a confusing homonym with Portuguese _faca_. Reflecting on the contrast in adoption of _cona_ and _naifa_ Pap suggests, and I would agree, "one may wonder whether Azorean immigrants in New England have been more anxious to avoid shocking Anglos . . . than to avoid shocking some recently arrived fellow Portuguese . . ." (Pap: personal communication).

Further examples, "knife, fork, and spoon" are in Portuguese: _a faca_, _o garfo_, _e a colher_. In New England it is not uncommon to hear instead: _a naifa_, _o garfo_, _e a colher_ -- the last two terms remaining unchanged but the English borrowing _naifa_ (from "knife") substituted for _faça_. The explanation of several Azorean informants was that _faca_ sounds like the English obscenity "fuck" so that its use in America was felt to be improper. This avoidance of inter-lingual word taboos is reported from a number of other bilingual situations (see Haas 1951).

In summary we see that there is neither conservative maintenance of donor community speech patterns nor simple substitution of English, but rather a shift to distinctive Portuguese-American patterns -- and in this the linguistic change reflects the general cultural change of the immigrant.

(2) _The importance of ox-carts_. Among the most important annual events in the Azores are the Holy Ghost Feasts (_Festas de Espirito Santo_ or _Imperios_). These feasts are given as fulfillment of promises made to the Holy Ghost in return for divine assistance. Many emigrants return to the islands to keep such promises or to attend the _Imperios_ of relatives. Culminating in a public feast in the summer, the complete ritual involves a series of preparatory steps throughout the year. The particular details and the organizational structure of the Holy Ghost Feasts vary from island to island. The incident described below occurred on the island of Santa Maria.

Participants stress the traditionality of the
Feasts and there is some documentary evidence that
present practice is largely unchanged from that of
several centuries ago. But while careful attention
is paid to ritual detail, no all activity associated with the Feasts and their preparations are
viewed as significant. Such non-prescribed activities include many of the pragmatic means to accom-
plish ritual ends.

One of the necessary steps preceding the public feast is the transportation of the bread, wine,
and meat from the house of the feast sponsor to the
feast site, often several kilometers distant.
Neighbors, friends, and relatives form a procession
and carry the large breads. The meat and wine,
and any remaining bread, are usually transported in
ox-carts specially decorated for the occasion with
flowers and ribbons. In Santa Maria, ox-carts are
still the prevalent means of heavy transport for
farmers. However, there are numerous trucks and
automobiles on the island, owned by members of the
middle class and the government, and if automobiles
happen to be present they are pressed into service
to carry breads to the feast grounds. Thus, a traditional procession is ritually required -- but,
when needed, alternative means of transport are employed.

Although the foregoing is the case for residents of Santa Maria, emigrants attending or spon-
soring Feasts do not all share this pragmatic view.
In 1974, at a procession in an isolated valley
there were too few people to carry all the breads
in a single trip to the feast site, a mile distant.
However, my offer of the use of my car was rejected
by an emigrant -- visiting after seven years in New
England -- who claimed that ox-carts were the only
permissable alternative to human transport, that an
automobile would be against tradition. He complained that things were different in America, that
there the Holy Ghost Feasts had commercial aspects,
were more like those of Sao Miguel (the island of
the majority of New England Portuguese), and the
break was not home-baked. He concluded by noting

with approval that a wealthy immigrant from Santa
Maria had purchased and sent to Massachusetts an
entire ox-cart, built in Santa Maria, so that in
one New England community there would be "authentic" Holy Ghost Feasts.

The emigrants' altered belief, in which a pro-
saic tool (an ox-cart) becomes a symbol of authentic
culture, is a good example of the nature of ethnic
boundary markers: while putatively "traditional",
their meaning and value in America may have little
or nothing in common with their significance in
the communities of origin.

(3) Women and work. If changes in language
and symbols appear superficial, the important area
of sex-roles provides a final example of Portuguese-
American culture.

In the District of Ponta Delgada only 10% of
the active, wage labor force are women and, with
the exception of those in skilled occupations or
professions (e.g., teachers) who may continue to
work after marriage, most working women are single.

Distribution of the active work force by type
of occupation in the District of Ponta Delgada,
1970:

	men	women
agriculture & fishing . . .	56.3%	1.7%
industry, factories, shops, public works	17.7	19.7
Government, offices, serv- ice transport, profes- sions.	26.0	78.6

(Computed from Distrito,
1973)

The fact that most working women are single is
due in part to the division of labor in peasant and
proletarian households in which the domestic work
of the wife is an essential and full-time activity,
and to little competitive demand for female labor

in an economy of chronic underemployment. This absence of women from extra-domestic work is rarely subject to criticism or even comment since it accords well with widely voiced judgements that it is improper for women to work outside the home and that the husband should be the principle wage-earner (with supplemental income from unmarried children). Of wage earning women perhaps the largest number are employed as domestic servants. Gossip concerning sexual liasons between maids and their employers suggests an underlying notion that working outside the home compromises a woman's reputation. Thus while the low percentage of working women reflects limited employment opportunities, this situation is positively valued.

Although statistical documentation is lacking, it can safely be said that among Portuguese immigrants in New England, it is the norm for women to work outside the home. Several factors are involved. In urban, industrialized America women have much greater opportunity for employment. Further, there is a perceived economic necessity for women to be wage earners. In part this is the case because a higher standard of living is maintained by the Portuguese in the United States than in the Azores and in part because the motive for emigration is economic, with family strategy explicitly oriented to improving economic status. It may also be that the small scale, unstable economy of New England mill cities and towns, with their frequent lay-offs, may require a diversified, dual-worker household to ensure subsistence. A recent paper by Lamphere (see Addendum to References Cited) explicitly poses this question of the relation between the nature of the New England economy and Portuguese immigrant family roles. My own research suggests that Lamphere is correct in her general statement of the problem but that much more research is needed to account for the variation in family patterns which her paper reports. Lamphere's analysis is weakened by her invocation of "traditional" Azorean patterns (i.e., pre-migration family roles and ideology) which are unsubstantiated and ignore variation in the islands. But of main interest to the present discussion is the absence of expressed opinions among immigrants that it is improper for women to work. This is in contrast to situations in Santa Maria, for example, where even when there was financial need and the wife had worked before marriage, the husband objected to her accepting available work and both husband and wife felt that to act otherwise would lower their family prestige as judged by their neighbors. The nature and source of this change in sex-role norms await further investigation.

A second way in which immigrants can be said to become Portuguese-American lies in the structuring of their social relations. Many new social categories become relevant to the immigrant (for example, 'factory worker') but of these "Portuguese-American" is the most pervasive. In this discussion, "Portuguese-American" is used as the category label for convenience. "Portuguese" and "Luso-American" (and their Portuguese equivalents) are commonly used labels and the somewhat denigrating "Portagee" or "Gee" also are used. Label and definition of the category would vary with user and context. As a social category it serves many functions: a criterion of recruitment to roles and to group membership; an idiom for cooperation and competition; and an explanation of behavior (by reference to ethnic stereotypes). The immigrants come to associate on the basis of this ethnicity -- or at least to justify association in terms of common ethnicity and find themselves treated as members of this category by others.

Ethnicity as a social category is often misunderstood by social scientists. Ethnicity is taken as a given and used to explain other phenomena. Ethnic enclaves and organizations are commonly explained as due to immigrants' innate preference to associate with their "own kind". Thus it is generally assumed that ethnicity is a conservative phenomenon, marking a persistence of Old World categories in America.

This widespread misconception of ethnicity has three sources. First, a tenet of the ideology of ethnicity is that ethnic identities are ascribed, immutable, primordial. For American social scientists -- as members of a society in which ethnicity plays a great role in structuring social relations -- such a tenet tends to be taken for granted. The situation is comparable to that of students of adolescence who tend to view their subject as a natural given rather than as a social category 'invented' during the Industrial Revolution (Musgrove 1964). Second, and closely related, is the fact that ethnic research subjects affirm that they really are, innately, by blood, "Portuguese" or "Italian", etc. Adequate social scientific understanding requires knowledge of social actors' definitions of situations. Anthropologists strive to apprehend the motives, goals, assumptions, and calculations of the people whose lives they observe. But it is difficult to gain this knowledge without impairing the distinction between folk realities and analytic interpretation. Third, the assumption that immigrants bring their ethnic identities with them is easy to maintain in the absence of studies of immigrants' communities of origin.

In the Azores, beyond individual (personal and role-related) and family identities, the most important social identities are as villager and islander. People are characterized as being of particular places. The island of Santa Maria, with only 37 sq. miles and 9,000 people, has five parishes each of which tends to be highly endogamous and to attribute negative stereotypes to other parishes. On the neighboring and much larger island of Sao Miguel (288 sq. miles, 150,000 pop.) the inhabitants of villages separated by as little as a mile hold themselves to be linguistically, culturally, and tempermentally distinct. After such local categories the next most common and significant social identities are insular: under most conditions one's own island marks the limits of chauvinism, we-feeling, patriotism. Between the larger islands (Sao Miguel, Faial, Terceira) there are long established rivalries over claims of

208

preeminence in the archipelago. Each island's inhabitants are known by a nickname, usually derogatory (e.g. those of Terceira are called by others "rabos tortos": "twisted rumps").

Portugal is a country of strong regionalism, and the regions are in fact marked by distinctive ecologies and histories. Portuguese-speakers can usually identify one another by regional dialect. Here again there are commonly known stereotypes, though the most frequent contrasts are between each region and the capital, Lisbon. This opposition reflects the very high degree of centralization under the fascist state and of the great socioeconomic contrast between an urban center like Lisbon and the largely rural districts of the rest of the nation. Though normally not a relevant category for identity or interaction, most islanders will readily assert that they are "Azoreans" when such a distinction is useful. In the Azores, officials and tecynicians usually come from continental Portugal and vis-a-vis them a person from, say, Sao Pedro parish, Santa Maria will be "Azorean" These non-islanders are usually high status and urban; and they tend to treat Azoreans as inferiors (the other non-Azorean Portuguese regularly present in the islands are soldiers who, though they may come from peasant villages, attempt to assert prerogatives over local civilians). "Azoreans" normally contrast themselves to "Continentals" -- a category which includes all regions of continental Portugal but in practice most often refers to people of Lisbon. Contacts with "Continentals" are not common so that being "Azorean" is not an aspect of day-to-day life. This in no way diminishes the reality of the identity. Conservative political elements in the Azores were able to mobilize a good deal of separatist sentiment following the April 1974 anti-fascist coup. Though the motivation of the organizers of the independence movement appears to have been economic (a strategy to retain privilege previously protected by the central government), followers and sympathizers of the movement genuinely rallied to the appeal of Azorean nationalism. The ease with

209

which "communist" and "continental" were equated
and the acts of terrorism against continentals in
the islands resulted as much from pre-existing
hostility toward non-Azoreans as from the anti-
communist sentiment inculcated under fifty years
of fascism.

But the one identity that is almost never employed is "Porguguese". It is rare, except among
those with higher education or those who have spent
time abroad, to hear "we Portuguese" used spon-
taneously. Even in interaction with or conversation about foreigners (e.g., Americans or French)
the in-group is most likely to be identified as
"we Azoreans".

For the immigrant, then, it is only in the
United States or Canada that "Portuguese" becomes
an important social category. Beginning with the
visa application, the immigrant interacts with
non-Portuguese who, ignorant of the distinctions of
regional and local identity, deal with him largely
in terms of nationality (age, sex, occupation and
class also affect interaction). In the United
States, use of Portuguese, or a Portuguese accent
in speaking English, surname, and neighborhood all
serve to identify the immigrant as "Portuguese" to
people to whom "Azorean" or "Micaelense" are mean-
ingless. The immigrant also finds that there are
"Portuguese" churches and associations with such
names as "Portuguese-American Social Club". Radio,
television, and newspapers address themselves to
"a comunidade portuguesa" ("the Portuguese community"). However strong his or her Azorean chauvinism may have been, in America no category other
than "Portuguese" seems appropriate in interaction
with non-Portuguese.

The category "Portuguese" in New England is
decidedly an American category. Portugal, until
the anti-fascist, anti-colonial coup of 1974, de-
clared itself a "Multi-continental" nation in which
inhabitants of "Overseas Portugal" (Cabo Verde,
Guinea, Angola, Mocambique, S. Tome, Principe,
Macao, Timor) were said to be as Portuguese as

residents of Lisbon. However much special laws, separate currencies, exploitation, and oppression qualified the claim, the assertion of common nationality was not empty rhetoric (it must be remembered that the Portuguese had been in Africa for five centuries). Thus, if asked, an Azorean would readily affirm that Cape Verdeans were Portuguese. But in the United States binary racial classification and discrimination against non-whites has influenced Azoreans to disassociate themselves from Cape Verdeans who also immigrate to New England. Not accepted by other Portuguese immigrants and wishing to distinguish themselves from American blacks, Cape Verdeans attempt to maintain a distinct ethnic category (see Machado, this volume, for an analysis of the Cape Verdean case).

Even though "Portuguese" is a relevant category for Azoreans in the U. S. and is viewed as homogeneous by non-Portuguese, pre-immigration distinctions are, in fact, maintained. Within areas of Portuguese settlement in New England there is clustering by community of origin. In smaller towns the "Portuguese" may be almost all from a single island. Pap (1949:10) provides the following examples:

> Some settlements have a rather distinct regional character; others contain a mixture of immigrants from different parts of Portugal. In New Bedford, for example, the Azoreans . . . form probably the largest group, but there are also relatively large contingents of Continentals, Madeirans (in the northern section), and Cape Verdeans (in the south). In Fall River the overwhelming majority of the settlers hail from the island of Sao Miguel. The small colony at Valley Falls, Rhode Island, has a mauority from Castendo (Beira Alta), but those across the bridge, in Central Falls, are almost in their entirety from Madeira. Most of the Continentals in Newark came from the town of Murtosa.

Ethnic organizations claiming to represent all
Portuguese-Americans exist but many of the recrea-
tional clubs, bands, and fraternal organizations
are associations of particular sub-groups, distinguished by island of origin. Rogers (1974:30)
writes that:

> In Cambridge, Massachusetts, where
> 2,521 Portuguese were reported to be liv-
> ing in the summer of 1971, there is a club
> of the Fayalese (Faialense Sport Clube),
> another of Michaelese . . . (Santo Cristo
> Center), and yet another of the Madeirans
> who boast they come from the Atlantic's
> pearl (Clube Recreio Madeirense). The
> different groups of Portuguese in the
> various areas of settlement have tended
> not to cooperate one with another over the
> decades, except in the Portuguese Catholic
> churches. Recently, however, they have
> manifested greater unity.

Another important division is between older and
newer immigrants (those arriving after the 1965
lifting of restrictive quotas). The more recent
immigrants come from a different Portugal than the
one the previous immigrants left. Most arrive in
America with more education and wider experience
(e.g. military service in Africa) than was usual
among the earlier immigrants. And they arrive at
a time when ethnic distinctiveness (rather than
cultural homogeneity) is popularly and officially
favored (Ussach 1975; Rogers 1974).

Talking with Portuguese-Americans, it is common to hear such statements as "Almost all of us
at the factory are Portuguese but we have a couple
Americans work there too." "American" is left undefined. It usually means non-Portuguese and, with
questioning, becomes non-foreign born. It is a
residual category, non-in-group, however this is
defined. An Azorean immigrant, describing a party
he attended in Boston at which 1st and 2nd generation Italians and Greeks as well as Portuguese-
Americans were present, said "We Latins know how

to have good parties, not like the Americans."

This vague positing of a "real American" category is not only a folk usage, but is embedded in American social science. Until the last decade, acculturation theory dominated the study of migration and ethnicity. Originally conceived as the investigation of the mutual adjustment occuring when 'cultures come in contact', acculturation studies tended to assume that the process was an inevitable, undimensional movement to conformity in which 'minority' culture was lost, replaced by 'mainstream' culture. From the perspective of the 1970's acculturation theory appears simply as a social science version of popular notions of America as a melting pot. This is not the only myth so enshrined in theory. "Common sense" can mislead the social theorist as much as explicit ideology does and is perhaps more difficult to detect. One such common sense assumption, imported into social science, is that there is a Mainstream America, a majority culture, to which sub-cultures are contrasted. It is in terms of this 'normal' America that behavioral pathologies are defined. It is to this American culture that immigrants are said to be acculturating. This mainstream culture is either left undefined, a matter of common knowledge between writer and reader, or identified variously as "Anglo-American" or "middle class". As in the folk usage discussed above, the content of the social scientists' "America" varies according to the category to which it is contrasted. An important difference between sociologists and immigrants/ ethnics is that the social scientists take "American" as their in-group.

A social category works because those using it treat it as internally homogeneous and as one member in a system of complementary 'us-them' dichotomies. A valid theory of ethnicity must account for such folk classifications without itself being based on their assumptions. Freed from the vision of Mainstream America, we can approach cultural consensus as an empirical question. And when we do encounter consensus we will not mistake it for the

natural state of society but as an achieved and
problematic state. As Hicks observed:

> When we discard the monolithic ver-
> sion of American culture, we are not left
> with the task of merely cataloguing sepa-
> rate cultures. As in the study of any
> heterogeneous or plural society, a major
> interest is how society hangs together in
> the absence of cultural agreement.
> (Hicks 1976: 8-9)

Conclusion

(1) <u>Psychology of change and the concept of culture</u>. Examining Azorean migration, with knowledge of life in the Azores, it has been possible to suggest that migration is not the 'uprooting' it is often thought to be. A larger question to be considered is what type of change does produce psychological or social stress. In part the answer depends upon how we conceptualize 'normal' social life and culture.

A useful example of this dependence is the "marginal man" concept. Robert Park formulated the concept as follows:

One of the consequences of migration is to create a situation in which the same individual . . . finds himself striving to live in two diverse cultural groups. The effect is to produce an unstable character -- a personality type with characteristic forms of behavior. This is the 'marginal man.'

(Park 1928:881)

The key to evaluating this concept is the implicit assumption that the normal state of affairs is cultural homogeneity. Park notes

There are no doubt periods of transition and crisis in the lives of most of us that are comparable with those which the migrant experiences when he leaves home to seek his fortune in a strange country. But in the case of the marginal man the period of crisis is relatively permanent.

(Park 1928:893)

If, in contrast, we take seriously the emerging anthropological paradigm which holds heterogeneity, ambiguity, and conflict to be normal to social life, then we must assert that all of us or none of us are marginal men. The formation, around various issues, of 'progressive' and 'traditional'

215

factions is widely reported and indicates that experience of competing reference groups is quite common. Current research suggests that even in areas where factions and alternatives are not recognized by the actors, the degree of actual consensus is problematic. Some degree of status inconsistency is probably always present as individuals shift roles or move from, for example, the private to public arena (e.g. to be a lord at home and a serf at work). Alternative, context-specific social identities also occur under normal conditions. In one context, a man of Sao Miguel can define himself as essentially "Micaelense" in chauvinistic rivalry with a "twisted tail" from Terceira, yet in another context find himself joining his brother "Azorean" to drive the Continentals from the islands. If migration creates marginal men, it is not the presence per se of cultural alternatives and multiple reference groups that constitutes the causal crisis. If it is the degree of heterogeneity that produces "unstable character", we need to investigate normal levels of heterogeneity and ambiguity and how they are dealt with before we can understand "crisis". (See R. Taft (1973:112-114) for a related critique of theories of marginality and culture conflict.)

In general, reports of social and personal disorganization among immigrants suffer from questionable definitions of pathology and a failure to consider alternative causes. The tendency to assume a mainstream standard against which other behavior is defined as pathological has already been mentioned. The error of, for example, viewing matrifocal families as pathological when health is ethnocentrically defined as patrifocal, is beginning to be recognized. Also, if certain conditions commonly exist among immigrants it may be because they are not only immigrants but working or lower class. It is easy to forget that the classic studies of immigrants were made in or concern the period before the 1926 "closing of the gate" and that this period was characterized by rapid urban and industrial growth. The lack of disorganization among immigrants to rural areas is usually explained

216

as the result of their being able to better maintain traditional lifeways in the relative isolation
of the countryside -- that they were not as exposed
to the stress of acculturation as their urban counterparts. They were, however, also not exposed to
slum and sweatshop.

Most sociological discussions of immigration
and ethnicity are developmental (e.g. Hansen's
'law' of 3rd Generation Return) with observed
characteristics accounted for as typical of one or
another stage in an on-going developmental process.
But in spite of the inherent time reference most
such theories are ahistorical, ignoring the particular conditions in which immigration, assimilation,
etc. were taking place.

(2) <u>Ethnic conservatism?</u> The present discussion of ethnicity counters the common-sense view
which might be termed "pluralism as preservation":
that members of ethnically defined categories are
drawn together by primordial sentiment, that both
the ethnic group boundary and its normative culture
in the United States are preservations of donor community culture. In contrast, immigration research
based on a familiarity with donor communities has
shown that common-sense fails in this case. The
view of Portuguese-American ethnicity developed
here parallels the position of students of African
urbanization (e.g. Cohen 1969, Mitchell 1966,
Southall 1975) who have argued against the prevalent idea that urban migrants are 'tribesmen' whose
ethnically based identities and associations are a
mere continuation in the city of a primordial rural
tribalism. They find instead, in Cohen's words,
that ethnicity "involves a dynamic rearrangement of
relations and of customs, and is not the outcome of
cultural conservatism or continuity" (1969:199).
A similar perspective is beginning to appear in
American ethnic studies. Schiller expresses this
point of view when she writes:

. . . it is possible to review the
literature and discover that many ethnic
groups never shared a common culture and

217

a common identity. They came from different regions and different social classes
and their loyalties and customs were more
local than national. Ethnic identities
were formed within the United States in
response to pressures generated by American society . . . . Moreover, one cannot
simply assume that people who share a common national origin desire companionship
with their fellow immigrants or seek to
preserve the behavior or beliefs they left
behind them. It can instead be demonstra-
ted that the members of an ethnic group
(or category) often differ greatly from
one another and can choose from a number
of different identities.
                                    (Schiller 1977:25)

    (3) <u>Non-linear development of social science</u>.
As this article neared completion I belatedly read
Volume 5 of Thomas and Znaniecki's classic <u>The
Polish Peasant in Europe and America</u> (1920). Fifty-
seven years ago, with a wealth of data, careful
analysis, and clarity of exposition, they argued
that the "situation /of Poles in America/ is really
much more complicated than most of the popular
American literature concerning immigration and
Americanization sees it" (viii). To demonstrate
that current ethnic research is rediscovering what
pioneers in the field clearly stated more than half
a century ago I will quote at length:

        . . . if we look at Poles in America
    not from the standpoint of Polish or Ameri-
    can national interests but from that of an
    objective sociological inquiry, we find
    that the problem of individual assimila-
    tion is at present an entirely secondary
    and unimportant issue . . . . The funda-
    mental process which has been going on dur-
    ing this period is <u>the</u> <u>formation</u> <u>of</u> a <u>new</u>
    <u>Polish</u>-<u>American</u> <u>society</u> out of those frag-
    ments separated from Polish society and em-
    bedded in American society . . . . And the
    striking phenomenon . . . is the formation

of this coherent group out of originally
incoherent elements, the creation of a
society which in structure and prevalent
attitude is neither Polish nor American
but constitutes a specific new product
whose raw materials have been partly drawn
from Polish traditions, partly from the new
conditions in which the immigrants live
and from American social values as the immigrant sees and interprets them. It is
this Polish-American society, not American society, that constitutes the social
milieu into which the immigrant who comes
from Poland becomes incorporated and to
whose standards and institutions he must
adapt himself.
(Thomas and Znaniecki 1920:viii-x)

With the single caution that we not posit an "America" that is anything more than the relations among
its parts, this is the viewpoint of the present
paper.

Afterword 1981

    "Azoreans in America" was written in 1976. By
the vagaries of publishing it is now coming to
press on short notice, largely unrevised. The more
opaque phrasings of the original have been edited
for clarity and an addendum to the bibliography
will lead interested readers to some recent works
on Portuguese migrants.

    Although I still stand by the positions taken
five years ago, if written today this paper would
address other issues. However, some topics not
considered in 1976 would also be omitted now. An
explanation of these 'silences' may be of use to
students of ethnic heritage.

    The intent of the paper -- which was directed
to non-anthropologists -- was to criticize views of
migration which saw it as disorganizing and to ad-
vocate a way of thinking about ethnicity. The posi-

tions taken are still valid, but the views criticized were almost passe at the time I wrote. More recent work has moved in other directions, further away from acculturation models. In particular, social historians have been examining the effects of industrial labor on the family and community life of immigrants. In these studies there is ample recognition of adaptation and strategizing, and of collective response. Understanding of ethnicity has advanced more unevenly. In educational, medical and other areas of applied research, ethnicity now commonly appears as a variable. But often 'what ethnicity is' is left unstated. Many social scientists have simply accepted ideological claims of cultural distinctiveness, so that ethnicity appears in their accounts as a form of cultural determinism. It is here that the Azorean examples provide useful cautions.

Before turning to a brief explanation of the paper's omissions let me underscore two related points. Ethnicity is too close to us to be easily understood. The perception-shaping power of ideology and political engagement must not be underestimated. The current redirection of Federal policy and the radical shift in political discourse may very well allow students of ethnicity to discern the selectivity of their perceptions: the inadequacies of cultural pluralism may soon stand out as sharply as the failings of assimilationism. The second point has to do with the symbolic and socially constituted nature of reality. Arguments concerning the genesis of ethnicity -- that the category "portuguese" gains salience for migrants after arrival in America and that the traditionality of Portuguese-American culture is problematical -- must not be taken to diminish the reality of sincerity of the experience of ethnic identity of Portuguese-Americans.

The paper does not offer much description of Portuguese life in the United States, nor does it deal at any length with non-migrant ethnics. It contributes little that can be used to enhance ethnic pride, little of the sort of material found in ethnic heritage programs. In part these omissions reflect the preliminary nature of my research. But they also reflect the current state of anthropology, specifically the status of the culture concept. Here, in condensed and perhaps cryptic form, are some of the considerations which explain these omissions:

(1) Ironically, at a time when "culture" has achieved wide currency as a popular explanation of behavior, anthropologists are finding their discipline's central concept inadequate, and have in some cases abandoned it. Characterizing the way of life of a people is no easy task for an anthropology that no longer posits cultural homogeneity as a basic social fact. The problem does not arise from intrasocietal cultural differences such as those between classes, men and women, young and old, or regions of a nation. These have been dealt with by invoking the notion of "subculture". But now anthropologists have come to question what it is that individuals in any group share, by virtue of which their behavior is coordinated and patterned. In developing a new understanding of culture, or an explanatory concept to take its place, anthropologists are discerning new types of sharing, of commonality: e.g., common arenas of action, common idioms of discourse, rather than shared values, norms, and beliefs. In another possible direction, ethnographic generalizations will no longer be phrased as absolutes but as probabilistic, statistical norms. In either case, ethnographers find themselves less certain what to make of their field impressions and faced with greater difficulty in documenting assertions about community culture or individual strategies.

(2) More concretely, I offered no ethnography of Portuguese-American communities because I could not answer the following questions. What is attributable to portuguese-ness? What is typical of Portuguese-American life? What does Portuguese-American culture include? (belief that the Holy Ghost is vengeful? working in factories? speaking Porguguese? pooling household wages?).

221

How should we interpret the frequent characterization of the Portuguese in New England as "hard working"? Is it simply an ethnic stereotype, a conventional judgment with little basis in fact? Should we look for its origin in Portuguese culture or personality? Or should we examine New England labor history? Comparison with Hawaii would be salutary. In Hawaii, with a different migration and occupational history, the Portuguese are stereotyped as "shiftless and lazy".

Listing dates, numbers and places of settlement of immigrants from Portugal is not at all the same sort of assertion as saying that Portuguese families are traditionally male-dominated or that Portuguese-Americans are religious. "Portuguese immigrant" is unambiguous in a way that "dominance" and "religiosity" are not. And head counts can be substantiated in ways that claims to traditionality cannot be. These are perennial problems for social science. I have belabored the obvious only because belief in ethnic culture has made observers credulous.

(3) When these difficulties are overcome, there remains the problem of attributing common behavior to shared culture. Structural constraints and opportunities can call forth similar individual responses without shared norms having been inculcated by socialization or legitimated by 'tradition'. This was illustrated in the discussion of the wage labor of Azorean immigrant women. This is the direction of my own research, but concern with structure does not solve the problem of characterizing Portuguese-American life. The problems, resources, and strategies of members of this ethnic category differ significantly.

(4) Why did this paper give no testimony to the accomplishments of the Portuguese? Why in a society where minority groups are objects of prejudice did I not document the admirable traits of the Portuguese? This omission is not justified by any belief on my part that judgment and science must be kept discrete. The findings of social scientists

have long played a part in creation of those negative and positive group images which legitimize domination in our society.

In large part the explanation here is the same as that offered above: how do we assign credit to a social category or ethnic group or nation or culture? This is not to say that I did not form such judgments during the course of my fieldwork, while living in the Azores and in New England. Ethnographers' impressions are as sincerely held and as apparently real as are ethnics' identities. My abiding impressions are of people of great hospitality, warmth, and dignity. I owe a great debt to many people for the openness and kindness with which they received me. But I also know, critically, that once constructed this view became a lens through which some experiences and individuals appeared as aberrant, exceptional, un-Azorean.

Finally, even if we allow ourselves to speak of "The Portuguese" and to take apparent facts at face value, clear-cut evaluations may be difficult to make. Students of ethnic heritage should ask themselves, for example, from what perspective 'being a good worker' is admirable. How is it to be distinguished from alienation, passivity, and exploitation? On another level of heritage, should we admire the Portugal of Camoes: a nation of explorers; or condemn five hundred years of Portuguese colonialism? Or, more to the point at the close of a paper on Portuguese migration, are we to judge Portugal as a state whose principal export commodity is human labor?

REFERENCES CITED

Antunes, M. L. Marinho
    1973 A Emigracao Portuguesa desde 1950: Dados
    e Comentarious. Lisbon: Gabinete de Inves-
    tigacoes Sociais.

Barth, Fredrik (ed.)
    1969 Ethnic Groups and Boundaries. Boston:
    Little, Brown and Co.

Bohme, Frederick G.
    1956 The Portuguese in California. California
    Historical Quarterly 35:233-252.

Borges, Nair Odete da Camara
    1960 Influencia Anglo-Americana no Falar da
    Ilha de S. Miguel (Acores). Supplemento II
    of Revista Portuguesa de Filologia. Coimbra:
    Instituto de Estudos Romanicos, Faculdade de
    Letras da Universidade de Coimbra.

Brettell, Caroline Bieler
    1977 Ethnicity and entrepreneurs: Portuguese
    immigrants in a Canadian city, in Ethnic En-
    counters: Identities and Contexts. George L.
    Hicks and Philip E. Leis, eds. pp. 169-180.
    North Scituate, Mass.: Duxbury Press.

Cohln, Abner
    1969 Custom and Politics in Urban Africa: A
    Study of Hausa Migrants in Yoruba Towns.
    Berkeley: University of California Press.

Cornwell, Elmer
    1970 Bosses, machines, and ethnic groups, in
    The Urbanization of America. A Wakestein,
    ed. pp. 276-282. Boston: Houghton Mifflin
    Company.

Distrito Autonomo de Ponta Delgada
    1973 Exposicao: Bases Preliminares para uma
    Participacao no Planeamento Territorial de
    Distrito Autonomo de Ponta Delgada. (Gabi-
    nette de Planeamento Territorial) Ponta Del-
    gade, Portugal.

Ferst, Susan T.
1972 The Immigration and the Settlement of the
Portuguese in Providence: 1890 to 1924.
Masters Thesis, Department of History, Brown
University.

Gordon, Milton
1964 Assimilation in American Life. New York:
Oxford University Press.

Haas, Mary
1951 Interlingual word taboos. American Anthropologist 53:338-341.

Handlin, Oscar
1951 The Uprooted: The Epic Story of the Great
Migrations that Made the American People.
New York: Grosset & Dunlap.

Hicks, George L.
1976 Ethnicity and utopianism in America. Paper
presented at the Northeastern Anthropological
Association Annual Meeting, March 25, 1976.
Middletown, Conn.

Mitchell, J. Clyde
1966 Theoretical orientations in African urban
studies in The Social Anthropology of Complex
Societies. Michael Banton, ed. pp. 37-68.
(A.S.A. Monographs 4) London: Tavistock Publications.

Musgrove, Frank
1964 Youth and Social Order. London: Routledge
and Kegan Paul.

Pap, Leo
1949 Portuguese-American Speech. Columbia University, N. Y.: King's Crown Press.

Park, Robert
1928 Human migration and the marginal man. American Journal of Sociology 33:881-893.

225

Portugal. Instituto Nacional de Estatistica
    1971   11° Recenseamento Geral da Populacao.

Portugal (I.N.E., Delegacao de Ponta Delgada)
    1974   O Distrito de Ponta Delgada: Sumula Esta-
    tistica (1963-1972). Instituto Nacional de
    Estatistica: Serie Estatisticas Regionais,
    n. 5. Lisbon.

Rogers, Francis M.
    1974   Americans of Portuguese Descent: A Lesson
    in Differentiation. Beverly Hills, Calif.:
    Sage Publications.

Schiller, Nina Glick
    1977   Ethnic groups are made not born: the Hai-
    tian immigrant and American Politics in Ethnic
    Encounters: Identities and Contexts. George
    L. Hicks and Philip E. Leis, eds. pp. 23-26.
    North Scituate, Mass.. Duxbury Press.

Serrao, Joel
    1974   A Emigracao Portuguesa: Sondagem Historica.
    2nd ed. Lisbon: Livros Horizonte.

Southall, Aidan
    1975   Forms of ethnic linkage between town and
    country in Migration and Urbanization: Models
    and Adaptive Strategies. Brian du Toit and
    Helen Safa, eds. pp. 273-283. The Hague:
    Mouton.

Szwed, John F.
    1974   An American anthropological dilemma: the
    politics of Afro-American culture in Rein-
    venting Anthropology.

Taft, Donald R.
    1923   Two Portuguese Communities in New England
    (Studies in History, Economics, and Public
    Law, CVII, no. 1). New York: Columbia Uni-
    versity.

Taft, Ronald
  1973 The concept of social adaptation of migrants
    in Migration: Report of the Research Confer-
    ence on Migration, Ethnic Minority Status, and
    Social Adaptation. United Nations Social De-
    fense Research Institute (Publication No. 5)
    pp. 105-114.

Thomas, W. I. and Florian Znaniecki
  1920 The Polish Peasant in Europe and America.
    Vol. 5: Organization and Disorganization in
    America. Boston: Richard G. Badger.

Trueblood, Marilyn A.
  1977 The melting pot and ethnic revitalization
    in Ethnic Encounters: Identities and Con-
    texts. George L. Hicks and Philip E. Leis,
    eds. pp. 153-168. North Scituate, Mass.:
    Duxbury Press.

U. N. Department of Economic and Social Affairs
  1953 Sex and Age Characteristics of Interna-
    tional Migrants: Statistics for 1918-1947.
    Population Studies No. 11.

U. S. Department of Justice
  1974 Immigra5ion and Naturalization Service An-
    nual Report. Washington, D. C.: Government
    Printing Office.

Ussach, Steven S.
  1975 The New England Portuguese: a plural so-
    ciety within a plural society in Plural Socie-
    ties 6 (2):47-57.

Valentine, Charles A.
  1968 Culture and Poverty: Critiques and Coun-
    ter-Proposals. Chicago: University of Chi-
    cago Press.

Vecoli, Rudolph J.
  1964 Contadini in Chicago: a Critique of The
    Uprooted. Journal of American History 51:
    404-417.

ADDENDUM 1981

Anderson, Grace and D. Higgs
    1976 A Future to Inherit: The Portuguese Commu-
        nities in Canada. Toronto: McGlelland and
        Steward Ltd.

Alpalhao, J. Antonio and Victor M. P. da Rosa
    1980 A Minority in a Changing Society: The
        Portuguese Community of Quebec. Ottawa:
        University of Ottawa Press.

Brettell, Caroline B.
    1978 Hope and Nostalgia: The Migration of Por-
        tuguese Women to Paris. Ph. D. dissertation,
        Anthropology Department, Brown University.

Brettell, Caroline G. and Colette Callier Boisvert
    1977 Portuguese Immigrants in France: Familial
        and Social Networks and the structuring of
        "Community" in Studi/Etudes, Emigrazione/Mi-
        grations. Centro Studi Emigrazione. Rome.

Cabral, Stephen
    1978 Portuguese-American Feasting: Tradition
        and Change in New Bedford, Massachusetts.
        Ph. D. dissertation, Anthropology Department,
        Brown University.

Cumbler, John T.
    1979 Working-Class Community in Industrial
        America: Work, Leisure, and Struggle in Two
        Industrial Cities, 1880-1930. Westport,
        Conn.: Greenwood Press. (Lynn and Fall
        River, Mass.; compares experience of French-
        Canadians, Poles, and Portuguese).

Da Rosa, Victor M. P.
    1980 Emigration portuguaise et developpement
        inegal. Les Acoreens au Quebec. Ph. D. Dis-
        sertation. Anthropology Department, McGill
        University.

DeMartino, George F.
1978 Immigrant Resistence: Portuguese Textile
Workers in Bristol County, Massachusetts.
Honors thesis, Harvard University.

Fernandez, Ronald
1977 A Logic of Ethnicity: A Study of the Significance and Classification of Ethnic Identity Among Montreal Portuguese. Ph. D. dissertation, Department of Anthropology, McGill
University.

Graves, Alvin R.
1977 Immigrants in Agriculture: The Portuguese
Californians, 1850-1970. Ph. D. dissertation,
Geography Department, U.C.L.A.

Lamphere, Louise
1980 Kin Networks and Family Strategies: Working Class Portuguese Families in New England
in the Versatility of Kinship. L. Cordell
and S. Beckerman, eds. New York: Academic
Press.

Like, Robert
1975 Portuguese Popular Health Culture: A Discussion of Three Case Histories. A Manuscript.

Maranhao, Tullio Persio
1981 Speech Acts in Their Social Context of Use
in a Community of Portuguese Immigrants. Ph.
D. dissertation, Department of Anthropology,
Harvard University.

McGowen, Owent T. P.
1976 Factors Contributing to School Leaving
Among Immigrant Children: The Case of the
Portuguese of Fall River, Massachusetts. Ph.
D. dissertation, Catholic University.

Meneses, Fernando de (pseudonym)
1977 Entre Dois Mundos. Vida quotidiana de cri-
ancas portuguesas na america. 2 vols. Text
and Teachers' Guide. Cambridge, Mass.: National Assessment and Dissemination Center.

229

(high school level text with nignettes of
school and home life of Portuguese immigrants
in New England; acute and insightful observa-
tions.)

Moitoza, E. and R. Coelho
1980 Ethnic Factors in the Delivery of Psychological Services to Portuguese Americans. Paper presented at the Annual Meeting of the
Northeast Anthropological Association, Am-
herst, Massachusetts, March 29, 1980.

Monteiro, Lois
1976 Immigrants and the Medical Care System:
the Example of the Portuguese. Paper presented at the Smithsonian Institute Bicentennial
Conference "The New Immigration: Implications for the United States and the International Community" Washington, D. C., November 16, 1976.

Nelson, Carl
1979 Health Care Behavior and Attitudes in a
Portuguese-American Community: Does Ethnicity Matter? Manuscript, Northeastern University.

Providence Journal
1980 Portugal/Cape Verde. Special Issue Sunday
Journal Magazine. May 18, 1980. Providence,
Rhode Island. (Report and photo essay on immigrant families in Rhode Island and donon
communities in Azores, Continental Portugal
and Cape Verde.)

Pap, Leo
1976 The Portuguese in the United States. A
Bibliography. New York: Center for Migration Studies.

Pinho, Helder
1978 Portuguese na California. Lisbon: Edi-
torial Noticias.

Rocha, Craig D.
   1979   Culture and Education in 'Comunidade': The
   Portuguese-American Community of San Diego,
   California. Ph. D. dissertation, United States
   International University.

Rogers, Francis
   1980   Portuguese. In Harvard Encyclopedia of
   American Ethnic Groups. S. Thernstrom, A.
   Orlov, and O. Handlin, eds. pp. 813-820.
   Cambridge, Massachusetts: Harvard University
   Press.

Serpa, Caetano Valadao
   1978   A Gente dos Acores. Identificacao: Emi-
   gracao e Religiosidade Seculos XVI-XX. Lisbon: Prelo.

Silva, Philip T.
   1976   The Position of "New" Immigrants in the
   Fall River Textile Industry. International
   Migration Review. 10:221-232.

Smith, M. Estellie
   1976   Networks and Migration Resettlement:
   Cherchez la Femme. Anthropological Quarterly
   49 (1): 20-27.

Trindade, Maria Jose Lagos
   1976   Portuguese Emigration from the Azores to
   the United States during the Nineteenth Century. In Studies in Honor of the Bicentennial of American Independence. pp. 237-295.
   Lisbon: Luso-American Educational Commission
   and Calouste Gulbenkian Foundation.

Wolfrom, Sandra
   1978   The Portuguese in America. San Francisco:
   R & E Research Associates, Inc.

CAPE VERDEAN AMERICANS

Deirdre Meintel Machado

This paper concerns the multiple social identities claimed by members of a small, racially
mixed ethnic category, Cape Verdean-Americans. Attention will be directed to the ways that the small
size of this population makes social identity problematic for its members. The following remarks are
based on findings from a year of research in the
Cape Verde Islands, as well as several years of
part-time research and contact with Cape Verdean-
Americans in the Providence, R. I. -- New Bedford,
Mass. area (These investigations were supported by
a grant from the National Institute of Mental
Health and by P. H. S. Research Grant No. 17216
from the Center for Urban Ethnography, University
of Pennsylvania.).

This people's homeland, the Cape Verde archipelago, comprises ten islands located some 400
miles off the coast of West Africa near the equa-
tor. Until July, 1975, the Islands were a Portuguese colony. Although poor and largely unknown,
the archipelago is characterized by a unique and,
in many ways, remarkable cultural tradition. Most
Cape Verdean-Americans reside in New England, although several concentrations are found in California, New York, Pennsylvania and Ohio. Informal
estimates of their number range as high as 300,000,
or forty thousand more than the population of the
Islands themselves. The actual figure is difficult to determine since there is no special category for Cape Verdean-Americans in the U. S. Census. Cross-tabulation of the 1970 census figures
gives 42,000 as the maximum possible number of
foreign born and first generation (I am grateful to
Professor Lois Monteiro, Brown University, for providing me with this information.). However, many
who consider themselves Cape Verdean are second,
third and even later generation individuals whose
mother tongue is English. Most work as manual
laborers in maritime, dockside, factory or service

233

jobs; however, some, even among the foreign-born, have become doctors, lawyers and university professors. In the century or so since Cape Verdeans began settling in New England they have carved out a niche of respectability for themselves while maintaining certain culturally distinctive traits.

In many ways this has not been easy. Most Cape Verdeans would be called "Black" in everyday American parlance, although in fact they exhibit a wide range of phenotypical variation, sometimes within the same family. Few Cape Verdeans willingly considered themselves Negro or black at the time of their arrival in the U. S., for reasons that will be made clear below. However, once here, they experienced discrimination at the hands of white Portuguese immigrants (from Portugal, Madeira and the Azores) as well as by other Americans. At the same time, Cape Verdeans' efforts to maintain their cultural distinctiveness and social separateness from American blacks (The term "American Black" is used herein to refer to Blacks not of Cape Verdean descent, in the U. S.) came to be resented as "racist" by the latter. A later section will treat some of the ways that Cape Verdean-Americans have dealt with these cross-cutting challenges to the social identity for which most of them were socialized; that is, Cape Verdean, Portuguese and not-black. First, however, I will briefly relate the history of the Cape Verdean immigration to the U. S.

Despite the Cape Verdes' location near Africa, they are socially and historically part of the New World. The discovery of these islands in 1490 under the sponsorship of Henry the Navigator marked an early step in the European expansion which culminated in the colonization of the Americas. When the Europens arrived, the archipelago was unhabited, but it may have been known to Arabs and Africans (Marques 1973:198-199). The Portuguese attempted to make the Cape Verdes a rich sugar-producing area, using the labor of African slaves, as other Europeans would do a few decades later in the Carribbean. Although small plantations were es-

234

tablished in several islands, agriculture proved to be a precarious enterprise in the arid climate of the Cape Verdes. Extensive miscegenation between the few Portuguese who came to settle in this unpromising colony and their slaves, resulted in a mixed population. Meanwhile a new culture and a Creole language, called Crioulo, developed, whose roots are both African and Portuguese.

Because of their convenient position relative to winds and currents near the Guinea coast, the Cape Verdes became an entrepot for goods flowing to the coast and for slaves being transported to the New World. The commercial value of agriculture was largely superceded by profits to be gained from slave running and other types of trade, both legal and contraband. Because the dry climate of the Cape Verdes was much more tolerable for the Portuguese than that of Guinea on the African mainland, they became the administrative center for that colony and a place of refuge for Portuguese working in Africa. Cape Verdeans themselves became middlemen in Portuguese efforts to exploit and colonize Africa, first as traders in Guinea securing slaves and trade goods for white merchants in the Islands and later as middle-level government administrators, teachers and missionaries in the African colonies.

In the 1960's hundreds of Cape Verdean agricultural laborers and their families were brought to Angola to form model agricultural settlements called colonatos, in a policy aimed at "the creation of a semi-literate population of Africans and Portuguese holding rural Portuguese values, industrious, dedicated to the land, and politically conservative" (Duffy 1963:169). The Cape Verdeans' role in Portugal's colonial efforts closely parallels that of French Antillians in French West Africa as described by Franz Fanon (1968, 1969, pp. 17-24) and others.

Two results of the historical factors outlined here were particularly significant for the adaptation of Cape Verdeans to the U. S. One is that miscegenation in the Islands produced a wide

variety of physical types in the population. For a
number of reasons Cape Verdean society was not
polarized into black and white caste-like divisions
as happened in the U. S. Instead a complex and
flexible system of phenotypical classification developed, with over 250 categories into which an
individual might be placed (Terms for phenotypes
were elicited through a testing device developed
by Professor Marvin Harris of Columbia University
who kindly provided me with the necessary materials.
These consisted of 72 full-face drawings, varying
in sex, hair, nose, color and lip type. They were
shown to 100 subjects in Brava, one of the Cape
Verde Islands. Details about Harris' use of the
test in Brazil can be found in his article (Harris
1970). Moreover, use of the categories varies according to social context, so that incertain situations considerations such as wealth, education and
background may be taken into account, as well as
minute phenotypical differences. In this respect
the Cape Verdes resemble societies such as Brazil
and stand in contrast to those like to the U. S.,
where most people's racial "calculus" includes only
two categories, "white" and "black".

Secondly, Cape Verdeans found themselves in an
ambiguous position in the Portuguese empire. On
one hand they were colonizers, feeling themselves
different from and superior to Africans living on
the continent, whose cultures and social organization showed far less European influence than did
their own. On the other hand, Cape Verdeans were
themselves colonized by the Portuguese. Economically they were exploited by metropolitan commercial
monopolies and laws designed to protect the latter.
While citizens of Portugal, they nonetheless suffered various forms of legal and extra-legal discrimination. For example, even as late as 1972,
a Cape Verdean could be prevented from leaving his
home island by the whim of the government admini-
strator there. Young men recruited in the Islands
(This does not include some of the upper class
white families who were sent to school in Lisbon
and were recruited there. Some of these eventually
entered the higher ranks of the military.) for the

Portuguese army could not rise above a rank equivalent to private, first class, until the colonial wars of the 1960's. Cape Verdeans were not subject to conscript labor as were the indigenous peoples of Angola and Mozambique. Nevertheless, threat of starvation in the arid archipelago resulted in large-scale labor migration to plantations in the Portuguese-owned islands of Sao-Tome and Principe, near the African coast. There, inhuman conditions frequently resulted in death or permanent disabilities.

Even in the Islands, then, Cape Verdean identity has been a matter of deep ambivalence. Prestige was accorded those things associated with the colonial power, such as the Portuguese language, certain customs believed to be of Portuguese origin and, of course, "white" skin and physical features. Correspondingly, anything deemed African was likely to be disparaged. All this was encouraged in the colonial educational system and in the government-sponsored press. But even though they were often denigrated, many of the "African" traits, such as Crioulo, certain customs, and dark skin color were seen as intrinsically Cape Verdean. Furthermore, the Portuguese, whose administration of the Islands was astonishingly shoddy and corrupt, were objects of bitter satire and ridicule. Often they were viewed as intellectual inferiors by Cape Verdeans; in fact, the general level of education and literacy in the Cape Verde Islands was probably equivalent to or better than that of Portugal during certain periods of the Islands' history. (The Cape Verdes may well have had less illiteracy than Portugal ca. 1878, when the latter had an illiteracy rate of nearly 80 percent, by official statistics (Oliveira Marques 1973 II:228). However, this figure diminished to 38.1 percent in 1960 (still the highest in Europe) (Oliveira Marques II:396). By this time the Cape Verdes probably had 80 to 90 percent illiteracy, according to school officials there, for the educational system had not expanded with the population and in certain areas had declined, in terms of schools and teachers available.)

In sum, being Cape Verdean, for those living in
Cape Verde was a potential source of both shame
and pride during the colonial era.

Cape Verdean immigration to the United States
probably began sometime in the early nineteenth
century, though scattered individuals are known to
have arrived earlier. (An interesting article by
Herman Mellville in Harper's Magazine (1856:507-
509) refers to "Gees" (Portuguese) from the island
of Fogo in the Cape Verdes serving under Nantucket
whaling captains since early in the nineteenth century and notes the presence of "sophisticated"
(i.e., acculturated) Cape Verdeans in Nantucket and
New Bedford. Although his description of the Cape
Verdean is strikingly racist in tone, Melville allows that "no well-attested educational experiment
has ever been tried upon him." "There has been
talk," he goes on, "of sending five comely Gees,
aged sixteen, to Dartmouth College; that venerable
institution, as is well known, having been originally founded partly with the object of finishing
off wild Indians in the classics and higher mathe-
matics" (509). Professor George Monteiro of Brown
University kindly brought this reference to my attention.) American whalers had been stopping in
the Islands for storm and shelter since the early
eighteenth century, occasionally taking on Cape
Verdeans as crew members. In the mid- and late
nineteenth century, textile mills in the old whaling ports such as New Bedford began attracting
labor away from seafaring; whalers put out from
port with a skeleton crew, counting on the extra
hands to be picked up in the Azores and the Cape
Verdes. Cape Verdeans were only too willing to un-
dertake the drudgerous and often dangerous toil of
whaling, since most were desperately poor. During
the droughts that periodically struck the Islands,
resulting in tens of thousands of deaths by starvation, passage on the whalers offered hope of survival. Some used the whalers for cheap transportation to North America; others, however, went on to
become harpooners, captains and even shipowners.

By the 1850's, the trickle of Cape Verdean seamen into ports such as New Bedford and Providence
was augmented by Cape Verdeans emigrating on a
longer-term basis to New England. Most of these
were working age men, though a few women and children also made the journey. Slaveowners sometimes
rewarded their chattels with manumission and passage to the U. S.; for a woman in social disgrace
for any reason, emigration offered escape from the
claustrophobic ambience of the small islands. At
this time the U. S. was viewed as a poor and even
hostile place, fit only for the dregs of Cape Verdean society. Yet even in the 1840's (Lima describes extensive use of American goods: wood,
tiles, furniture, dishes, clothing, etc. 1844:108),
if not earlier, schooners were arriving in the islands laden with food, clothing, and all manner of
household furnishings sent by the emigrants.

From the turn of the century, until the restrictions on immigration imposed two decades later,
Cape Verdeans were arriving in New England by the
hundreds, sometimes thousands, each year, most of
them leaving from the small island of Brava which
had been a favorite stopping place for the whalers.
These immigrants were still, for the most part,
young men intending to stay only a few years, but
the shift from sea to land occupations was beginning and with it a gradual change in the pattern of
migration.

As early as 1905 Cape Verdean men were doing
backbreaking labor in cranberry bogs of the Massachusetts and Rhode Island littoral, where manpower
was always in short supply. A few families were
turning rejected farmland in the same areas to productive use. Others were employed by textile mills
and many continued in maritime occupations. Cape
Verdeans often held steward and cook jobs on river
or seagoing vessels, probably because these were
the jobs traditionally open to blacks. Typically,
a man spent most of his working years in the U. S.,
visiting his wife and family in Cape Verde every
few years. Most of his earnings were sent home,

239

with his wife supervising the purchase and cultivation of properties. Especially after the introduction of social security in the U. S., the immigrant
could look forward to a retirement of gentlemanly
leisure, as well as a certain prestige, in his island of origin. Yet even during this early phase
of Cape Verdean settlement in the U. S., a few of
the immigrants were entering prestigious occupations
notably law, and would later become leaders of the
ethnic community.

With the change to land occupations, more and
more Cape Verdean men began bringing their families
to the U. S. This tendency became the norm by the
end of World War II; during the 1940's the Islands
suffered several particularly devastating droughts,
one of which took some 30,000 lives. The postwar
prosperity of the U. S. made it doubly attractive
as a permanent home, though many families continued
to hold property in the Islands. Today most Cape
Verdeans able to come to the U. S. through close
relatives here or through marriages of convenience,
do so with the intention of remaining permanently.
After all, immigrants from Brava, as well as some
of those from other parts of the archipelago, are
likely to have more relatives in the new country
than in the old. While most Cape Verdean-Americans
today work in factory of service occupations, increasing numbers in the second and third generations are completing college and taking white collar jobs.

As described earlier, social identity was
problematic for Cape Verdeans even in the Islands;
however, outside, the two urban centers of the
archipelago, Mindelo and Praia, Cape Verdeans had
little contact with Portuguese or other outsiders.
In the rural areas, whence most of the immigrants
originate, the question of identity remained implicit rather than a felt concern of everyday life.
In this country, it became one of immediate importance. Here the immigrant was expected to fit into
one of two categories: black (Negro) or white.
Not only bureaucrats but the society at large employed this binary system of racial classification,

one of whose corollaries is that an individual with
any known African ancestry is to be classified as
"Negro" no matter what his appearance. By American
terms, the Cape Verdean could appropriately be assigned a social identity that, to use Goffman's
term, is a "stigmatized" one; that is, an identity
comprised of one or more attributes deeply dis-
crediting to the one who holds it (Goffman 1963:3).
Most importantly, it was an identity stigmatized in
Cape Verdean terms as well, one that, if accepted,
no matter how grudgingly could be an occasion of
shame and self-denigration.

Many Cape Verdeans, when initially confronted
with this choice, called themselves "white". After
all, in the Cape Verdes, "white" was as much a
social as a racial designation. That is, a respec-
table person of color would be called "white" in
many social contexts. Also, the term "Negro" in
Crioulo is an odious racial slur meaning "nigger",
one that no Cape Verdean would willingly accept no
matter what his or her color. If individuals of
dark complexion often describe themselves as a
"people of color", but never as "black" or "Negro".
By their own reckoning, Cape Verdeans were "Portuguese", culturally superior to Africans and to American blacks as well. Certainly the undesirability
of being considered "Negro" in the new society
quickly became apparent. Protests arose, for example, ca. 1905 with the entry of Cape Verdean children into schools in certain Massachusetts towns
(Gaw 1905). Many journalistic accounts of the day,
probably reflecting widely held stereotypes, portray the Cape Verdean as primitive, dirty, a menace
to the local community and certainly a "less desirable" immigrant than the white Portuguese.

The Cape Verdean who called himself "Portuguese" and "white" found that those claims were not
accepted by the white Portuguese, whose numbers
were always substantially larger than those of Cape
Verdeans in New England. Few Portuguese clubs
would admit Cape Verdeans; the Portuguese congrega-
tions of Catholic churches were so hostile to Cape
Verdeans that many of the latter converted to

Protestant sects or, as in New Bedford, formed a
new Catholic congregation of their own. The white
Portuguese considered Cape Verdeans to be Africans,
primarily because of color, and secondarily because
of language and other cultural differences.

In response, most Cape Verdeans attempted to
set themselves apart as a separate social category,
closed to American Blacks by preference and segre-
gated from white Portuguese by necessity. To be
sure, some Cape Verdeans whose appearance allowed
them to do so "passed" as Spanish, Puerto Rican or
some other ethnicity, but usually at the cost of
severing family ties. Others, arriving without
friends or relatives in the U. S., became lost in
the larger American black population. This was especially true of lower-class immigrants from the
islands of Santiago and Fogo, whose inhabitants
tend to be considerably darker than those of Brava.
These darker Cape Verdeans suffered discrimination
and rejection from their own compatriots as well
as from the host society.

Most of the immigrants grouped together in an
endogamous community whose boundaries were social
rather than geographical. The amorphous entity
called "the Cape Verdean community" now encompasses
the whole eastern seaboard from Boston to Philadelphia, as well as Cabo Verde, France, Lisbon and
other places in Europe, Africa and South America
where Cape Verdeans are found. This network of
friendship and kinship ties based on assertion and
acknowledgement of common identity is sustained by
various forms of communication across a wide geographical area. People, messages, goods and services (e.g., obtaining spouses or employment) move
with amazing frequency and rapidity between the
various localities mentioned.

Culturally, the defining features of this community in the U. S. most often cited by Cape Verdean-Americans themselves are language (Crioulo),
music and cuisine. In the American context, all
of these "ethnic markers" have been somewhat
transformed from the versions originally brought

from the Island. For example, the types of Cape
Verdean music played on guitar and mandolin, whose
roots are thought to be European, have been refined
and elaborated upon in the U. S. The more "African" sounding forms, some of which are sung and
chanted to the accompaniment of drums, did not survive in this country, though since Cape Verdean
independence, interest in these types of music has
increased, especially among younger Cape Verdean-
Americans. Similarly, the Crioulo spoken in the
U. S. is distinguished by certain archaisms and
neologisms not found in the Archipelago. More importantly, the social significance of Crioulo
changed completely; under the colonial regime in
the Islands it was commonly regarded as rather em-
barrassing evidence of African origins and illiteracy; in the U. S. it became a means of salvaging
the Cape Verdeans' sense of self-worth, for it un-
questionably distinguished them from American
Blacks. Moreover, there was certainly some practical utility in maintaining the mother tongue, since
American whites often regard foreigners of color
as "not the same as" or "better than" American
Blacks and accord them more benign treatment.

Perhaps the greatest importance of these cultural traits lies in their collective symbolic
value. Cape Verdean-American children are usually
socialized to believe that they are not the same
as American Blacks, despite appearances, because as
Cape Verdeans, they have a "culture". (This is
often linked with the idea that "Cape Verdeans were
never slaves", although they were indeed slaves in
the Islands and some were exported to the New
World.) Exhibition or practice of the group-defin-
ing traits mentioned above is far less important
for an individual's inclusion in the community than
giving the appearance of positively valuing them.
Even more crucial is the fulfillment of certain
normative prescriptions for social behavior incum-
bent on anyone who would be part of the community.

Because of its geographical vagueness, the
Cape Verdean-American community seems to be characterized by a certain fluidity and openness. A Cape

243

Verdean can change residence many times and still remain part of it. Any Cape Verdean festivity typically attracts friends and relatives across city and state lines. Yet the boundaries are, in behavioral terms, rather rigid. Perhaps most important is the requirement of endogamy: while marriage with a Portuguese or with any other white does not necessarily affect an individual's standing (though marriage within the Cape Verdean category is often preferred), marriage to an American Black has traditionally resulted in social ostracism, sometimes even from close relatives. I would suggest that the necessity for marrying within the Cape Verdean category (since marriage with whites was rarely a possibility) partially accounts for the continuing extensive contact between those in the U. S. and those in the Islands. For a long time, the unbalanced sex ratio in the immigrant group necessitated a man's findings a spouse in the Islands, if he were not to marry a black American. In contrast, the Cape Verdean seamen who settled in Hawaii, where race relations were quite different from those in New England, were able to marry into the local population and eventually lost contact with Cabo Verde.

Second only to the requirement of endogamy are the obligations of kinship attendant on membership in this community. These include mutual aid of various sorts: e.g., offering financial help, shelter, assistance in finding a job, etc. Many crises such as death, childbirth and illness are the occasions of mandatory social visiting, especially for women. An active gossip network, facilitated by modern technology of communication and transportation, keeps the individual aware not only of the doings of others, but the eyes of the community upon himself.

Traditionally, Cape Verdean-Americans are expected to be hardworking, politically inconspicuous, to stay off welfare, and to seek as much schooling as possible, for his children if not for themselves. (It is important to note that these are ideals, not necessarily reality in many cases.) These are all

244

ideas brought from the Islands, where education was
the only hope for upward mobility, where hard work
and mutual aid were prerequisites for physical survival, and where to "make politics," as the Crioulo
phrase puts it, was to jeopardize the safety of
family and friends. By maintaining these ideals as
well as the racial ideology brought from the Cape
Verdes, which among other things included the con-
viction that to be Cape Verdean was to be different
from, and better than, being black and African,
Cape Verdeans succeeded amirably in effecting certain changes in their new social mileu. That is,
in the areas were they are numerous, Cape Verdeans
have come to be viewed as a "special case", not
white and yet not the same as American Blacks.

Early in this century when Cape Verdeans were
still suspect because of their color, Yankees recognized the fear and respect these immigrants held
for the police, and their reluctance to use violence. By an account of this period, Yankee employers found the "Bravas", as Cape Verdeans were
called (after the island so many of them embarked
from), "docile, obedient, willing to work, not
over-fastidious with regard to food or shelter or
the discomforts of the weather" (Bannick 1917:65).
Already Cape Verdeans were seen by New Englanders
as a "better breed than our own Negroes". Apparently the physical hardships of Cabo Verde along with
the psychological ones of colonialist repression
were quite adequate preparation for Cape Verdean-
Americans to become a so-called "successful" and
"desirable" ethnic group. Today in the Providence-
New Bedford area, many employers and landlords consider Cape Verdeans (commonly referred to as "black
Portuguese") desirable clients and distinguish them
from American Blacks. Even the latter, it seems,
recognize the higher status Cape Verdeans have se-
cured for themselves: it is said that occasionally
non-Cape Verdean blacks have tried to "pass" for
Cape Verdean.

Yet the "success" of Cape Verdean attempts to
create a special category for themselves has not
been without its costs. Not all forms of racial

discrimination could be avoided: Cape Verdean
children, like Afro-American children generally,
were usually channelled into manual occupations
by school authorities. Cape Verdeans moving into
strange neighborhoods often encountered hostility.
Yet many Cape Verdeans who remained in the New
England community continue to deny the existence of
racism in their experience or, in the extreme case,
to attribute it to outsiders' ignorance of the differences between Cape Verdeans and blacks. Accord-
ingly, the burden of failure for one who does not
manage to realize the ideals mentioned earlier --
the welfare case, the high school dropout -- can
fall only upon the individual himself.

For the very young child, the ethnic community
offers a kind of protective capsule that allows in-
sulation from stigmatized definitions of himself
and thus allows him "to see himself as a fully
qualified ordinary human being, of normal identity
in terms of such basic matters as age and sex"
(Goffman 1963:33). For the adult it affords refuge
and counterpoint to the denigrating definitions of
self he may encounter as a person of color in a low
status occupation. However, for some individuals
the price is too high; the strictures on behavior
and the gossip network that supports these may be
felt as claustrophobic, stultifying. Moreover, the
fragile protection of the community is likely to
fail the geographically or socially mobile individual. For many Cape Verdean men, World War II
was a critical biographical event. Some, antici-
pating possible discrimination, asked to be sent to
black regiments, only to be informed by recruiters:
"You're not black; you're Portuguese". Those who
went to white regiments often found themselves in
the South where for the first time they began to
experience life as black persons and to see themselves as black. Such individuals, removed from
the home community, is confronted with the fact
that "Cape Verdean" means nothing to most Americans.
There is no category into which they can be readily
placed except the "Black" category. Although they
themselves often did not accept the rigid black-
white distinction current in the wider society,

they could not usually enforce their own view of their identity. Many of those who, for whatever reason, found themselves beyond the shelter of the community's protective umbrella have concluded, like the informant who had been stationed in Georgia, "If I'm American, I'm black."

Until quite recently the resolution of the dilemmas posed by the wider society and by his own background has been the burden of Cape Verdeans as individuals. Each of the compromises available to him has implicated certain demands unknown to those who fit neatly into the two major racial categories of this society. Some whose phenotype enables them to do so have passed for white at the cost of disowning friends and family while disguising their own personal history. One who decided to identify himself as Black risked the wrath of relatives and others in the community, who have regarded such affiliation as a denial of one's heritage, and by extension, of one's family. At the same time, acceptance by others of a purported "Black" identity was by no means assured. The example of the recruit described above suggests that, at least in the Providence-New Bedford area, whites themselves may not accept such a claim. American blacks have interpreted Cape Verdean claims to cultural distinctiveness as a form of racism, a view that was not, as we have seen, entirely without foundation. Gaining acceptance as Black has, in some cases, involved the kinds of information control about oneself that is commonly associated with passing an ascribed status for such Cape Verdeans, but one that must be achieved. With the growth of Black movements in the 1960's, Cape Verdean-American students, for example, found themselves pressured to ally themselves with black students' struggles, and yet had constantly to prove themselves free of the taint of racism.

The case of "Johnny" (pseudonym), a stevedore in his early thirties living in Providence suggests some of the dilemmas and contradictions faced by the individual who would choose a Black identity.

To the dismay of his family who berated him for "denying your Cape Verdean culture", John had come to look at himself as Black. Lunching on the job one day, John met up with a Cape Verdean friend and began conversing with him in Crioulo. One of his coworkers reacted by saying "You're not really black, then you're Portuguese" and began referring to him as "the 'Portagee'". Some weeks after that an Azorean joined the work group and when told that John was also Portuguese, responded with "No, he's a black African".

The following passages taken from an interview with a Cape Verdean-American college student, Terry, reveal some of the difficulties faced by the young person who, as she puts it, feels "sociologically" Black but who resents "having to give up my whole culture". Terry is medium of dark complexion, with naturally straight hair and so-called 'white' features. Her mother was brought up in this country by "very traditional" Cape Verdean-born parents; her father was born in Brava and came to America as a young man. Both parents work in factories. Terry "admires" Malcom X and says: "I don't feel white -- forget the whites".

Terry: It's hard on the people whose grandparents came from the Islands. They want to be Americans and they are, they're Americanized . . . but they're subjected to the opinion of other Cape Verdeans especially older ones . . . Say they walk into a house with a 'fro' -- somebody's aunt is going to say "Ugh! That hair!"

Deirdre: Have you ever joined any Afro-American groups at school, for example?

Terry: Not really. I went to one or two of the Afro society meetings just to see what it was like, but they just sit there, they shuck and they jive . . . the kind of group where one's trying to be blacker than the other one. For most Cape Verdean kids either you're in or your're

248

out . . . And if you go to school with them and your name's Carvallo or Santos, you can be as black as you want to be, you can wear an Afro, but you're still a Portuguese to them. They might not say it to your face, but you always know what they're thinking.

Deirdre: What about Rose? (Rose is a friend of Teresa's, also about 20 years old, who identifies as black).

Terry: She'll always try to disown Cape Verdeans' being Portuguese in any fashion. Like when she moved to _____ college and her brother was helping her, a black guy said to her, "Oh you have a nice accent, Rose. Your last name's Lopes?" She said "Yeah, it's a Cape Verdean name but it don't mean nothin". Don't pay any attention -- I'm really a sister." . . . Or take my cousin, he was the nicest kid, and he had real straight hair, he really looked Cape Verdean, and the kids would never accept him because he had an accent . . . So he turns around, went and cut his hair and made a 'fro' and stuff to be accepted . . . After a while he started imitating the (black) kids to a "T" but they never, ever accepted him, 'cause the minute he'd turn around, they'd say, "oh you know Tony, that Portuguese kid."

Deirdre: Why are the black kids so resentful when you show anything Cape Verdean -- remember when you spoke Crioulo in front of that guy, and he wouldn't speak to you after that?

Terry: It's because they figure that it weakens their force -- the more people they can get behind them the better, right? I believe that the only thing Cape Verdeans share with the black people is the socio-

249

logical aspect, in America . . . the same
social problems, and that's the only
place where I think they should unite
. . . they're trying to deculture every-
one of color so they'll be exactly like
them, so they'll be more unified . . .
Like they say we should wear dashikis --
but they don't wear them in Cape Verde
. . . The only soul food I've ever had
is chicken and corn bread . . . I don't
think we should take their culture, we
preserve what we have.

Deirdre: Did you ever have anybody give you a bad
time because of your color?

Terry: When we first moved to _____
(a suburb of Providence), a bunch of
English-type people would call us nigger,
they would ask my sister "What color are
you?" I was maybe four or so and I was
walking to the store with my father, and
a bunch of hoods started shoving him
around . . . He couldn't speak English
and they made fun of him and they hit
him -- I'll never forget that . . . but
my father said he never hated them. He
said, "just because they're ignorant,
don't be like them" . . . My father always said it's worth anything to make a
friend, it's not worth anything to make
an enemy . . . It was really bad. Those
same guys used to throw big hard apples
at me and my sister, she was about two
and a half . . . They used to break win-
dows on us, sic dogs on us. I know a lot
of Afro-Americans who probably didn't
have the experiences we had. After a
while we weren't "niggers" to them, we
were (in a mincing voice) "Por-tyu-guese
. . . Oh they're not black, we don't have
black families, we have a Portuguese
family".

250

Cape Verdeans who continued to cling to a non-black identity could only do so in the face of overwhelming evidence that they were, to most Americans, Black. Pursuit of a non-Black identity has usually involved denial or reinterpretation of certain Cape Verdean cultural items and historical experience. Crioulo was passed off as Portuguese, African-inspired musical forms largely forgotten, the experience of slavery denied. The body, of course, did not escape criticism and modification. A darker child was a disappointment, Afro hair styles, anathema. To the extent that traits considered racially indicative could be controlled (e.g., by use of hair straightners and complexion lightners, avoiding exposure to sun), they were.

Still other Cape Verdeans have taken on a Black identity for certain social contexts; among Cape Verdeans and certain whites he might emphasize his Cape Verdean-ness, while to other audiences, particularly Blacks, he would display a black identity, and the speech patterns and gestures assumed to be part of that identity. Anti-poverty programs in New Bedford and Providence often attracted such Cape Verdeans, to the irritation of American Blacks who accused them of profiteering on an identity they had never accepted before. It is quite possible that Cape Verdeans, with their ideals of education, etc., presented a particularly acceptable demeanor to those in charge of hiring for such programs. Such individuals are often conscious of their own situational shifts of identity and view these as a compromise required by the circumstances.

The year 1972 saw the beginnings of active proselytization by the P. A. I. G. C. (Movement for the Independence of Guinea and the Cape Verde Islands, American Support Committee). Now the problem of identity, carefully denied or submerged in public contexts in the past, became a subject of intense debate. The P. A. I. G. C. supporters explicitly rejected the old polarity of Cape Verdean versus African or Black. Attempts were made to re-educate Cape Verdean-Americans' views of their own history by stressing the heritage of slavery and colonialism. Rejected elements of Cape Verdean culture, such as the African types of music mentioned earlier, were given positive valuation.

The practical success of the Committee's endeavors was minimal; however the significance of their ideological platform cannot be doubted. With Cape Verdean independence in 1975, most Cape Verdean-Americans were alarmed at the severance of dependency tied with Portugal and at the new Republic of Cabo Verde's close ties with Guinea-Bissau on the African mainland. However, these developments also made it evident to some, especially those of the postwar generations that their identification as Afro-Americans and their support for Black liberation movements no longer need to be seen as contradicting their sense of cultural distinctiveness.

It cannot be denied that the American community remains the least supportive of the homeland's new status of all the Cape Verdean emigrant enclaves across the globe. Rumors run rife as to the alleged evils of the new system; influential figures from the old regime have become comfortably installed in the American community, even at times trying to mobilize followers for an offensive against Cabo Verde's government, though without much success. At present many, probably most, Cape Verdean-Americans distrust that government as "communist", though it has never presented itself as such. Many continue to bring up their children in the norms of social and cultural identity described earlier. But there have been at the same time undeniable changes in the public and institutional life of the New England ethnic community.

With independence the pro-Portuguese leadership of the ethnic community lost the support it had enjoyed from the old regime, support expressed in prestige-conferring "perks" such as subsidized trips to Portugal and her colonies, special attention from government officials prominent under the dictatorships of Salagar and Castano, etc., and backed up by fears (justified over, by this writer's personal experience) of Portuguese police agents in the ethnic community. This allowed the emergence of a new set of potential leaders who see themselves as Afro-American without denying the Portuguese element of their background. One concrete result is shift in political orientation of the Cape Verdean newspaper most widely read in the New Bedford-Providence area. Cape Verdean Independence Day (July 5) is celebrated with picnics, speechmaking and music that attract animated crowds. Slowly, new possibilities -- social, political and cultural -- are developing for the community and her members.

In conclusion I would like to delineate some of the implications of the small size of the Cape Verdean-American population for the problem of social identity (This term is used herein as Goffman has developed it in Stigma 1963:2 et passim). Cape Verdean-Americans comprise a kind of minority among minorities, given their numbers relative to, say, Italian or Irish-Americans. While Cape Verdeans are considerably smaller than certain other ethnic categories in the Providence-New Bedford area, they are virtually invisible in the wider society. This has certain material consequences in a society. Where political strategies are typically designed along ethnic lines, that is it will be more difficult for such a small population to secure recognition and rewards as an interest group. For example, Cape Verdeans were only recognized as a separate category in the census in 1980 after years of effort by members of the community. There were numerous bilingual English-Portuguese programs in Massachusetts and Rhode Island, before such facilities existed as they do now for Cape Verdean children, whose first language, if not English, is normally Crioulo. These recent changes suggest that independence for Cabo Verde has highlighted and given new legitimacy to Cape Verdean cultural distinctiveness for the public at large as well as for Cape Verdean-Americans.

"Invisibility" is nothing new in the Cape Verdean experience. In the Islands one encounters, instead of the ethnocentrism commonly found among isolated peoples, a strange cosmopolitanism born of economic dependence on the outside world. Individuals who have never left the archipelago nevertheless see their homeland as "the end of the end of the world". In material terms, the insignificance of the Islands in the Portuguese imperial constellation was made clear in many ways. One minor but revealing example is the matter of educational materials: before the wars in Africa, the Cape Verdes, like the other colonies received textbooks completely oriented to the metropole. With Portugal's struggle to maintain the African territories, new social science texts were introduced giving considerably more attention to those colonies. Aside from their objections to the political message of the books ("We are all Portuguese"), Cape Verdeans were particularly resentful of their equally obvious orientation to the much larger (and more lucrative) colonies on the African mainland.

If wider society has been slow to offer rewards for Cape Verdean-Americans as an ethnic group, it has on the other hand stimulated the development of a Cape Verdean social identity that is providing a basis for eventual mobilization as an ethnic interest group. That is, "Cape Verdean" became the primary social identity for individuals only in the U. S. Most Cape Verdeans came from rural areas of small islands and defined themselves as being from a certain village or, in other contexts, from a certain island, just as Italian immigrants, for example, initially identified themselves by village and regional affiliation. It is the host society that places persons from Brava and those from other islands in the same category.

In this case, it was also the host society that forced a choice of self-definition as "black" or "white". Unlike members of certain larger ethnic categories, such as Japanese-Americans or many Puerto Ricans, who may also be viewed as falling in-between or outside the black/white categories. Cape Verdeans cannot expect that to identify them-

selves as "Cape Verdean" will be self-evident,
except in quite restricted geographical areas of
the United States. While Cape Verdeans vary in
the identities they try to claim, they share the
experience of disjunction between their felt social
identity and the category to which others assign
them.

Only the strenuous creation of a distinctive
subculture and of a rather restrictive community
allowed Cape Verdeans a special place even in New
England. Elsewhere, social placement by outsiders
often proved definitive, forcing acceptance of an
identity that Cape Verdeans could come to cherish
only by a vigorous process of self-re-education
involving a redefinition of their whole past.
Cape Verdeans who identified as Black have often
felt required to disown their cultural distinctiveness from other Afro-Americans; yet this distinctiveness comprises not only a certain language,
music and cuisine but also the historical experience of slavery, starvation and colonial exploitation. They could expect fellow Cape Verdeans to
berate them as a "traitor" to their own heritage;
yet the position of these others was itself ten-
able only by revising their own history and culture.

The collective and individual experience of
Cape Verdeans holds many ambiguities and ironies,
only some of which have been set forth here. It
is perhaps the desire to make sense of the past
that explains the surprising number of Cape Verdean-Americans who have attempted to write their
own memoirs or biographies. And perhaps it is the
tentative quality of their personal solutions to
the dilemmas of social identity that has made
these works closet creations.

REFERENCES CITED

Bannick, Christian John
    1917 Portuguese Immigration to the United States:
        Its Distribution and Status. Berkeley: The
        University of California. (Printed in 1971 by
        R. and E. Research Associates, 4843 Mission
        Street, San Francisco, California.

Duffy, James
    1963 Portugal in Africa. Baltimore: Penquin
        Books, Inc.

Fanor, Frantz
    1968 Black Skin, White Masks. New York: Grove
        Press, Inc.

Gaw, Cooper
    1905 "The Cape Verde Islands and Cape Verdean
        Immigrants," New Bedford Evening Standard.
        July 29, p. 3.

Harris, Marvin
    1970 "Referential Ambiguity in the Calculus of
        Brazilian Racial Identity", Southwestern Jour-
        nal of Anthropology 26:1-13.

Lima, Joaquin Lopes da
    1844 Ensaio Sobre a Statistica das Possessoes
        Portuguezas. Lisbon: Imprensa Nacional.

Oliveria Marques, A. H. de
    1973 Historia de Portugal, Vols. I and II.
        Edicoes Agora, Lisbon.

CONTRIBUTORS

ETHEL BOISSEVAIN (Ph. D. The University of Prague, Czechoslovakia) is Associate Professor Emeritus of Anthropology, Herbert Lehman College of the City University of New York. She has done field-work with Mohegan and Scatacook Indians, Narragansett Indians, Pequot Indians and Wampanoag Indians -- all New England tribes.

LEON FRANCIS BOUVIER (Ph. D. Brown University) is Director, Demographic Research and Policy Analysis, Population Reference Bureau, Washington, D. C. He has published articles on French-Canadians, Catholics and population growth.

MARK J. HANDLER (Ph. D. Brown University). Handler spent two years doing field research in the Azores. He was able to follow some of the immigrants from their habitat in the Azores to their adjustment in the United States following immigration. His special interests, in addition to ethnicity, include migration, sex roles, social history, philosophy of social science and peasant and industrial society.

DEIRDRE A. MEINTEL MACHADO (Ph. D. Brown University) is Visiting Assistant Professor of Anthropology at McGill University. She has conducted fieldwork in the Cape Verde Islands and in the Azores.

JOAN H. ROLLINS (Ph. D. The University of Oklahoma) is Professor of Psychology at Rhode Island College. Drug abuse, family violence and group dynamics are included among her areas of research interest.

WILLIAM S. SIMMONS (Ph. D. Harvard University) is Professor and Chairman, Department of Anthropology, The University of California at Berkeley. He is the author of Cawtantowit's House (Brown University Press) which is based on archaeological excavations of Jamestown Island, Rhode Island and includes an explanation of the Narragansett Indian religion.

257

MARLENE KOURY SMITH (M. A. Providence College) is
Executive Director of Common Cause of Rhode
Island. Her interest in studying the Arabic
community in Rhode Island stems from her own
Syrian heritage on her paternal side.

FRANK ANDREWS STONE (Ed. D. Boston University) is
Professor of International Education and Director, the I. N. Thut World Education Center, The
University of Connecticut. He spent the years
1953-1966 at the American College, Tarsus, Turkey and from 1969-1970 as Visiting Professor at
Hecettepe University in Ankara, Turkey. These
years in Turkey provided him with the opportunity for extensive research of Armenian history
and culture.